CHAIN 10
translucinación

editors
Jena Osman
Juliana Spahr

and
Thalia Field
Cecilia Vicuña

Honolulu, Philadelphia

Chain 10, summer 2003.
Chain appears annually.
$12 for one issue; $20 for two issues.
Please make checks payable to Chain Arts. Send orders to:

Chain (c/o Jena Osman)
Department of English
Temple University
10th floor, Anderson Hall (022-29)
1114 West Berks Street
Philadelphia, PA 19122-6090

This issue is made possible with monetary support from the National Endowment for the Arts, the Pennsylvania State Council on the Arts, 'A 'A Arts, Chain Arts, generous contributions from several individuals, and subscribers. Thanks also to the University of Hawai'i at Mānoa and Temple University for office space, Web space, and some postage.

NATIONAL
ENDOWMENT
FOR THE ARTS

Thanks to Kevin Davies.

Special thanks to Andrés Ajens for the word *translucinación*.

Distributed by Small Press Distribution, 1341 Seventh Street, Berkeley, CA 94710-1409, http://www.spdbooks.org

Indexed by the *Index of American Periodical Verse* (Lanham, MD: Scarecrow Press), the *American Humanities Index*, and partially by the *MLA Bibliography of Periodical Literature*.

Cover and frontispiece by Gaye Chan.
Typesetting by Deirdre Kovac.

Archive . . . http://www.temple.edu/chain

ISSN: 1076-0520
ISBN: 1-930068-20-4

EDITORS' NOTES

The topic for this issue was Cecilia Vicuña's idea originally. And it was she who brought us to the word "translucinación," a word made up by Andrés Ajens to describe how translation is a form of reading and writing that creates new work, new conversations. Translucinación is, like dialogue (the topic of *Chain* 9), a cross-cultural encounter loaded with hope and yet always in danger of going wrong. While translation, post-Walter Benjamin, is no longer presumed to contain or clarify another language (or its accompanying culture), what interested us was the relentless utopian drive within any act of translation. For no matter what translation does, it still represents the need for one culture to speak and learn about another through the other culture's words.

As we edited this issue, we thought about these issues: What happens to a language when it is brought into English (or any other tongue)? What gets lost and what is added? How can a translation present its alterations with consciousness? How can a translation be shown as the creation of something new rather than a distortion of an original? Can translation be an act of dialogue rather than an act of imperialistic plunder?

We didn't want an issue that just collected works from around the world. And as we edited, we avoided fake translations, machine translations, homophonic translations, and oulipo-inspired translation procedures. We believe these methods do have some value (and we have included a few examples of such translations to represent the many that were submitted to us), but we wanted an issue that explored how translation might be a starting point for something that remained in explicit dialogue with the original work while at the same time transforming this work into something new. As we worked on this issue, Ammiel Alcalay and Larry Venuti sent us some emails that pushed us hard to think about the ethics of translation, an ethics of remaining attentive to what a work from another culture has to say. We like to think of translation as a collaborative act with many options. The translator might choose to remain intimate with the original and attempt a reproduction that emphasizes meaning or s/he might choose to spin off and explore intent or sound or any other aspect of the work. But we wanted work that made it clear that the translator and the author both matter. The translator is not just an invisible worker who only deserves a name in italics at the end of the piece. The translator is a visible creator who also has a responsibility to be in dialogue with the author and to not treat the original work as a completely knowable object, or as simply an interesting excuse for word play. Because we see translation as the result of such a rigorous conversation, we decided to put the author and translator names beside each other.

We also decided to include, whenever possible, the work in the original language (there are several exceptions where either the translator refused or it just didn't make sense). We are very grateful to the translators for providing the originals, for obtaining permission to reprint them, and for their help with typesetting them. If the original piece was previously published, the translators have made all reasonable efforts in good faith to obtain permission from copyright holders. Any permission omissions will be corrected in future issues. Deirdre Kovac, who typeset this issue, also deserves our thanks for her patient and attentive work with so many different fonts and languages.

—JO & JS

CONTENTS

翻訳

TRANSLUCINACIÓN

CHAIN

№ 10

ANDRÉS AJENS & ERIN MOURÉ

Poematriz en 3 papáginas y un(a) aparte /
Wombpoem in 3 papages and one a-part

I

a morosos abrevaderos (de) a **a**
m
l lllloviera **antes**

dudo du**da**
mos nos, entre veráceas
paginoscuras blablancas (entre
menudas medialunas
dudo: antes

d

y alterófilo *ya* dado conveniente—d e s nudo mudo
inasímil, bipicante)

y d
udando sin d u d a a
fuera calza y descalza la sin
táxis caí
da
de bandera—a es
quina d d d d d
lirios de inundados aamantes, a

Carache, por Trujillo, roxa la vía, y a Santiago por Rosal—e indudablementes).

I

to the a-morous watertroughs (of) a **l**
o
te rrrrain ho**vers** before

doubts **doubt**
full we, between **veraceous**
blablablank obscuropages (between
bitty parentheses
I doubt: before

d

and alterofilial *yay* dice-given convenient—de nuded muted
in-assimilable bi-biting)

and d
oubting w/o do ub t ou t
there softsoled and soleless the syn
tax is fl
agged
down—to cor
ner d d d d d
liriums of inundated lovers: to

Carache, via Trujillo, red-roaded—and to Santiago via Rosal, and undoubtablies).

II

EN CAMADAS tras
versales comisuras, encendidas
comas, telenamoráceas comillas, sus
tajos nímios, s u s
amor e s a distancia—

de cierto avanza
en la región de las imágenes pá-
trias, raíz (matriz) de pueblos nombres.

ansia de distancia en la d i s t a n c i a
antes que cita **(ciega)** de 'amor', temblor
de un beso dado
que llega sólo cuando no llega—adestino
transespacial de cuerpos, remotos cada vez, exorbitancias

teleterruños en sueños, geoBío-Bíografías, fluidas solares infancias
—y en entreveraz frontera un río timotocuica confluye: Táchira.

II

COUCHED IN COHORTS, trans
versal contiguities, incendiary
commas, teleamorous quotations, their
tiny slashes, th ei r
love ' s a t distance—

advances surely
in the image region of father-
lands, root (womb) of namepeoples.

anxiety of distance in the d i s t a n c e
before the blaze ("blind") of love, tremble
of a kiss-dice given
that arrives only when it doesn't arrive—transspatial
undestiny/ation of bodies, remote every time, exorbitances

tele-homesoils in dreams, geoBio-Biographies, fluent solarsoil infancies
—and at the betruthtween frontier a timotocuican river converges, Táchira.

III

a Lzo. Ayllapán

POR CLARO SOLAR A MAR,
solar austral, claro biíntimo,
inescrita empedernía a
bierta va, viene
Carahue camino a Puerto

y aún más y menos que austral (si austro
imperial), Mocha
Puaucho mar adentro,

de almas en pena, almácigo, de
a m o r e s s i n d i s t a n c i a—

llama la *ü* de *kütral* de *ül,*
l l a m a la *a* en alta mar
y pajarácea doblez en *ü ñ ü m, Üi, l a* ***c u r v***
a oscura *en despoblado* tal;

camino estrecha distancias
y aun al volver no hay camino, poe-
mar, *ül-*
kantuln, dichten:
nomás disponer finao dizque el Peñi Malo de Puerto, cadáver
cada ver en re-, tal *Re-*
trato oval: the scene
was heightened by contrast in dress: e
nd wore a loose chili jacket of dark velvet, beginning a
strange house with strange inmates in a s t r a n g e l a nd . . .

•

Cadencianonadas, incandescencias—

no cómo guardar silencio capitanías estrías si-
no si lencio silencio (‘,) al na d a r tantísimo *Farewell vn-*
hallowed cues y entrevEros tantOs.

III

for Lzo. Ayllapán

FROM CLEAR HOMESOIL S UN TO SEA,
austral homesoil, bi-intimate clearing,
an unwritten stoniness open
ly goes, comes,
Carahue on the road to Puerto,

and even more and less than austral (so austral-
imperial), to Mocha
via Puaucho, sea-borne

by souls in anguish, *soulsweeping*, of
l o v e s w i t h o u t d i s t a n c e—

so call u p the *ü* of *kütral* and of *ül*,
so c al l up the *a* of the high seaa
and the wingfold of *ü ñ ü m, Üi, t h e* ***d a r k c***
u r v e so *deserted;*

roadway makes distance smaller
so that, upon return, there's no way; to poe
mize, to *ül*
kantuln, to *dichten*:
solely presents the end-all, Peñi (comrade) Malo from Puerto says, a cadaver
can't a-ver in re-, such an Ov-
al Portrait: *the scene*
was heightened by the contrast in dress: the e
nd wore a loose chili jacket of dark velvet, entering a
strange house with strange inmates in a s t r a n g e l a nd . . .

•

Cadencestrifling incandescences—
not as harbours keep silence ripples but
si lence silence (',) having swum so long *Farewell un-*
hallowed cues and so much betruthtwe/Eros.

The art of losing isn't hard to master.
GEOGRAPHY *III*, E. Bis-.

una vez, desvezada: una frase, sí
laba a sílaba des
co y un tad
a—nomás un tipo, su
funicular carácter de fondo prototípico, queda
mimándola (el tipo: "no significa nada").

otra vez, vid a vid, otro sarmiento, misma mata:
"perder una é (ya perd una í) en el injerto
—prueba perder más rápido, perdiendo
más estrechamente todavía".

una y otra, vez tal: sustraída
—encriptado en el tiempo, el tipo—(al mito),
abre campo al campo de los desgajados, d es
par r amad os n om br
e s salares, atópicos bultos insepultos.

—y—una roza temporera desbroza
antes del antes del después y del ahora,
de las solares imperdidas pérdidas—a un art e.

The art of losing isn't hard to master.
GEOGRAPHY *III*, E. Bis-.

once, sundered, one sentence, syl
labial to syllable dis
join ted, sev e
red—just one type of guy, his
funicular character of prototypical founding, still
mimicking it (the type: "it doesn't mean anything").

once again, one vine to vine, another vine-shoot, same vineyard
"to los an e (an y alread lost) in the grafting
—tries losing faster, losing
more closely still."

once and again, such a time: taken away
—the type, time-encrypted—(to myth),
opens the field to the field of the disengaged, d is
per sa l over name s salt fl
ats, atopical hummocks uncrypted

—and—as clearing temporarily razes clear
before the before of the after and the now,
sunclarities' clearing's unlost lost, *unit—ed* to one art.

"THUS 'FABRICATION' IS HERE UN LITTLE BIT *HECHIZO-LESS": SOME NOTES BY ERIN MOURÉ ON TRANSLATING ANDRÉS AJENS: South-Chilean poet Andrés Ajens' work is of a density that is nearly untranslatable, or that* is *translatable,* if *English will bend to its will and pleasures, its amplitude, its extravagations. And if there is a way to make present the "culture" of which Ajens is part, and not simply the strangeness of my reading of that culture.*

Which is a risk I bear. For my work on Ajens is a translation not of "his text"—for there is no "his text" I have access to, and this is so for any translation—but of a reading practice, a translation of my *reading practice, focussed on a text that is his but is also one that by my very reading of it is already wrenched from its dizzyingly open context and culture, and is read, through my eyes, into mine.*

Yet his work (dizzyingly!) resists assimilation into "my culture." I never feel so "northern" as when I read Ajens. His work is so powerfully "south," southern. Even in Chile, it is "south," south of the metropolis of Santiago de Chile, off in the barren lands, and of the barren lands. In truth, I am as ignorant as any of us when it comes to details of the southern hemisphere. I only know enough, from reading Ajens, to realize that the world seen from south of the equator in the americas is very different from the world we are given to see in the north.

Yet Canada has corporeal similarities with Chile . . . we too are a narrow country (for the vast majority of our population resides in a thin belt close to the 49th parallel) but we are one stretched from east to west, with no North (in most of our white urban lives) except as Myth, or south, except as Huge Neighbour. Chile's body is all north and south, and no East and West. To go east or west in Chile is to leave it. A literal translation into Chilean Spanish of "go west, young man!" would be an invitation to drown. And to translate his "norte" by "north" is to see much of the weight of that word vaporize.

Our colonizations by the Europeans were likewise different: ours a tussle between English and French over fur and territory, that ignored or killed aboriginal peoples, theirs more intensely a tussle over religion, and gold, and territory, and conversion of aboriginal peoples, of "salvation"'s bitter head-vise. My knowledges of colonization can't be transposed to the south, and through my northern optic, I can't help but miss so much in Andrés's work. Intensities, sounds, repetitions, stutters, hauntings, histories: all these I've tried to draw on in my translation, but I couldn't have done it without Andrés' interventions, wrenching me out of my conceptions and ideological and linguistic framework constantly.

Allowing me to bend and stutter English differently, to try to open it to Andrés' speaking.

Andrés' intensities: we work so I can translate his work from Spanish (mostly—he's also got aymara, quechua, mapuche, brasileiro, deutsch in his work) into English. We talk in English un peu, in French muito, and lately, he writes in Brasileiro and I write in Galego, all to make an English. For this is what it takes, really, to make English, not just to use it, but to make it.

As Ajens said, early on in our discussions, to convince me why "fabrication" was not enough to translate "hechizo"—and here you'll get the flavour of our exchanges:

> *a. something is hechizo (or hechiza), if it is made precariously, only with that you have in this moment at hand*
>
> *on parle donc d'un . . . moteur hechizo s'il est fait avec des morceaux de moteurs anciens ou en désuetude, ou d'une caña de pescar hechiza . . . d'un vestido hechizo . . .*
>
> *mais . . . dans ce cas-ci l'affaire est doublement hechiza, puisque pour faire tomber l'accent dans la première de trois syllabes (para hacerla esdrújula) j'ai eu à faire d' 'hechizas' un mot . . . hechiza (héchiza)*

> *b. on peut comprendre aussi à l'anvers . . . ! laisser 'esdrújulos' comme adjectif du nom 'héchizos' (enchantements), tout proche d'hechizar, d'hechicería . . . (et tout cela du verbe . . . hacer, facere) (then 'fabrication' is there un little bit hechizoless)*

These translations, then, are "hechizas" not "fabricated." And are, also, "enchantments."

Elizabeth Bishop, in a poem to which Ajens refers, "One Art," seems to me to speak (unknowingly) of the process of translation:

> *Then practice losing farther, losing faster:*
> *places, and names, and where it was you meant*
> *to travel. None of these will bring disaster.*

Encouraging, don't you think? That we travel, though not where we meant to. It's wonderful, not a disaster at all. One art.

To Erin's Notes, Andrés Ajens Adds:

a. Canada and Chile, while not on the same "tropic," do share a . . . Meridian (the 73rd).

b. In "Chile," if you head toward the East, yes, you leave the country, or if you have a good compass, or a lot of luck, you'll get to . . . either to the (Chilean, otherChilean) Easter Island, or . . . Rapanui!!!!!, either to the (Chilean) island of Robinson Crusoe or maybe even right to "Crusoe's England."

c. [And again, Vicentre Huidobro said: "In Chile there are only three cardinal points: north and south."]

Last Word from Erin . . . Meridian *is a Celan reference of course . . . to C's speech upon receiving the Georg Büchner Prize in 1960,* The Meridian, *which concludes, in Rosmarie Waldrop's translation:*

> *Ladies and gentleman, I find something which consoles me a bit for having walked this impossible road in your presence, this road of the impossible [interruption from EM: i.e. this red-road]. I find the connective which, like the poem, leads to encounters. I find something as immaterial as language, yet earthly, terrestrial, in the shape of a circle which, via both poles, rejoins itself and on the way serenely crosses even the tropics: I find . . . a* meridian.

Here's to the shared meridian!—EM

SHIMON BALLAS & AMMIEL ALCALAY

from *Outcast*

אין אדם היכול להצביע על הסתירות ב"היהודים בהיסטוריה" כמוני, ואף־על־פי־כן אני מתיצב מאחורי כל משפט בו. זה נשמע מקיאבליסטי כלשהו, אבל ספר היסטוריה, מעצם מהותו, נועד למלא שליחות, וכזהו ספרי. חקר ההיסטוריה אינו מדע אובייקטיבי כמדעי הטבע; הוא מתיחס לבני־אדם, וכל העוסק בו לא יכול להיות משוחרר מנטיות אישיות. ואיזו דוגמה מאלפת לאי־אובייקטיביות זו מאשר ספרי ההיסטוריה של היהודים? אבל איך לענות על השאלה המתבקשת מאליה: האם רק הם סילפו?

זה עתה חזרתי מפגישה עם תלמידי החוגים להיסטוריה ולשפות שמיות באוניברסיטה, ואני חייב להודות שאך בקושי נחלצתי ממלכודת. בכלל לא קל ליצור קשר של אמון עם צעירים אלה, ודומה שאחדים מהם לא באים אלא כדי להפגין את השגותיהם ולהציק למרצה. אני מתכוון לקומץ קטן, שלושה או ארבעה בסך הכל, הפזורים בתוך למעלה ממאה איש באולם, אשר מאלצים אותך להפנות את דבריך אליהם ולנהל מעין דו־שיח אתם. השאר מגיבים בהנהוני ראש ובחיוכים, או שומרים על ארשת אטומה של פסיביות או אדישות. בכל פגישה עם סטודנטים בולטים במיוחד הקומוניסטים ודומיהם, שכל הסבר מקבלים בהרמת גבה או בהתנגדות מפורשת; והמרגיז הוא שהם מצליחים להדביק את סביבתם ויוצרים מצב של עימות לא רק אתם, אלא עם ציבור שלם. הם גם כמעט היחידים הבאים עם שאלות מוכנות, וכאילו בלי כל כונה להביך, מציגים את שאלותיהם בנימוס של תלמיד אל מורה. כך עשה אותו בחור שהציג לי קושיה הנשמעת הגיונית, ואמנם היא הגיונית בלי כל ספק, לאמור: אם על־פי המחקר המדעי אפשר לבטל בקלות את הטענה הסלפנית של היהודים שאברהם היה יהודי ואבי האומה העברית, כיצד נוכל להוכיח שהוא היה מוסלמי כפי שכתוב ב"קוראן"? מה יכולתי להשיב על שאלה זאת? לומר לו שאברהם לא היה מוסלמי כפי שלא היה יהודי, אם בכלל היה קיים? היושר המדעי מחייב להשיב כך, אבל האם אנו בתחום המדע הצרוף, או בזירת המאבק נגד אויב מתוחכם ורב תושיה?

מזל היה לי שמישהו מסר לי לפני ההרצאה חוברת שהוצאה מטעם לשכת ההסברה של מפלגת אל־בעת' הסורית ובה נטען בין השאר, כי עוד במאה השמונה־עשרה לפני הספירה נמצאו בדרום עיראק שבטים יהודיים שנדדו מחצי האי הערבי והמשיכו בנדידתם צפונה ומערבה עד שהגיעו לארץ כנען. לא האמנתי למראה עיני. מנין הביאו דברי הבל אלה? האם העתיקו מפרסומי תעמולה ציוניים, שכל מגמתם להחדיר לתודעת העולם שליהודים חזקה לא רק על פלסטין, אלא על כל האדמה הערבית מהפרת ועד הנילוס? התעלמתי משאלתו של הבחור ופתחתי בהתקפה על מחברי החוברת הזאת המפיצים תעמולה של האויב בשעה שמתכוונים כביכול

להזהיר מפניו. דיברתי גם על מדיניות ההסברה שלנו החוזרת בלי הרף על סיסמאות נדושות ואינה יורדת לשורש הבעיה, והיושב־ראש סמך ידו על דברי ואף הוסיף, כי ספרי ימנע מעתה משגים חמורים כאלה.

רוצה אני להאמין שכך אכן יהא, אם־כי ספר אחד, ואפילו עשרה ספרים לא ישנו מציאות. רק כוח ישנה מציאות, והכוח אינו לצידנו. זאת האמת. ובינתיים אנו טרודים במאבקים הקטנים שלנו ואיש נועץ צפורניו בגרון רעהו. חברה סוציאליסטית, מארכסיזם־לניניזם, מאויזם, כל אחד וספרי הקודש שלו. והצעירים עטים על כל תבשיל, ויהא באוש כאשר יהא, הבא מן החוץ! צברי התהלך בלונדון עם "הספר האדום" בכיסו וכל שאלה מצא לה שם תשובה. כך גם זוהייר. בחור עדין נפש, שבניגוד לצברי הוַכְחָן הבלתי־נלאה, הוא מקשיב בנימוס, אבל מדעותיו לא יזוז כמלוא הנימה. משחר ילדותו נטע בו קאסם את השקפותיו המרדניות והכניס אותו למסדר האמונה בגן העדן עלי אדמות! וכלוֹם עם קאסם אפשר היה להתוכח? שום דבר לא הסיט אותו מאמונתו, ולמרות כל האכזבות המשיך ללהג על תפקיד הפרולטריון במהפכה הסוציאליסטית! מאסרים, עינויים, פעם בפנים פעם בחוץ, ואיפה הוא עכשיו? אומרים בפראג, בודד בזקנתו.

אני את שלי עשיתי. מילאתי את חובתי. כלפי עצמי אולי יותר מאשר כלפי ציבור הקוראים. בדפים האלה אני יכול להיות גלוי־לב, ומה שלא אמרתי בספרי ובפרסומי האחרים, אומר כאן ללא חשש. בתקופת מעבר אנחנו, ובתקופה כזאת של חוסר יציבות, מן הנמנע להיות החלטי ורצוי לומר דברים לחצאים ולרביע, לעשות שעטנז, אחד בפה ואחד בלב, לפעמים שניים בפה ואחד בלב או להיפך. כזה הוא "היהודים בהיסטוריה". ספר לתקופת מעבר, מאמץ לגיבוש תודעה לאומית הנשענת על יסודות אותנטיים. ספר מחקר הוא, אך גם נושא שליחות. אם ישיג את מטרתו, אבוא על שכרי ולא אתגונן מפני מי שיאשימני בחוסר עקביות, באמירת דברים המשתמעים לשתי פנים. מי שממלא שליחות, שומה עליו לשאת בתוצאות.

הרהרתי בכל זה בדרך חזרה ונדמה לי שבות׳יינה היתה שותפה להרהורי, אבל היא שתקה, ורק כשהגענו הביתה אמרה: "אתה נראה עייף, הפגישות האלו מעייפות אותך." ברמזים היא מדברת. בטוחני שחשבה גם על המכתב של המורה שלה. עשיתי טעות ואין לי אלא להצטער על שנתפתיתי לשגר אליו את המבוא. לחצו עלי לקבל חוות־דעת של מומחים, ומשרד ההסברה הכין תרגום נאמן למבוא לאנגלית ולצרפתית. קיוו, כפי שגם אני קיויתי, לקבל תגובות מחמיאות כדי להביאן בהקדמות לספר, אבל לבד מפרופ׳ ארנסט גרסמוק מברזיל, ידידי משכבר הימים, אשר שלח מכתב שופע שבחים, איש לא השיב תשובה שיש בה ממש. התחמקו מתגובה, או הודו בנימוס על משלוח החוברת. רק המורה היהודי שלה לא ויתר על תגובה מעליבה. נודע לי שאתה מהנדס ועצתי לך שתלמד היסטוריה בטרם תגש לכתיבת היסטוריה! גסות כזו. הוא לא טרח אפילו לקרוא את מהלך החיים שלי, כי אז היה נוכח שהיסטוריה למדתי כשהוא היה עודנו נער. בות׳יינה היתה במצוקה וחשבה להשיב לו, אבל עצרתי

בעדה. לא רציתי שידע שהיא בתי. חוקר חשוב ומכובד, לידיד הערבים נחשב, והיא אך בראשית דרכה בעולם האקדמי. אמרתי לה אילו ידע מי אני ומה עברי היה מגיב בחריפות יותר. השתדלתי להעמיד פנים שאין הדבר מרגש אותי, אבל העלבון צורב ומחלחל בנשמה. אמרה לי שבפגישה הראשונה אתו תספר לו. לא עניתי. עד שתפגוש אותו, אם בכלל, לא יהיה לזה כל חשיבות. הוא אמר את דעתו והיא ודאי לא תצליח להפריך אותה. אני גם מנחש מה היא חושבת על הספר ומה היא חשבה היום בפגישה עם הסטודנטים. אתה עייף, הפגישות האלו מעייפות אותך. את מחשבותיה לא תגלה ואני מעדיף שלא לדעת אותן.

—SB

There is no one more qualified than me to point out the contradictions in *The Jews in History*, even though I stand behind every sentence in it. This might sound somewhat Machiavellian, but a book of history, through its very existence, has a mission to fulfill, and my book is no exception. Historical research is not an objective science like the natural sciences; it deals with people, and whoever deals with people cannot free themselves from personal predelictions. And what better example for a lack of objectivity could one provide than books on Jewish history? But how is one to respond to the obvious question that comes up—are they the only fabricators?

I've just come back from a meeting with students from the departments of History and Semitic Languages at the university and, I must admit, I just barely escaped a well-laid trap. It isn't at all easy to create a sense of trust with these students, and it almost seems like some of them just show up to demonstrate their expertise in harrassing the lecturer. I'm referring to a small number of them, three or four all in all, dispersed among more than a hundred in the lecture hall, who force you to turn your attention to them and conduct some sort of a dialogue with them. The rest respond with nods and smiles, or else just maintain an impermeable expression of passivity or indifference. In every encounter with students, the communists and their like especially stand out, bristling at every explanation or explicitly defying them. The most aggravating thing is that they manage to infect the whole atmosphere and create tension not only through themselves but among everyone else as well. They're also the only ones who come prepared with questions, but they aren't really interested in the answers even though they present them politely before their professors. That's what one guy did to me when he came up with a conundrum that seemed logical enough, and perhaps it even was: if, according to scientific research we can readily dismiss the fabricated contention of the Jews that Abraham was a Jew and father of the Hebrew nation, how can we prove that he was a Muslim, as it is written in the Quran? How could I possibly answer such a question? Should I have told him that Abraham was neither a Muslim nor a Jew, if he even existed? Scientific honesty would compel one to answer in this manner, but are we in the field of refined sciences here or in the theater of struggle against a cunning and resourceful opponent?

Luckily enough for me someone had given me a pamphlet before the lecture put out by the Syrian branch of the Ba'ath Party's Ministry of Information which claimed, among other things, that in 1800 B.C. there were already Jewish tribes in Southern Iraq that had migrated from the Arabian peninsula and simply continued north and west until they arrived to the Land of Canaan. I couldn't believe my eyes. How did they come up with such drivel? Had they just slavishly copied Zionist propaganda whose sole purpose was to penetrate the consciousness of the world with the notion that Jews laid claim not only to Palestine but to all the Arab lands from the Euphrates to the Nile? I avoided the student's question and instead began attacking the authors of the pamphlet for disseminating enemy propaganda at the same time that they claimed to be cautioning us against it. I also spoke about our own public relations policies which relentlessly kept repeating the same hackneyed slogans without tackling the roots of the problem; the chairman gave his full consent and even added that my book would prevent such drastic mistakes in the future.

I'd like to believe that's how it will be, but I don't think one or even a dozen books can change anything. Only power can change things, and power isn't on our side. That's the truth. And in the meantime, we're all wrapped up in our petty struggles while someone digs their nails into their fellow's throat. Socialism, Marxist-Leninism, Maoism, everyone has their holy book. And the young partake of every dish, no matter how spoiled, as long as it comes from someplace else! Sabry walked around London with the *Little Red Book* in his pocket and he found the answer to every question in it. The same with Zuhair. A refined young man, quite the opposite of the contentious and indefatigable Sabry, he always listened politely while never straying an iota from his opinions. Kassem nurtured the seeds of rebellion in him from an early age and when the time came he fell right into an earthly paradise of believers. And how could you possibly argue about anything with Kassem? Nothing budged him from his beliefs, despite all the disappointments and failures he continued prattling on about the role of the proletariat in the socialist revolution! Imprisonment, torture, he was always in and out—and now where is he? Some say he's in Prague, alone in his old age.

I did what I could. I fulfilled my obligation. Maybe more to myself than to my readers. In these pages I can be open and freely express whatever it is I wasn't able to in my other books. We're in a period of transition, and at times like this, when things are unstable, it's impossible to be decisive and preferable to say things that can be halved and quartered, to mix wool and linen, to say things that aren't in your heart, or not say the things that are. That's how it is with *The Jews in History*. A book for a time of transition, an effort to crystallize a national consciousness based on authentic premises. A scholarly text, but one bearing a message. If it achieves its goal, I'll have earned my keep and I won't have to defend myself before those accusing me of any lack of consistency, of saying things that can be interpreted ambivalently. Anyone setting out to fulfill a mission is obligated to bear the consequences.

I mulled all this over on our way back and it seemed like Butheina joined me in my ruminations, even though she kept quiet until we got home: "You look tired," she said, "these meetings are tiring you out." She spoke in allusions. I'm sure she was also thinking of the letter from her professor. I made a mistake and there is nothing I can do about it except regret that I let myself be persuaded to consign the introduction to him. They pressured me into accepting the reader's report, and the Ministry of Information prepared a faithful translation of the introduction into English and French. They hoped, as I too had hoped, to get supportive responses that could be included in the foreword but, other than Prof. Ernst Grassmok from Brazil, an old friend who sent a letter full of praise, no one responded with anything worth quoting. They either evaded it or politely thanked us for sending the introduction. Only her Jewish professor couldn't resist an insulting response. I'm well aware that you're an engineer, but I would advise you to teach some history before you start writing it! And so on. He didn't even bother reading my biography since he would have realized that I had studied history when he was still a kid. It disturbed Butheina and she wanted to write something back to him, but I stopped her. I didn't want him to know she was my daughter. An important and well-respected scholar, considered a friend of the Arabs, while she was just beginning her academic career. I told her that if he knew who I was and knew something about my past, his comments would have been even more virulent. I made out like it didn't bother me, but I felt the affront scathe me to my very soul. She told me that she would tell him everything at their next meeting. I didn't answer. By the time they met, if ever, it wouldn't even matter any more. He gave her his opinion and she certainly wouldn't be able to disprove it. I'm also trying to figure out what she thinks about the book and what she thought today at the student meeting. You're tired, these meetings tire you out. She won't reveal what she thinks and I prefer not knowing.

—*AA*

Outcast *is narrated by Haroun Soussan, a Jewish convert to Islam. Soussan's character is based on a historical figure, Ahmad (Nissim) Soussa, who converted to Islam in the 1930s and whose work ended up being used as a certain kind of propaganda during Saddam Hussein's regime. The narrator is a civil engineer and historian who has completed his life's work,* The Jews in History. *The book opens with him getting an award from the President (Saddam Hussein), during the period of the war between Iran and Iraq. The text we are reading, the novel, is his autobiography written at the age of seventy, the book he writes after having completed* The Jews in History, *and the book where he feels he can explore his own personal and political history more openly, particularly his relationship to his daughter, Butheina, and two friends, Kassem Abd al-Baki, a militant communist in political exile in Eastern Europe, and Nissim Assad, loosely based on the Iraqi Jewish writer Anwar Shaul.*

The novel contains many narrative issues that will be altogether too familiar in most parts of the world but which may present real problems to many American readers. To begin with, there are a number of entryways into the book itself, "fictional" suppositions that structure our relationship to the text and the world it depicts. The original text is in Hebrew, but the fictional narrator is telling his story in Arabic. The fact that this fictional narrator is a Jew who has converted to Islam and the author, Shimon Ballas, is an Arab Jew from Baghdad who emigrated to Israel in 1951 and only began writing in Hebrew in the mid 1960s, makes this entryway more like a hall of mirrors. So the text itself is already *a translation, in several senses: to begin with, it is a "fictional" construct, but it is also an intralinguistic text that has an Arabic basis even though it is written in Hebrew. Ballas has spoken about this in an interview I conducted with him in the mid 1990s:*

> *I think that for me the transition to another language is crucial, the use of language as a means. Yet language is not only a tool, language is also part of the personality. That's what makes this transition so difficult: you have to literally reconstruct yourself, you recreate yourself through a borrowed language. But I'm a Jew by chance—the realm of ideology, ideology as a world view, of Judaism, of Israel, of Hebrew, and the total identity between Hebrew and the Jews—none of that plays that much of a role with me. Zionist ideology is essentially an Ashkenazi ideology that developed in a different culture, in different surroundings, in a different world and which came to claim its stake here in the Middle East through alienation and hostility towards the surroundings, with a rejection of the surroundings, with no acceptance of the environment. I don't accept any of this, this is all very different from what I am. I am not in conflict with the environment, I came from the Arab environment and I remain in constant colloquy with the Arab environment. I also didn't change my environment. I just moved from one place to another within it. The whole project of a nationalist conception, of Zionist ideology, of the Jewish point of view, the bonds between Jews in the diaspora and Israel, all of this is quite marginal for me and doesn't play a major role, it's not part of my cultural world. I am not in dialogue with the nationalistic or Zionist point of view, nor am I in dialogue with Hebrew literature. I am not conducting a dialogue with them. If anything, I am in dialogue with language itself. On the one hand, I am trying to fend off, avoid or neutralize ideological connections or associations within the language. On the other hand, I think that I am probably trying to bring my Hebrew closer and closer to Arabic. This isn't done through syntax, but maybe through some sense of structure or way of approaching things. It is very abstract and I don't do it in a way that is completely conscious either. That's the problem, and it is extremely difficult to describe or quantify.*

As in all of Ballas's other works, the apparently conventional narrative masks extremely radical approaches to ideological and historical assumptions, particularly regarding the context of Zionism, the mystified relationship of Jews to language and the diaspora, but also to the history of Jews in the Arab world and their participation in the production of modern political life there. The passage excerpted here, for example, covers an enormous amount of shifting ground. To begin with, it was fairly standard practice for historians and academics living under such a totalitarian system to sustain covert or surrogate political and intellectual discourse by encoding historical works with messages pointing far beyond the materials under examination. In this case, we are presented with a group of students, identified as communists, questioning the Biblical narrative of Abraham. The novel's narrator then refers to a pamphlet put out by the Syrian Ba'ath party, an entity fiercely opposed to the Iraqi branch of the party, which seems to "slavishly" copy Zionist propaganda, allowing Jews to lay claim "not only to Palestine but to all the Arab lands from the Euphrates to the Nile" There are many levels at which we can read this, from the narrator's own point of view as a convert to Islam, whose relationship to the ruling Ba'ath party is always permeated by a certain aura of fear, or as a commentary injected by the author who was himself a communist and whose assumptions about Jews and Israel are definitively not based on any form of Zionist ideology. The narrator's own relationship to his daughter is affected by the publication of The Jews in History*—he himself is unsure of what she thinks about her father's position and how his position and public prominence might affect her own professional and public standing as an aspiring academic. Here, as throughout the novel, Ballas, the Iraqi exile, manages to provide an intimate history of the major events of a country he hasn't lived in since 1951, a narrative that also delineates his own sense of exile and attempts to translate and reconfigure his life in a language that might both embrace his former self and allow new selves to emerge. While our horizons in this country are very much geared towards literary texts that appear formally complex or technically innovative,* Outcast *never surrenders itself to any facile or fashionable rendering of the experience of exile. On the contrary, Shimon Ballas's insistence on historical specificity in a novel that is itself a clearly fictionalized construct, opens a very new and different space for politics, one that requires a reader to recalibrate their own assumptions about what radical writing might look like.—AA*

CHARLES BERNSTEIN, HAROLDO DE CAMPOS, LEEVI LEHTO, ERNESTO LIVON-GROSMAN, & TRADUCTION COLLECTIVE À ROYAUMONT

A Test of Poetry

A Test of Poetry

What do you mean by *rashes of ash*? Is *industry*
systematic work, assiduous activity, or ownership
of factories? Is *ripple* agitate lightly? Are
we *tossed in tune* when we write poems? And
what or who *emboss with gloss insignias of air*?

Is the *Fabric* about which you write in the epigraph
of your poem an edifice, a symbol of heaven?

Does *freight* refer to cargo or lading carried
for pay by water, land or air? Or does it mean
payment for such transportation? Or a freight
train? When you say a *commoded journey*,
do you mean a comfortable journey or a good train
with well-equipped commodities? But, then, why
do you drop the 'a' before *slumberous friend*? And
when you write, in "Why I Am Not a Christian"
You always throw it down / But you never
pick it up—what is *it*?

In "The Harbor of Illusion," does *vein*
refer to a person's vein under his skin or
is it a metaphor for a river? Does *lot*
mean one's fate or a piece of land?
And does *camphor* refer to camphor trees?
Moreover, who or what is *nearing*. Who or
what has *fell*? Or does *fell* refer to the
skin or hide of an animal? And who or what has
stalled? Then, is the *thoroughfare of*
noon's atoll an equivalent of *the template*?

In "Fear of Flipping" does *flipping* mean
crazy?

How about *strain*, does it mean
a severe trying or wearing pressure or
effect (such as a strain of hard work),
or a passage, as in piece of music?
Does *Mercury* refer to a brand of oil?

In the lines
shards of bucolic pastry anchored
against cactus cabinets, Nantucket buckets
could we take it as—pieces of pies
or tarts are placed in buckets (which
are made of wood from Nantucket)
anchored against cabinets (small
rooms or furniture?) with cactus?

What is *nutflack*?

I suppose the *caucus of caucasians*
refers to the white people's meeting
of a political party to nominate candidates.
But who is Uncle Hodgepodge?
And what does *familiar freight*
to the returning antelope mean?

You write, *the walls are our floors.*
How can the *walls* be floors if the floors
refer to the part of the room which forms
its enclosing surface and upon which one
walks? In *and the floors, like balls,*
repel all falls—does *balls* refer to
nonsense or to any ball like a basket ball
or to guys? Or to a social assembly for
dancing? *Falls* means to descend
from a higher to a lower
or to drop down wounded or dead?
But what is *the so-called overall*
mesh?

Is the *garbage heap* the garbage heap
in the ordinary sense? Why does
garbage heap exchange for *so-called*

overall mesh? Since a *faker* is
one who fakes, how can
arbitrary reduce to *faker*?

Who or what are disappointed
not to have been?

Does *frames* refer to form, constitution,
or structure in general? Or to a
particular state, as of the mind?

In the sentence,
If you don't like it
colored in, you can always xerox it
and see it all gray
—what is *it*? What does
colored in mean?

A few lines later you write,
You mean, image farm when you've got bratwurst—
Does *bratwurst* refer to sausage?
Does the line mean—the sausage
you saw reminded you of a farm which you imagined?

Does *fat-bottom boats* refer to boats with thick bottoms?
Is *humble then humped* used to describe the actions of one
who plays golf? In the phrase *a sideshow freak*—
the *freak* refers to a hippie? *Sideshow* refers to secondary
importance? Or an abnormal actor in the sideshow?
Then, who or what is *linked* with *steam of pink*. And
how about *the tongue-tied tightrope stalker*—
does the *stalker* refer to one who is pursuing
stealthily in the act of hunting game? The stalker
is a witness at first and then a witless witness?

You write *The husks are salted*:
what kind of nut husks can be salted for eating?
What does *bending* mean—to become curved,
crooked, or bent? Or to bow down in submission
or reverence, yield, submit? Does *bells*
refer to metallic sounding instruments or
a kind of trousers?

Just a few lines later you have the phrase
Felt very poured. Who felt poured? Toys?
Is *humming* in the sense of humming a song?
Stepped into where? *Not being part of* what?

In "No Pastrami" (*Walt! I'm with you in Sydney / Where the echoes of Mamaroneck howl / Down the outback's pixilating corridors*)—does the *pastrami* refer to a highly seasoned shoulder cut of beef? Is *Mamaroneck* a place in the U.S. where wild oxes howl? I take it *corridors* refers to the passageway in the supermarket? Could I read the poem as— The speaker is doing shopping in a supermarket in Sydney; he is walking along the eccentric passageways among the shelves on which goods are placed; he does not want to buy the pastrami as he seems to have heard the echoes of wild oxes howling in the U.S. while he addresses Walt Whitman?

In *No end to envy*, does the envy refer to admire or in the bad sense?

—*CB*

Um Teste de Poesia

O que você quer dizer com *impinges de cinzas*? *Indústria* é
um trabalho sistemático, uma atividade assídua, ou alude à posse
de fábricas? Encrespar é agitar levemente? Nós
entramos *em estado de transa* quando escrevemos poemas? E
que ou quem *gofra com glosas lustrosas insígnias de ar*?

A *Fábrica* sobre a qual você escreve na epígrafe
de seu peoma é um edifício, um símbolo do céu?

Frete refere-se a carga ou mercadoria carreada
mediante pagamento por mar, barra ou ar? Ou se reporta
ao preço do transporte? Ou a um trem
fretado? Quando você diz uma *viagem cômoda*
está querendo dizer uma viagem confortável ou um bom trem,
bem-equipado, com todas as comodidades? Mas, então, por
que você elimina o "um" antes de *amigo sonolento*? E
quando você escreve, em "Por que não sou cristão",
você sempre o deixa cair / Mas nunca o
apanha do chão esse *o* é o quê?

Em "Porto da Ilusão", *veia*
refere-se à veia de uma pessoa sob sua pele ou
é uma metáfora para rio? *Lote*
tem a ver com loteria-da-fortuna
de cada um ou com loteamento de terreno?
E *cânfora* refere-se a canforeiras?
Ademais, quem ou que se está *acercando*? Quem ou
que tem *felpas*? Ou felpa refere-se a
pelame ou tosão de um animal? E quem ou que
atolou? Então, a *rodovia* do atol do meio-dia é
equivalente a *molde ou módulo*?
Em "Pavor de Piparotes" *piparote* é o mesmo
que biruta?

Á propósito de *tensão*, significa
esforço intenso ou suportar pressão ou
efeito de (como em impacto de um trabalho duro),
ou uma passagem melódica numa peça musical?
Mercúrio refere-se a uma certa marca de óleo?

Nas linhas
parcelas de pastéis bucólicos ancorados
a gabinetes cactáceos, gamelas de Nantucket,
devemos entender isso como pedaços de empadas
ou tortas estão contidos em gamelas (que
são feitas de madeira de Nantucket)
acopladas a gabinetes (pequenas
salas ou peças de mobília?) guarnecidos de cáctus?

O que é *querela de matusquela*?

Suponho que o *caucus de caucasianos*
refira-se a cauto concíliábulo de adeptos brancos
de um apartido político para o fim de escolher candidatos.
Mas quem é Tia Mixórdia?
E o que quer dizer *vagão fretado familiar*
para antílope de torna-viagem?

Você escreve as *paredes são nossos assoalhos.*

Como podem *paredes* ser assoalhos se assoalho
refere-se à parte do aposento que forma
sua superfície inclusiva e sobre a qual a gente
pisa? Em *e assoalhos como bolas*
repelem todas as carambolas bolas refere-se
a quem não é bom da bola
ou a qualquer bola como uma bola de basquete
ou a um cara gabola? Ou a um clube de dança
onde se rebola? *Bola* em *carambola* é algo que baixa
de um ponto superior para um inferior
ou um corpo que ferido ou morto rola?

Mas o que é *a assim chamada geléia*
geral?

Um *monte de lixo* é o monte de lixo
no sentido comum? Por que
monte de lixo dá ideia de permutar com a chamada
geléia geral? Uma vez que *falsário*
é aquele que falsifica, como se pode
reduzir *arbitrário* a *falsário*?

Que ou quem está desapontado
por não ter sido?

Molduras refere-se a forma, constituição,
ou a estrutura em geral. Ou a um
estado particular, como o de espírito?

Na sentença,
Se você não gosta dele
colorido, você pode sempre xerocá-lo
e vê-lo inteirinho cinza
o que é esse *o*? O que quer
dizer *colorido*?

Algumas linhas adiante você escreve,
Você quer dizer, fazenda de imagens, quando conseguiu bratwurst—
Bratwurst refere-se a salsicha?
A linha significa a salsicha
que você viu lembrou-o de uma fazenda que você tirou da imaginação?

Botes com fundos fofos refere-se a botes com fundilhos balofos?

Usa-se *desbunda dando uma tunda* para descrever os atos de uma cara
que joga golfe? Na frase *um vagabundo de shows de segunda*
Vagabundo refere-se a bicho-grilo? *Show de segunda* refere-se a
de importância secundária? Ou a um ator anormal num show marginal?
Então, que ou quem entrosa com *vapor cor-de-rosa*? E
o que me diz do *espia-a-presa língua-perra na corda tesa*
espia refere-se a alguém que persiste contumaz na tocaia da caça?
O espia-a-presa é uma testemunha com toda a certeza,
mas, logo, vira uma testemunha que não sabe das mumunhas?

Você escreve: *As cascas estão salgadas*:
que tipo de cascas de nozes deve ser comido com sal?
O que significa *inclinar* ficar curvo,
corcunda ou inclinado? Ou curvar-se em submissão
ou reverência, render-se, sujeitar-se? *Sinos*
refere-se a instrumentos metálicos de som ou
a calças boca-de-sino?

Algumas linhas a seguir surge a frase
Sentiu-se muito encharcado. Quem sentiu-se encharcado? Brinquedos?
Cantarolando está usado no sentido de cantarolar uma toada?
Metido em quê? *Não-fazendo parte de* quê?

Em "Não temos Pastrami" (*Walt! Estou com você em Sidney / Onde os ecos do berro do Mamaroneck / Ao longo dos corredores abilolados dos cafundós de judas*) será que *pastrami* se refere a um bem-condimentado corte de bife de boi? Será que *Mamaroneck* é um lugar nos E.U.A. onde bois bravios berram? Devo entender que *corredores* refere-se às passagens no supermercado? Posso ler o poema como
O sujeito que fala está fazendo compras no supermercado em Sidney; está caminhando pelas excêntricas passagens entre prateleiras nas quais os produtos estão dispostos; não quer comprar pastrami uma vez que lhe parece ter ouvido os ecos de bois bravios berrando nos E.U.A. enquanto ele se dirige a Walt Whltman?

Em *A inveja não tem fim*, inveja refere-se a admiração ou tem sentido pejorativo?

—*HdC*

Runoustesti

Mitä tarkoitat *tuhkan pahkuroilla*? Onko *tuotanto*
organisoitua työtä, uutteraa askarrusta vaiko tehtaitten
omistamista? Onko *karehduttaa* yhtä kuin kevyesti sekoittaa? Ja kun
runoilemme, onko meidät silloin *singottu sointuun*? Entä
mitä tai kuka *pakottaa ilman kimaltavin arvonmerkein*?

Onko *Kudos* josta kirjoitat runosi
epigrafissa
rakennelma, taivaan symboli?

Viittaako *rahti* lastiin vai vesitse, maitse tai ilmateitse
korvausta vastaan kuljetettuun kuormaan? Vai tarkoittaako se
tällaisesta suoritettua maksua? Vaiko rahti-
laivaa? Ja kun sanot *tavaroitu matka*,
tarkoitatko miellyttävää matkaa vai hyvää junaa,
jossa on hyvin varustettuja tavaroita? Mutta miksi, näin ollen,
panet ilmaisun *unelias ystävä* nominatiiviin? Entä
kun kirjoitat runossasi "Miksi en ole kristitty?":
*"Aina sinä paiskaat sen alas / Etkä koskaan
nosta ylös"*, mikä on *se*?

Viittaako *suoni* runossa "Lakkaan satamasta" ehkä
henkilön ihon alla olevaan suoneen vai onko se
joen metafora? Tarkoittaako *osa*
ihmisen kohtaloa vaiko maaplänttiä, tonttia?
Kamferi kamferipuuta?
Edelleen: kuka tai mikä *lähestyy*. Kuka tai
mikä *vuotaa*? Vai tarkoitatko sittenkin
eläimen nahkaa tai turkkia? Ja kuka tai mikä on
kartellut? Niin, ja onko *keskipäivän atollin
läpikulkureitti* kenties sama asia kuin *malline*?

Mikä on *hiiteetuli*?

Entä kuka on Setä Sekameteli?
Ja mitä *palaavan antiloopin tuttu
rahtimaksu* mahtaa tarkoittaa?

Onko *roskaläjä* roskaläjä
tavanomaisessa merkityksessä? Miksi
roskaläjä vaihtaa paikkaa *niin sanotun*
yleisverkoston kanssa? Koska huijarin
työnä on huijata, kuinka
mielivaltainen voi pelkistyä *huijariksi*?

Ketkä tai mitkä ovat pettyneitä koska
eivät ole olleet?

Muutamaa riviä myöhemmin kirjoitat:
"Elikkä mielikuvamaatila kun lievä bratwurst on"—
tarkoittaako *bratwurst* makkaraa?
Tarkoittaako rivi: näkemäsi
makkara muistutti sinua kuvittelemastasi maatilasta?

Tarkoittaako *lösöpohjapaatit* veneitä joissa on paksut pohjat?
Kuvaako ilmaisu *nöyristeli, kyttyröityi* golfia pelaavan henkilön
toimintoja? Tarkoittaako *friikki* ilmaisussa *täytepalafriikki*
ehkä hippiä? Ja viittaako *täytepala* johonkin
toissijaiseen? Vai onko kyse välinäytöksessä esiintyvästä
epänormaalista näyttelijästä?
Entä kuka tai mikä liittyy *vaaleanpunan höyryyn*? Entä
sitten *änkyttävä nuorallaväijyjä*?—
viittaako *väijyjä* henkilöön joka etenee salakähmäisesti
riistaa metsästäessään? Tämä väijyjä on ensin
silmin-, sitten *silmitön* näkijä?

Muutamaa riviä myöhemmin käytät sanontaa
Tuntui kaadetulta kuin kannusta. Kenestä tuntui? Leluista?
Tarkoittaako *hyräillä* niin kuin laulua hyräillään?
Astui sisään mihin? *Olematta osa* mitä?

Runossa "Ilman pastramia!" (*"Walt! Olen kanssasi Sydneyssä / Missä*
Mamaroneckin kaiut / Takamaan
hourukäytävistä ulvahtaa")—tarkoittaako *pastrami* voimakkaasti
maustettua häränpalaleikettä? Onko
Mamaroneck yhdysvaltalainen paikkakunta jossa villihärät ulvovat?
Tulkitsen että *käytävät* viittaavat supermarketien
kulkuväyliin? Voisinko lukea runon näin:
puhuja on ostoksilla sydneyläisessä

supermarketissa ja kävelee pitkin eksentrisiä
kulkuväyliä hyllyjen lomitse joille tavarat on
aseteltu; hän ei tahdo ostaa pastramia
koska vaikuttaa kuulleen Yhdysvalloissa ulvovain
villihärkäin kaikuja puhutellessaan Walt Whitmania?

—*LL*

Una prueba de poesía

¿Qué quiere decir con *rusos rasos*? ¿Es *industria*
trabajo sistemático, trabajo intenso, o una
fábrica? ¿Es *ondular* agitarse levemente? ¿Cuando
escribimos poemas terminamos *transportados por el tono*? ¿Y
quién o qué *lleva labradas brillantes insignias de aire*?

¿La *Fábrica* que menciona en el epígrafe
de su poema es un edificio, o un símbolo celeste?

¿*Flete* se refiere a cargamento o al transporte de una carga
por tierra, aire o agua? ¿O se refiere al
pago por ese transporte? ¿O aun tren de carga?
¿O a un caballo? ¿Cuando dice un *viaje cómodo*
se refiere a una travesía confortable o a un tren
equipado con muchos servicios? Pero, entonces ¿por
qué suprime "un" justo antes de *amigo somnoliento*? Y
cuando en "Por qué no soy cristiano" escribe
Siempre lo tiras / pero nunca lo levantas ¿De qué se trata?

En "La bahía de la ilusión", *vena* se
refiere a la vena sanguínea o es una
metáfora de río? ¿Y la palabra *loteo* se
refiere a un pedazo de tierra o a
la suerte asociada con la lotería? ¿Y la palabra *alcanfor*
se refiere a los árboles del alcanfor? Aun más importante, ¿quién o
qué está *acercándose*? ¿Quién o qué ha *caído*? O *caído* ¿se refiere al cuero
o piel de un animal? ¿Y quién o qué se ha
detenido? ¿Entonces, el *atolón de la avenida*
al mediodía es el equivalente a *un patrón o modelo*?

En "Miedo a rayarse" ¿*rayarse* quiere decir
enloquecer?

¿Y en el caso de *forzar*, quiere decir
una prueba severa o una tensión o pasaje
desgastante (como en trabajo desgastante),
o un pasaje en una pieza de música?
¿La palabra *Mercury* refiere a una marca de aceite?

En los versos
Escamas de masas bucólicas ancladas
contra gabinetes de cactus, baldes de Nantucket
¿se trata de pedazos de tortas o
tartas colocadas sobre baldes (que están
hechos de madera de Nantucket)
anclados a gabinetes (¿pequeños ambientes o
muebles?) con cactus?

¿Qué es un *nutflack*?

Supongo que *asamblea caucásica*
refiere a la congregación de personas blancas
reunidas en un partido político para nominar candidatos.
Pero quién es el Tío Mescolancha
¿Y qué quiere decir un *envío familiar*
para el antílope que regresa?

Usted escribe que *las paredes son nuestros pisos.*
¿Cómo pueden las *paredes* ser los pisos si los pisos
son la parte de la habitación que limita ese
espacio y a la vez la superficie sobre la que se
camina? En *y los pisos, como bolas, repelen*
todas las olas—*bolas* es una referencia al
sinsentido o se trata de cualquier bola como en bola de billar
o bolas de hombres? ¿O a un rumor que se esparce
subrepticiamente? ¿Y *olas* quiere decir algo que se
eleva y luego baja o una moda transitoria?
¿Pero qué es *el supuesto tejido*
general?

¿Es la *pila de basura* la pila de basura
en el sentido corriente? ¿Por qué
cambiar *pila de basura por supuesto*
tejido general? Dado que *falsificador* es
aquel que falsifica, ¿cómo puede lo *arbitrario*
asimilarse a *falso*?

¿Quién o qué está desilusionado
por no haber podido ser?

¿El término *encuadres* se refiere a la forma,
a la constitución o a la estructura en general? ¿O a un
estado en particular como al hablar de estados mentales?

En la frase,
Si no te gusta
coloreado, lo puedes fotocopiar y
verlo todo en gris
¿A qué se refiere? ¿Qué quiere
decir *coloreado*?

Unos versos más tarde usted escribe,
Quieres decir, imagen de granja cuando has conseguido un
bratwurst. ¿*Bratwurst* se refiere a una salchicha?
¿El verso quiere decir que, la salchicha
que vio le recordó una granja imaginaria?

¿Botes con *fofos fondos* quiere decir botes con fondos gordos?
¿*Achaparrado por lo tanto jorobado* se utiliza para
describir a alguien que juega al golf? ¿En la frase *un loquito*
en un espectáculo de segunda el *loquito* es un hippie? ¿*De segunda* indica
que es de menor importancia o que el actor
que participa en el espectáculo es subnormal?
¿Y entonces quién o qué está *conectado a un vapor rosado*? ¿Y
qué pasa con *el acechador de la lengua tensa en la cuerda floja*?
¿El *acechador* es una persona que persigue furtivamente durante
la caza de una presa? ¿El acechador
es primero un testigo y luego un testigo tonto?

Usted escribe *Las cáscaras están saladas*:
¿qué clase de cáscaras se salan para ser comidas?
¿Qué quiere decir *doblarse*—volverse curvo,
encorvado, doblado? ¿O inclinarse en un gesto de sumisión
o en una reverencia, ceder u obedecer? *Campana* se
refiere a un instrumento metálico o a un
tipo de pantalones?

Unos versos más tarde usted escribe la frase
Se sintieron muy vaciados. ¿Quiénes se sintieron vaciados? ¿Los juguetes?
¿Es *canturrear* utilizado en el sentido de tararear una canción?
¿*Entrado en* dónde? ¿*No siendo parte de* qué?

En "Sin Pastrami" (*¡Walt! estoy contigo en Sydney / Dónde los ecos del Mamaroneck aúllan / A lo largo De los alocados corredores del llano*)—¿*Pastrami* se refiere A un corte de carne roja muy condimentado? ¿*Mamaroneck* Es un lugar de los EEUU donde aúllan los bueyes salvajes? ¿Debo suponer que los *corredores* son los pasillos de un supermercado? ¿Puedo leer el poema como que, El narrador está haciendo compras en un supermercado en Sydney, caminando por entre los excéntricos pasillos que separan las diferentes góndolas donde se encuentran productos, y no quiere comprar el pastrami porque le parece escuchar los ecos de bueyes salvajes aullando en los EEUU, mientras que le habla a Walt Whitman?

En "No hay fin para la envidia" ¿la palabra envidia se refiere a admiración o a una connotación negativa?

—*ELG*

Un test de poésie

Que veux-tu dire par *urticaire de cendre*? Est-ce qu'*industrie*
désigne le travail systématique, l'activité assidue ou la propriété
d'usines? *Onduler*, est-ce remuer légèrement? Est-on
porté par le ton quand on écrit des poèmes? Et
qui ou quoi *estampe avec les insignes brillants de l'air*?

Et cette *Fabrique* dont tu parles dans l'épigraphe
du poème, est-ce un édifice, un symbole céleste?

Est-ce que *fret* a rapport à cargaison ou acheminement
par mer, terre ou air? Ou s'agit-t-il
du prix du transport? Ou d'un train
de marchandises? Quand tu dis *un voyage commode*,
est-ce un voyage confortable ou un train
bien aménagé? Et aussi, pourquoi
éliminer l'article devant *ami dormeur*? Et
quand tu écris dans "Pourquoi je ne suis pas chrétien"
Tu le fais toujours tomber / Mais tu ne le
ramasses jamais—c'est quoi ce *le*?

Dans "Le port de l'illusion", est-ce que *veine*
désigne la veine de quelqu'un sous la peau ou
est-ce une métaphore pour fleuve? Par *lot*,
entends-tu sort ou bien lotissement?
Est-ce que *camphre* a rapport au camphrier?
Et puis, qui ou quoi *s'approche*? Qui ou quoi
est *tombée*? Ou est-ce que *tombée* fait référence
à la peau ou au pelage d'un animal? Et qui ou quoi
a *calé*? Et est-ce que le *boulevard*
de l'atoll de midi équivaut à *gabarit*?

Dans "La peur de flipper", est-ce que *flipper* veut dire
fou?

Et, pour *tension*, s'agit-il
d'une pression forte ou d'un effet d'usure
(comme un momentum de travailler dur)
ou un passage, comme en musique?
Mercury, est-ce une marque d'huile?

Dans les vers
fragments de pâtisserie bucolique ancrés
contre des cabinets de cactus, seaux de Nantucket
peut-on imaginer que—des parts de gâteau
ou de tarte sont mises dans des seaux
(en bois de Nantucket) ancrés contre des cabinets (petites
pièces ou meubles?) avec cactus?

Qu'est-ce que c'est *nutflack*?

Je suppose que le *bloc des Caucasiens*
fait allusion aux blancs réunis
en parti politique pour désigner des candidats.
Mais qui est Oncle Hodgepodge?
Et que veut dire *fret familier*
pour l'antilope qui revient?

Tu écris *les murs sont nos planchers.*
Comment les *murs* peuvent-ils être des planchers si les planchers
désignent cette partie de la pièce qui constitue
sa surface délimitée et sur laquelle on
marche? Dans *et les planchers, comme des boules,*
repoussent toutes les chutes—boule, c'est ici
n'importe quoi ou une boule comme aux boules
ou chez les mecs? Ou bien une soirée
dansante? *Chute* veut dire descendre
de haut en bas
ou tomber blessé ou mort?
Et quel est ce *prétendu réseau*
général?

Le *tas d'ordures*, est-ce le tas d'ordures
au sens habituel? Pourquoi échanger
tas d'ordures contre *prétendu*
réseau général? Puisqu'un *faussaire*
fabrique du faux, comment
arbitraire se réduit à *faussaire*?

Qui ou quoi est déçu
de ne pas avoir été?

Cadres renvoie-t-il à forme, composition
ou structure en général? Ou bien à
un état particulier, d'esprit par exemple?

Dans la phrase
Si tu ne l'aimes pas
en couleurs, tu peux toujours le photocopier
et le voir en gris
—c'est quoi ce *le*? Que veut dire
en couleurs?

Quelques vers plus bas tu écris
Tu veux dire: élevage d'images là où tu as bratwurst—
Est-ce que *bratwurst* renvoie à saucisse?
Est-ce que ce vers veut dire—la saucisse
que tu as vue te rappelle un élevage de ton imagination?

Les *bateaux culés* sont-ils des bateaux à gros cul?
Baissé-baisé sert-il à décrire
un joueur de golf en action? Dans l'expression un *monstre de foire*—
le *monstre* est-il un hippie? *Foire*, de banlieue?
Ou un anormal, acteur dans une foire?
Ensuite, qui ou quoi est *lié* à *vapeur de rose*? Et
ça, *le tueur sur fil bouche bée*—
le *tueur*, est-ce celui qui traque
furtivement le gros gibier? Le tueur
est-il d'abord un témoin puis un témoin béat?
Tu écris *les cosses sont salées*:
Quelle sorte de cosses de pois mangez-vous salées?
Que veut dire *courber*—s'incurver,
se tordre, se pencher? Ou bien s'incliner par soumission
ou respect, céder, se soumettre? Est-ce que *cloches*
renvoie à des instruments au son métallique ou
à un genre de pantalon?

Un peu plus bas tu emploies l'expression
senti très versé. Qui s'est senti versé? Les jouets?
Fredonner au sens de fredonner une chanson?
Entrer dans quoi? *Ne pas être des* quoi?

Dans "No pastrami" (*Walt! Je suis avec toi à Sydney / Où hurlent les échos de Mamaroneck / dans les couloirs pixélisés de la brousse*)—est-ce que *pastrami* renvoie
à une épaule de bœuf très épicée?
Mamaroneck, est-ce un endroit aux E.U. où hurlent les bœufs sauvages?
Les *couloirs*, ce sont bien les allées
du supermarché? Je propose cette lecture—
Le narrateur fait ses courses dans un supermarché
à Sydney; il se promène dans les allées
excentriques entre les rayons où sont disposés
les produits. Il ne veut pas acheter le pastrami
parce qu'apparemment il entend l'écho des bœufs sauvages
hurlant aux E.U. tout en s'adressant à Walt Whitman?

Dans *Pas de fin à l'envie*, est-ce que l'envie renvoie à l'admiration ou
à son sens mauvais?

—*Traduction collective à Royaumont dans le cadre de l'Atelier Cosmopolite*

"A Test of Poetry" was written in 1992 and published in My Way: Speeches and Poems *(University of Chicago Press, 1999). The poem is based on a letter from the Chinese scholar Ziquing Zhang, who translated poems from* Rough Trades *and* The Sophist *for* Selected Language Poems *(Chengdu, China: Sichuan Literature and Art Publishing House, 1993); quotations from the poems are italicized. It seemed to me that Ziquing Zhang's questions provided both an incisive commentary on my poems and also raised a set of imponderble yet giddy, not to say fundamental, translation issues. Several poets have taken up the task of translating this poem, and we here compile the results: Haroldo de Campos into Portuguese, Leevi Lehto into Finnish, Ernesto Livon-Grosman into Spanish, and Traduction collective à Royaumont dans le cadre de l'Atelier Cosmopolite into French (originally published in 1995 as a chapbook in the Format Américain series).—CB*

INGER CHRISTENSEN, SUSANNA NIED, & DENISE NEWMAN

Sommerfugledalen: Et Requiem / Butterfly Valley: A Requiem

II

I Brajčinodalens middagshede luft,
hvor al erindring smuldrer, og det hele
i lysets sammenfald med plantedele
forvandler sig fra duftløshed til duft,

går jeg fra blad til blad tilbage
og sætter dem på barndomslandets nælde,
naturens mest guddommelige fælde,
der fanger hvad der før fløj væk som dage.

Her sidder admiralen i sit spind,
mens den fra forårsgrøn, forslugen larve
forvandler sig til det vi kalder sind,

så den som andre somres sommerfugle
kan hente livets tætte purpurfarve
op fra den underjordisk bitre hule.

—IC

II

In the noon-hot air of Brajčino Valley
where all memory disintegrates, and everything
in the blending of plant parts and the light
transforms itself from scentlessness to scent,

I walk from leaf to leaf, going back,
setting them on the nettles of my childhood land,
nature's most divine traps,
which capture what once flew away as days.

Here sits the admiral in its cocoon
as from a spring-green, glutted caterpillar
it transforms itself to what we call a spirit

so that, like other summers' butterflies,
it can bring the dense crimson color of life
up from the bitter underground cave.

—*SN (literal translation)*

II

In Brajčino Valley's heated air of noon,
where memories disintegrate, and everything in sight
in the merging of parts of plants and light,
transforms itself from scentless to perfumed,

backward from leaf to leaf I make my way
placing them on nettles from that childhood land of mine,
of all nature's traps, the most divine
capturing there what once flew away as days

Here in its cocoon the admiral sits
once a spring-green greedy caterpillar
transforms itself into what we call spirit

so that like butterflies of summers long ago
it can bring life's dense crimson color
up from the bitter underground grotto.

—*DN (rhyming translation)*

Glare

Noonheated white stucco across the street
watering the dead plant like trying to remember
how to wake. Some color would avenge—
a lemon-headed, red-handed girl slip-
ping on a tongue-wave back to
where the interminable invisible music plays:
"it's over here. no, it's over here . . ."

—DN (recast translation)

This poem is the second in Butterfly Valley: A Requiem, *a fifteen-sonnet sequence by contemporary Danish poet Inger Christensen. In Danish, these sonnets sound simple and conversational, despite their unusual structural complexity. (The last line of each of the first fourteen sonnets is also the first line of the next. The fifteenth poem, the master sonnet, is made up on the first lines of each of the previous poems.) Christensen weaves images together in unpredictable patterns while keeping her rhyme and meter so natural that readers may barely notice them. Our first impulse as translators was to avoid compromising content, even if we had to forego rhyme and meter. Yet we found omitting these sound elements as problematic as including them. The content did not easily separate from its music. Through our collaboration, we discovered that simultaneous, multiple translations may provide the best representation of complex work such as Inger Christensen's.—DN & SN*

CHUANG TZU, ALLISON COBB, JEN COLEMAN, & BURTON WATSON

Come Out of Works: A Physical Translation

【今译】

颜渊要东行到齐国去，孔子面有担忧之色。子贡走下座位向前问道："学生斗胆问一下，颜回东到齐国去，先生面有忧色，是为什么呢？"

孔子说："你问得很好！从前管仲有句话，我十分赞同。他说：'袋子小就装不下大东西，绳子短就汲不起深井的水。'这样说来，认为性命各有它的形成之理，而形体各有它的适宜之处，这是不可改变的。我担心颜回去跟齐国国君讲尧舜之道或跟他重申燧人氏神农氏的圣言。齐国国君听了以后，会自己反省却不能领悟，不能领悟就会起疑心，起了疑心，就有杀身之祸了。

"你难道没有听说过吗，古时有只海鸟飞落在鲁国国都郊外，鲁侯把它迎进太庙，给它敬酒，奏《九韶》名乐给它取乐，宰牛羊给它吃。海鸟目光迷惑而心中悲哀，不敢吃一块肉，不敢饮一杯酒，到了第三天就死了。这是鲁侯用养他自己的东西去养鸟，不是用养鸟的东西去养鸟。用养鸟的东西去养鸟，就应该让鸟在深茂的树林里栖息，在沙滩上漫游，在江湖中漂浮，吃白鱼和泥鳅，随鸟群行列活动止息，自由自在地生活。鸟类最怕听到人类的声音，为什么还要这般喧哗呢！如果在洞庭的野外演奏《咸池》、《九韶》的音乐，鸟听见了就会飞走，野兽听见了就会逃走，鱼听见了也会沉入深水中，然而人听见了，却会围过来观赏。鱼在水中才能生存，人在水中就会淹死，人和

【原文】

恶故异也。故先圣不一其能，不同其事。名止于实，义设于适，是之谓条达而福持。"

列子行食于道从，见百岁髑髅，攓蓬而指之曰："唯予与汝知而未尝死，未尝生也。若果养乎？予果欢乎？"

种有几，得水则为继，得水土之际则为蛙蠙之衣，生于陵屯则为陵舄，陵舄得郁栖则为乌足。乌足之根为蛴螬，其叶为胡蝶。胡蝶胥也化而为虫，生于灶下，其状若脱，其名为鸲掇。鸲掇千日为鸟，其名为干馀骨。干馀骨之沫为斯弥，斯弥为食醯。颐辂生乎食醯；黄軦生乎九猷；瞀芮生乎腐蠸。羊奚比乎不箰，久竹生青宁；青宁生程，程生马，马生人，人又反入于机。万物皆出于机，皆入于机。

【今译】

鱼的生存必备条件各自不同，所以好恶也就不同了。因此圣人不要求人具有同等的才能，不要求他们做同等的事。名要和实际相符，事理的确定应该适合于各自的特性，这就叫做'条理通达而福气长存'。"

列子旅行中在路旁吃饭，看见一个上百年的骷髅，拔一根茅草指着它说："只有我和你知道你没有死，也没有生。你果真忧愁吗？我果真欢乐吗？"

生物中有一种极小的种类叫做"几"，它得水滋养便成为断续如丝的继草，在水土的交界处便长成青苔，生长在高地就变成车前草，车前草得到粪土滋养就长成乌足草，乌足草的根变成蝎子，它的叶变成蝴蝶。蝴蝶不久就化为虫，生在火灶底下，形状就像蜕化下来的皮，它的名字叫鸲掇。鸲掇虫过了一千天以后又化成鸟，名叫干馀骨。干馀骨的唾沫又变成斯弥虫，斯弥虫又变成酒缸里的蠛蠓虫。颐辂虫生于蠛蠓虫，黄軦虫生于九猷虫，瞀芮虫生于萤火虫。羊奚草和久不长笋的竹子结合就生出青宁虫，青宁虫生出豹，豹生出马，马生出人，人又复归于自然。万物都生于自然，又复归于自然。

—*CT*

Once a sea bird alighted in the suburbs of the Lu capital. The marquis of Lu escorted it to the ancestral temple, where he entertained it, performing the Nine Shao music for it to listen to and presenting it with the meat of the T'ai-lao sacrifice to feast on. But the bird only looked dazed and forlorn, refusing to eat a single slice of meat or drink a cup of wine, and in three days it was dead. This is to try to nourish a bird with what would nourish you instead of what would nourish a bird. If you want to nourish a bird with what nourishes a bird, then you should let it roost in the deep forest, play among the banks and islands, float on the rivers and lakes, eat mudfish and minnows, follow the rest of the flock in flight and rest, and live any way it chooses. A bird hates to hear even the sound of human voices, much less all that hubbub and to-do. Try performing the Hsien-ch'ih and Nine Shao music in the wilds around Lake Tung-t'ing—when the birds hear it they will fly off, when the animals hear it they will run away, when the fish hear it they will dive to the bottom. Only the people who hear it will gather round to listen. . . .

Lieh Tzu was on a trip and was eating by the roadside when he saw a hundred-year-old skull. Pulling away the weeds and pointing his finger, he said, "Only you and I know that you have never died and you have never lived. Are you really unhappy? Am I really enjoying myself?"

The seeds of things have mysterious workings. In the water they become Break Vine, on the edges of the water they become Frog's Robe. If they sprout on the slopes they become Crow's Feet. The roots of Crow's Feet turn into maggots and their leaves turn into butterflies. Before long the butterflies are transformed and turn into insects that live under the stove; they look like snakes and their name is Ch'ü-t'o. After a thousand days, the Ch'ü-t'o insects become birds called Dried Leftover Bones. The saliva of the Dried Leftover Bones becomes Ssu-mi bugs and the Ssu-mi bugs become Vinegar Eaters. Yi-lo bugs are born from the Vinegar Eaters, and Huang-shuang bugs from Chiu-yu bugs. Chiu-yu bugs are born from Mou-jui bugs and Mou-jui bugs are born from Rot Grubs and Rot Grubs are born from Sheep's Groom. Sheep's Groom couples with bamboo that has not sprouted for a long while and produces Green Peace plants. Green Peace plants produce leopards and leopards produce horses and horses produce men. Men in time return again to the mysterious workings. So all creatures come out of the mysterious workings and go back into them again.

—BW

Translation of Chuang Tzu with the Noise of the Shower Running

Haven't you heard of the suburb seabird
that capitals and temples entertains
with its meat and listing?

Feasted-on bird looks dazed. Three days
and it was dead. Don't feed the bird
what you would eat. Let it eat mud

fish, minnows and the sound of human voices.
You shall music in the wild. Fly off or dive
to the fish and thrive. Or die.

Eat by the roadside: a 400-year-old
skull and finger that never died.
Am I really enjoying myself? Mysterious

slippers enjoy cow feet, rabbits
and dragonflies. Bugs under the stove.
Bug munches bug from rat nearby.

Produce green peace plants,
leopards produce horses, men. All creatures
come out of works and go back again.

—AC & JC

Translation of Chuang Tzu from Behind Smeared Glasses

Hiving you heaved toward the sea. A capital
three. Canned meat lists toward fists. Eat

minnows, wild flies, fly off to dine.
Die at the bottomfish and thrive.

The former man had good Reason.
Eat by the road skull and finger.

I am really enjoying myself. Figs and slippers feel
crowd feels. Rabbits and dragonflies dried after bone shy.

Creatures come on to the mysterious works and go back in again.

—AC & JC

Translation of Hearing Chuang Tzu While Not Looking at the Writing Page

Living you hewed toward the sea
Three lists to feast
Dazed three days

Don't feed the bird, turned
Let it eat this minnow
The bottomfish thrive or die

Mysterious seeds fly from the rat
Produce produce produce
Mysterious works go back to them

—*AC & JC*

Translation of Hearing Chuang Tzu from a Cell Phone on Street

Near-living hewed to the feed.

Birds suffer free and inert.

A bird look day.

What would you eat?

Minnows, the sound and fly-off autumn fish.

The summer is food, eat by the road.

A fingerlet seeds and slips murder.

Fucked murder.

Steal a rabbit and dragon.

Feet, dried leftover bones.

Leopards, meat creatures of the mystery of works and back.

—*AC & JC*

Translation of Hearing Chuang Tzu from a Cell Phone in a Check-Cashing Office

Lying never hued
to the bird look.
Days, voices in
the summer food
fingerlet. Never food
produces feet
mysterious and go
back to them:
peace pants and dress
feet dried left mango
bones and email.
Man food died of
hammer voices borne
to the fed bone immute.

—AC & JC

Translation of Chuang Tzu from Pictographs (omitted)

Nesting to keep from flood
leads the sun to be buried, not swallowed
sun flooded to love bleeding seed-sun.

And country of sun. Going out
a tidal wave of leaving
safe countries undo.

The sun has babies,
countries,
cars plus stop and go.

A big belly leads to babies, to suckers,
lollipops, basketball pants and geometry.
Countries border diseases, stop guy lollipop.

Bone friends and mail.
Sun, sunburn, lollipop guy and what?
The mysterious spot near the nose:

Disease in the mail, or on it, touching it
like jellyfish or suns leaking leads
to diseases of bones, not leaving.

—*AC & JC*

For this collaborative translation project, we chose a text attributed to the Chinese philosopher Chuang Tzu who lived around 350 B.C. *and who is credited with helping found the Taoist school. Chuang Tzu interprets the workings of the Tao through the physical qualities of the world—animals, landscapes, physical objects. In this spirit, we interpreted the lessons of Chuang Tzu through the physical qualities of our bodies: hearing, sight, physical movement. As the lessons of Chuang Tzu are shaped and obscured by the passing of time and boundaries of language, so our translation is obscured by the boundaries of our senses. We heard the poem through the noise of a shower, challenged our vision with smeared glasses, challenged our physical abilities as draftspeople by translating into pictographs, and in other ways "translated" Chuang Tzu's lessons through the fog of the physical world. The text from which we worked was translated into English in 1964 by Burton Watson. He notes that Chuang Tzu's text is "doubtful at many points." If, as Lao Tzu says, the Tao is incommensurable, a doubtful text is the best interpretation. Our "physical" translation attempts to honor the unknowable nature of the Tao.—AC & JC*

MICHAEL CUEVA

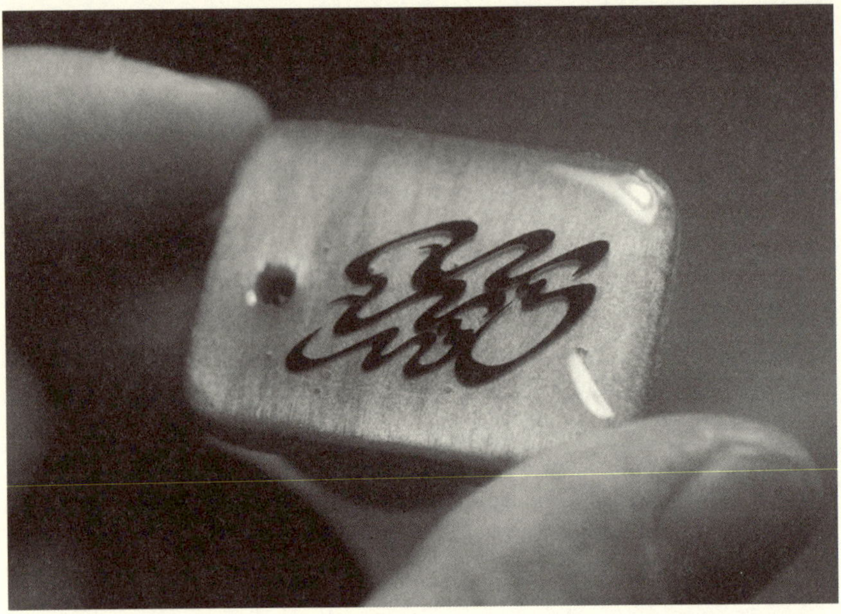

*A*RT: *These amulets were a part of an exhibition called "Invoke:Evoke," a two-man show with Philippine artist Perry Mamaril and myself. It was held in New York in November 1998 at a place called Cendrillon and curated by Jeff Baysa.*

The idea of the show was about superstition, belief, motivation, and a person's faith. This was specifically based on the idea that there are Filipinos all over the globe, even in the most unlikely places. How would they deal with new culture? This is how we came up with the physical forms for the art: altars and amulets.

*A*MULETS: *These amulets were derived from ancient Philippine script called Alibata or Baybayin. These scripts were often associated with secret prayers that gave the user special abilities. With these amulets, I based the script on a single word and stylized the form to make it almost indecipherable to others.*

Alaala: *to remember*
Kalingain: *to endure*
Lahi: *nation or ethnicity*
Makatiis: *to endure (to be able to)*
Matibay: *strong; like a material (metal, stone, wood . . .)*

*S*IZE: *approximately 1.75" x 1"*
*M*ATERIALS: *wood, resin, overhead transparencies, laser toner*

DANTE & CAROLINE BERGVALL

VIA (48 Dante Variations)

Nel mezzo del cammin di nostra vita
mi ritrovai per una selva oscura
che la diritta via era smarrita

—Dante, *The Divine Comedy*, Part 1, Inferno, Canto I (1-3)

First Series

1 Along the journey of our life half way
I found myself again in a dark wood
wherein the straight road no longer lay
2 At the midpoint in the journey of our life
I found myself astray in a dark wood
For the straight path had vanished.
3 Half over the wayfaring of our life,
Since missed the right way, through a night-dark wood
Struggling, I found myself.
4 Half way along the road we have to go,
I found myself obscured in a great forest,
Bewildered, and I knew I had lost the way.
5 Halfway along the journey of our life
I woke in wonder in a sunless wood
For I had wandered from the narrow way
6 Halfway on our life's journey, in a wood,
From the right path I found myself astray.
7 Halfway through our trek in life
I found myself in this dark wood,
miles away from the right road.
8 Half-way upon the journey of our life,
I found myself within a gloomy wood,
By reason that the path direct was lost.
9 Half-way upon the journey of our life
I roused to find myself within a forest
In darkness, for the straight way had been lost.
10 In middle of the journey of our days
I found that I was in a darksome wood
the right road lost and vanished in the maze

11 In midway of the journey of our life
I found myself within a darkling wood,
Because the rightful pathway had been lost.

12 In our life's journey at its midway stage
I found myself within a wood obscure
Where the right path which guided me was lost

13 In the middle of the journey
of our life
I came to myself
in a dark forest
the straightforward way
misplaced.

14 In the middle of the journey of our life I came to
myself in a dark wood, for the straight road was lost

15 In the middle of the journey of our life I came to myself
within a dark wood where the straight road was lost.

16 In the middle of the journey of our life
I found myself astray in a dark wood
where the straight road had been lost sight of

17 In the middle of the journey of our life, I found myself
in a dark wood; for the straight way was lost.

18 In the mid-journey of our mortal life,
I wandered far into a darksome wood,
Where the true road no longer might be seen.

19 In the midtime of life I found myself
Within a dusky wood; my way was lost.

20 In the midway of this our mortal life,
I found me in a gloomy wood, astray,
Gone from the path direct:

21 I was in the middle of my life when I found myself in a
dark wood, for I no longer knew the way

22 Just halfway through this journey of our life
I reawoke to find myself inside
a dark wood, way off-course, the right road lost

23 Midway along the highroad of our days,
I found myself within a shadowy wood,
Where the straight path was lost in tangled ways.

24 Midway along the journey of our life
I woke to find myself in some dark woods,
for I had wandered off from the straight path.

25 Midway along the span of our life's road

I woke to a dark wood unfathomable
Where not a vestige of the right way shewed.

26 Midway in our life's journey I went astray
from the straight road & woke to find myself
alone in a dark wood

27 Midway in the journey of our life I found myself in a
dark wood, for the straight road was lost.

28 MIDWAY life's journey I was made aware
That I had strayed into a dark forest,
And the right path appeared not anywhere.

29 Midway on our life's journey, I found myself
In dark woods, the right road lost.

30 Midway on the journey of our life I found myself within
a darksome wood, for the right way was lost.

31 Midway the path of life that men pursue
I found me in a darkling wood astray,
For the direct way had been lost to view

32 Midway this way of life we're bound upon,
I woke to find myself in a dark wood,
Where the right road was wholly lost and gone

33 MIDWAY upon the course of this our life
I found myself within a gloom-dark wood,
For I had wandered from the path direct.

34 MIDWAY upon the journey of my days
I found myself within a wood so drear,
That the direct path nowhere met my gaze.

35 MIDWAY upon the journey of our life,
I found me in a forest dark and deep,
For I the path direct had failed to keep.

36 Midway upon the journey of our life,
I found myself within a forest dark,
For the right road was lost.

37 MIDWAY upon the journey of our life
I found myself within a forest dark,
For the straightforward pathway had been lost.

38 Midway upon the journey of our life
I found that I had strayed into a wood
So dark the right road was completely lost.

39 MIDWAY upon the journey of our life
I woke to find me astray in a dark wood,
Confused by ways with the straight way at strife

40 Midway upon the pathway of life
I found myself within a darksome wood
wherein the proper road was lost to view.
41 MIDWAY upon the road of our life I found myself within
a dark wood, for the right way had been missed.
42 On traveling one half of our life's way,
I found myself in darkened forests when
I lost the straight and narrow path to stray.
43 Upon the journey of my life midway,
I found myself within a darkling wood,
Where from the straight path I had gone astray
44 UPON the journey of our life half way,
I found myself within a gloomy wood,
For I had missed the oath and gone astray.
45 Upon the journey of our life midway
I came unto myself in a dark wood,
For from the straight path I had gone astray.
46 Upon the journey of our life midway,
I found myself within a darksome wood,
As from the right path I had gone astray.
47 When half-way through the journey of our life
I found that I was in a gloomy wood,
because the path which led aright was lost.
48 When I had journeyed half of our life's way,
I found myself within a shadowed forest,
for I had lost the path that does not stray.

Second Series

20 Rev. Henry F. Cary, 1805
17 John A. Carlyle, 1844
46 Cayley, 1851
34 Thomas Brooksbank, 1854
8 F. Pollock, 1854
11 William Michael Rossetti, 1865
12 David Johnston, 1867
37 Henry Wadsworth Longfellow, 1867
44 Warburton Pike, 1881
10 James Sibbald, 1884
43 James Innes Minchin, 1885

35 John Augustine Wilstach, 1888
41 Charles Eliot Norton, 1891
3 George Musgrave, 1893
6 T. W. Parsons, 1893
30 Sir E. Sullivan, 1893
36 Marvin R. Vincent, 1904
23 C. E. Wheeler, 1911
18 Gauntlett Chaplin, 1913
19 Edith Mary Shaw, 1914
40 Edward J. Edwardes, 1915
9 Henry Johnson, 1915
47 Courtney Langdon, 1918
31 Melville B. Anderson, 1921
45 Jefferson Butler Fletcher, 1931
28 Laurence Binyon, 1933
33 R. T. Bodey, 1938
15 John D. Sinclair, 1939
32 Dorothy Sayers, 1949
39 Geoffrey Bickersteth, 1955
25 Fr. Kenelm Foster, 1961
27 Charles S. Singleton, 1970
24 Mark Musa, 1971
38 Kenneth MacKenzie, 1979
48 Allen Mandelbaum, 1980
4 C. H. Sisson, 1980
22 Tom Phillips, 1983
2 Patrick Creagh and Robert Hollander, 1989
21 Kathy Acker via Don Quixote, 1986
6 Seamus Heaney, 1993
42 Stephen Wentworth Arndt, 1994
29 Robert Pinsky, 1994
7 Steve Ellis, 1994
26 John Ciardi, 1996
1 Peter Dale, 1996
14 Robert Durling, 1996
5 Elio Zappulla, 1998
13 Armand Schwerner, 2000

Translations into English of Dante's Inferno as archived by the British Library—spring 2000 (700 years after the date fixed by Dante for the start of the journey).—CB

RUBÉN DARÍO & FRANCISCO ARAGÓN
Walt Whitman

Walt Whitman

En su país de hierro vive el gran viejo,
bello como un patriarca, sereno y santo.
Tiene en la arruga olímpica de su entrecejo
algo que impera y vence con noble encanto.

Su alma del infinito parece espejo;
son sus cansados hombros dignos del manto;
y con arpa labrada de un roble añejo
como un profeta nuevo canta su canto.

Sacerdote, que alienta soplo divino,
anuncia en el futuro, tiempo mejor.
Dice al águila: "¡Vuela!"; "¡Boga!", al marino,

y "¡Trabaja!", al robusto trabajador.
¡Así va ese poeta por su camino
con el soberio rostro de emperador!

—*RD*

Walt Whitman

In his country of iron lives the great old man,
beautiful like a patriarch, serene and saintly.
He has in the olympic furrow of his brow
something that rules and wins with noble charm.

His soul of the infinite resembles a mirror;
his tired shoulders merit a cloak;
and with a harp carved from ancient oak
like a new prophet he sings his song.

Priest, who feeds a divine wind,
announces a future of better times.
He says to the eagle: "Fly!"; "Row!," to the seaman,

and "Work!," to the robust worker.
This is how that poet goes down his path
with his magnificent emperor's face!

—*FA*

His Country of Iron Where He Lives

His country of iron where he lives: an older man, fatherly, strong,
wholesome, calm,
his appearance impressive—the furrow of his brow persuades and
charms, no end

to his soul that mimics a mirror, the tired curve of his shoulders
draped with a cloak;
and with his harp—carved from ancient oak—he sings his song
like a prophet. He's a priest

fueling a wind that promises and promises . . . *Fly!*, he says to an
eagle, to a seaman: *row!*
while a chiselled, robust worker hears: *put your shoulder to the
wheel!* This is the path

our poet takes
—magnificent

majestic face.

(on Walt Whitman)

—*FA*

My father boarded a plane in Nicaragua. Six months after he landed in San Francisco, he sent for my mother, who arrived in time to give birth to my sister. I was born ten years later, the youngest of four. Any "note on methodology," where my work with Rubén Darío is concerned, must begin with this fact. In other words, it is a very personal project—one that has evolved over the years and has only recently matured. A number of things had to happen along the way.

Before I became interested in poetry at UC Berkeley, my identity as a Latino of Nicaraguan descent was an integral part of how I viewed myself. This included knowledge of Rubén Darío. Before I read him, I heard him: lines my mother would recite . . . La princesa está triste. Qué tendrá la princesa . . . Dichoso el árbol que es apenas sensitivo . . . *when I was a child.*

There were crucial mentors. The late hispanista, John K. Walsh, took me under his wing as his co-translator of Lorca's homoerotic sonnets. Poet Francisco X. Alarcón made me his translator—a collaboration that produced four books. In the interim, I lived, taught, and traveled in Spain for ten years. Among the work I did there was render the creationist verse of Gerardo Diego, under the tutelage of Louis Bourne, one of the best but least known translators of modern Spanish poetry.

Upon my return to California, I revisited Rubén Darío—exclusively in Spanish this time. (I had been familiar with him in lackluster English as a teenager.) Given the conceptual nature of his work, I concluded that conventional modes of translation just weren't going to produce pleasurable poems in English. One day I decided to "rewrite" or, for lack of a better term, "imitate" my favorite poem of his, "Lo Fatal." The result was "The Inevitable," which was published in the Latino magazine, El Andar. *But the question nagged at me. Was this a legitimate literary endeavor? Another part of me, given my background and trajectory, felt that I had every right to approach Darío's work in this way—to approach it with reverence, affection, and make something new . . . for English readers.*

All doubts vanished when I met John Matthias. The poem that appears in Chain *was done in his class at Notre Dame. His workshop was organized around the idea of translation as a paradigm for apprenticeship to poetry writing. My method, finally, was something between translation and imitation—purely intuitive and organic. The long lines in the final version felt right, given the subject matter of the poem—Walt Whitman.*

During the many years Darío spent in Europe, before returning to die in his native Nicaragua in 1916, he was known by his first name, and first name alone. The working title of the collection I envision is "Versions of Rubén."—FA

ALBERT FLYNN DESILVER
Mto Mwivi / River Thief

Mto Mwivi

hatuna fedha. kizu kikali.
hana akili. vipandi vingi.
kisima hakina maji. mzigo myepesi.

una mayai?
mikia mifupi.
wana kalamu?
wevi werevu.
vipofu wachache.
sina.

wanazo. nchi pana.
mna taa? mke mvivu.
hatuna. kuku mwekundu.
hakuna jibu!
jino jeupe.
hamna kitu ndani.
kalamu ndefu.
hapana nafasi!
maziwa safi.

masanduku yaliyokuwa na nguo.
miti myembamba.
vitu vyote alivyo navyo.
wino mweusi. mbegu zote nilizokuwa nazo.
ndimi nyekundu.
kila kuku aliyekuwa naye.
askari hodari.
yule aliyekuwa na ndizi.
nyama mbichi. watu watakaokuwa na majembe.
maswali magumu.

vitabu ulivyo navyo;
nchi isiyo (kuwa) na mvua

maneno matupu;
mahali pasipo maji.

River Thief

we have no money. a sharp knife.
he has no sense. many pieces.
the well has no water. light loads.

have you any eggs?
short tails.
have they pencils?
cunning thieves.
a few blind men.
i have none.

they have. wide country.
have you lamps? an idle wife.
we have not. a red hen.
there is no answer!
a white tooth.
there is nothing inside.
a long pencil.
there is no time!
pure milk.

the boxes which had clothes.
slender trees.
all the things which he had.
black ink. all the seeds which I had.
red tongues.
every fowl which he had.
brave soldiers.
that (man) who had bananas.
raw meat. the men who will have hoes.
hard questions.

the books you have;
a rainless country

empty words;
a waterless place.

A collaged translation from the Swahili of D. V. Perrott in Teach Yourself Swahili, *English University Press, London, 1951.*

RAINER GANAHL

My First 500 Hours Basic Arabic, 2002
500 hours video, 250 VHS tapes of 120 minutes in 25 boxes

This work consists of studying Arabic. I film myself studying Arabic, by myself or with the help of somebody. This work is part of my study series that I started in the early 1990s with Japanese, followed by Modern Greek (the German Orient), Russian, Korean, and Chinese.

Basic Arabic, Slides (part of approximately 250 slides that I take of myself while studying—each day I study at least 2 hours a slide)

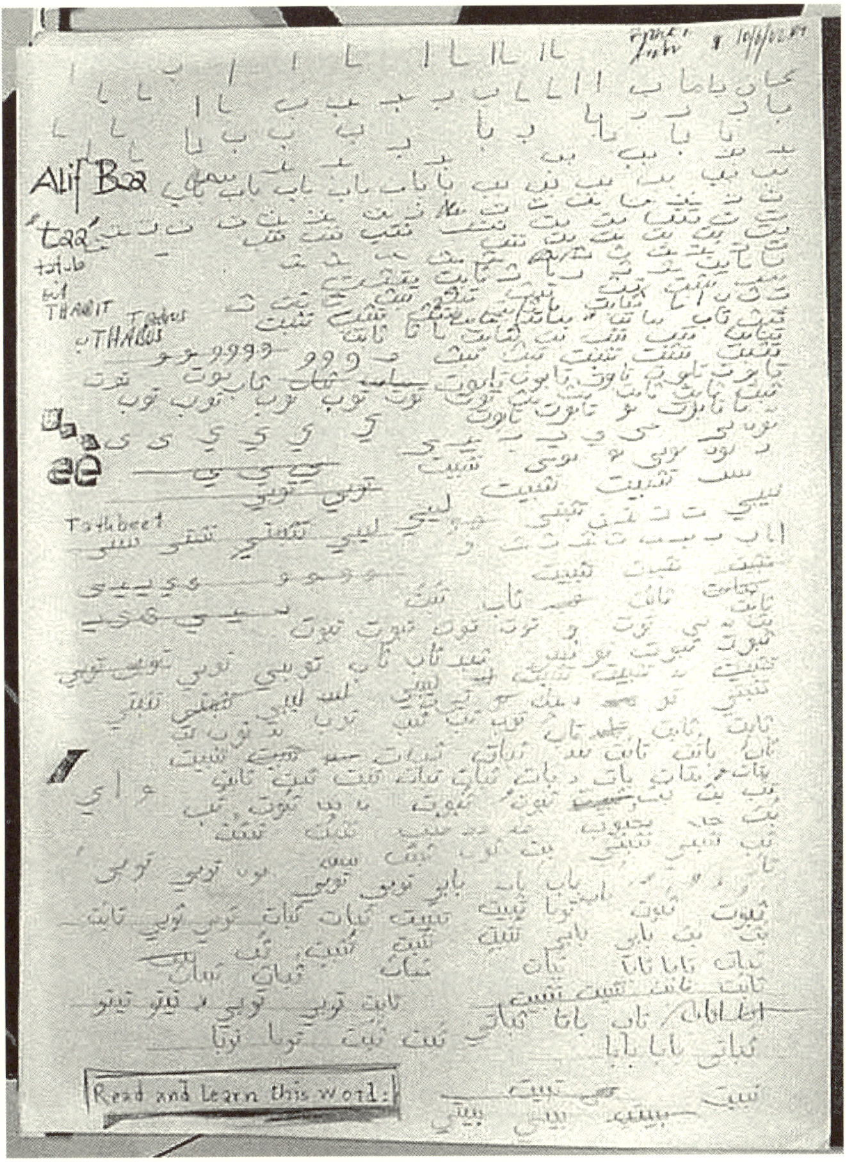

Basic Arabic, Study Sheet, 10/6/02, NYC, work on paper, 9 x 12 inches, 2002

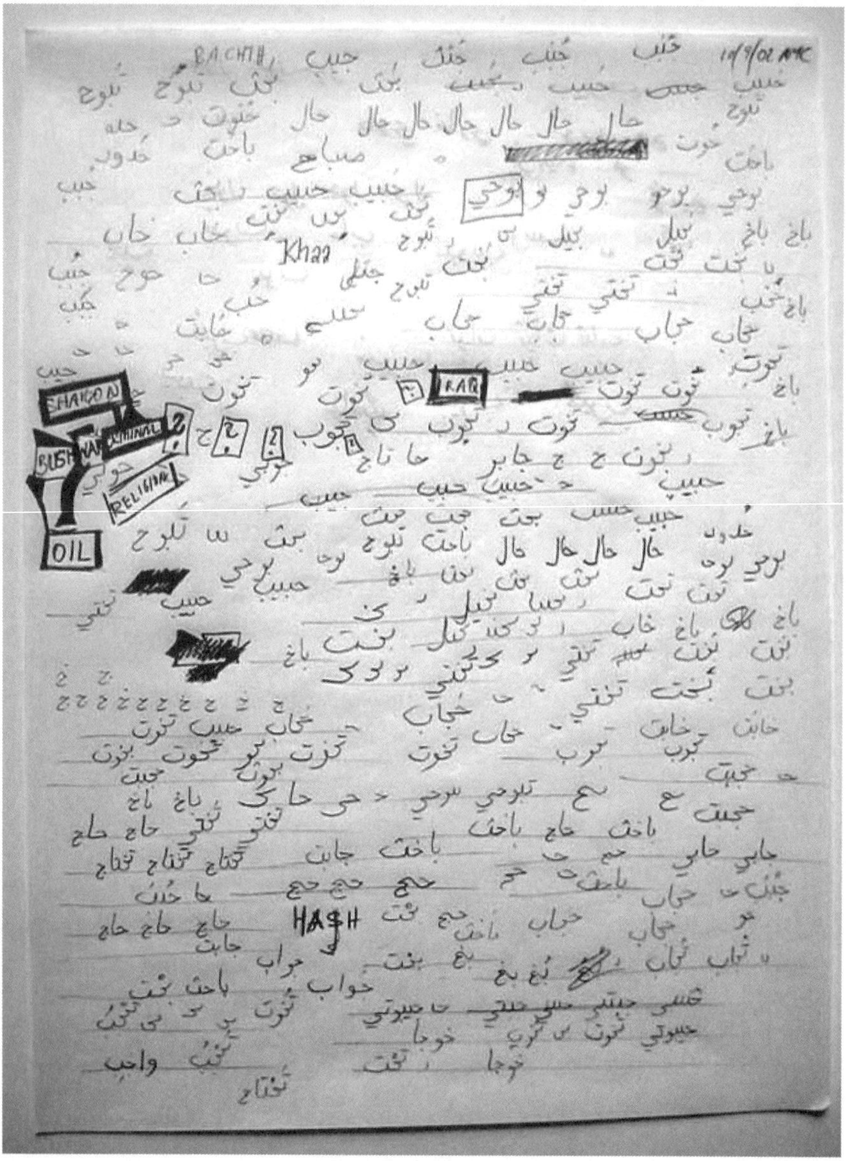
BACHTH
Khaa
IRAQ
SHARON
BUSH
WAR
RELIGION
OIL
HASH

JVC
VHS
SX
Premium Quality
GOLD
T-120 SX
120
SX
Rainer Ganahl
My First 500 Hours Basic Arabic
New York, 10/14/02
assisted by:
1/2
JVC
SX
Rainer Ganahl
My First 500 Hours Basic Arabic
New York, 10/13/02
assisted by:
1/2
JVC
SX
Rainer Ganahl
My First 500 Hours Basic Arabic
New York, 10/11/02
assisted by:
1/2
JVC
SX
Rainer Ganahl
My First 500 Hours Basic Arabic
New York, 10/10/02
assisted by:
1/2
JVC
SX
Rainer Ganahl
My First 500 Hours Basic Arabic
New York, 10/9/02
assisted by:
1/2
JVC
SX
Rainer Ganahl
My First 500 Hours Basic Arabic
New York, 10/8/02
assisted by:
1/2
JVC
SX
Rainer Ganahl
My First 500 Hours Basic Arabic
New York, 10/7/02
assisted by:
1/2
JVC
SX
Rainer Ganahl
My First 500 Hours Basic Arabic
New York, 10/6/02
assisted by:
1/2
JVC

Arabic: Each date represents one VHS tape = 2 hours studying; 10 dates = 1 box
10/6/02 New York
10/7/02 New York
10/8/02 New York
10/9/02 New York
10/10/02 New York
10/11/02 New York
10/12/02 New York
10/14/02 New York
10/13/02 New York
11/1/02 New York
20 hours
11/2/02 New York
11/3/02 New York
11/4/02 New York
11/5/02 New York
11/6/02 New York
11/7/02 New York
11/8/02 New York
11/9/02 New York
11/10/02 New York
11/11/02 New York
40 hours
11/12/02 New York
11/14/02 New York
11/16/02 New York
11/18/02 Utrecht, assisted by Hikmat Hemary
11/19/02 Utrecht
11/19/02 Utrecht, assisted by Hikmat Hemary
11/20/02 Utrecht, assisted by Hikmat Hemary
11/21/02 Utrecht, assisted by Hikmat Hemary
11/22/02 Utrecht, assisted by Hikmat Hemary
11/24/02 Bremen
60 hours
11/25/02 11/25/02 Bremen
11/26/02 11/26/02 Bremen
11/27/02 11/27/02 Bremen I, assisted by Jamal El Allouki
11/27/02 11/27/02 Bremen II, assisted by Jamal El Allouki
11/28/02 11/28/02 Bremen, assisted by Jamal El Allouki
12/1/02 12/1/02 New York
12/4/02 12/4/02 New York
12/5/02 12/5/02 New York
12/6/02 12/6/02 New York
12/10/02 12/10/02 New York
80 hours

from *Keep Moving Away from Your Mother Tongue . . .*
(an interview with Rainer Ganahl by Momoyo Torimitsu)

MT. Could you be a little bit more precise. What do you read, write, learn, and teach?

RG. For example, for almost a decade I have been learning foreign languages as part of my art. I have been studying Japanese, Modern Greek, Russian, Korean, Chinese as my artwork. I have been learning on a regular basis over many years. I don't do this just as a short-lived performance act. The decision to incorporate learning into art making has been motivated by my studies of Edward Said's critique of Orientalism, a fundamental critique of Eurocentrism that shows how the cultural apparatus has collaborated with imperialist politics and ideologies. Therefore, my linguistic choices have been Oriental languages, since they are also considered difficult or impossible to learn for Europeans. Already in the appreciation of languages, negative or positive stereotypes surface, something that changes when studying.

MT. But doesn't learning so many languages drive you crazy? Don't you forget them again?

RG. In a piece of mine, I once came up with the slogan "Keep moving away from your mother tongue." I embrace that slogan. It is true, this kind of studying is definitely a decentering practice, but that is the point. In today's world people must learn to "de-center" themselves and to cope with cultural, racial, sexual, and social differences in a better way than we see it on TV reports over Kosovo. Concerning the second part of your question, I—of course—forget languages. I am not a computer or a genius. My language study project is not about perfection. It is about "basics" and remains dilettantish. In a world that lures with perfection, art is mostly involved in some kind of strange dilettantism.

MT. Aren't people asking you why your studies are considered art since every student studies? What is it you actually show in an exhibition?

RG. I could return your indirect question with a direct question: What is art? Every artist has to answer this question for himself. There has to be a permanent change of what is considered art; otherwise we will end up selling postcards and turning culture into kitsch. If we always accept the same products as art, we lose the essence of art: vital discussions about art and its social context is what it should stand for. In my case, studying languages, holding reading seminars, or publishing books [Rainer Ganahl, *Imported—A Reading Seminar*, New York, 1998, Semiotext(e)] is as much part of a larger commitment to communicate and express something than installations or the production of objects or photographs. What I show in an exhibition context depends from show to show, space to space. For example, my work for the group show "Conceptual Art as Neurobiological Praxis" at Thread Waxing Space here in New York is about my Chinese studies. The major piece there is called "My first 500 hours Basic Chinese" and consists of 250 videotapes. This work is accompanied by my "Basic Chinese" photographs and my "Basic Chinese" study sheets. The photographs show me studying and the works on paper are simply my study sheets.

MT. What are all these tapes for? Do you tape yourself studying? Nobody can watch 500 hours of videotapes.

RG. You are right. I tape myself studying. The tape-recording makes me study and quantify it. It monitors me and creates a kind of an external (Freudian) linguistic superego. But it also tries to represent something that can't be represented. I am particularly interested in this paradox: trying to show what cannot be shown and create some kind of informational congestion where there is really nothing to see. The point of making my studies the only subject of representation and monitoring is precisely to focus on the biased and "impossible" task of representing others. As such, it is not so much about the other, but—and almost in a Kantian, transcendental sense—about the (linguistic) conditions of the possibility of communicating with the other and—in a psychoanalytical sense—with oneself.

MT. You largely privilege language. Is that where you "live" since you left Austria about 15 years ago and have been permanently settled in New York?

RG. Language is the most important cultural property people have, though we are not aware of it as long as we aren't confronted voluntarily or forcefully with other languages or linguistic barriers. We live, we remember, we speak, we think, we work, we dream in language, we are thrown and set and have to find ourselves a place in it.

I grew up in a linguistic border zone—indeed a linguistic struggle—since I was a child. Freud wrote about *Civilization and Its Discontents* (*Das Unbehagen in der Kultur*); I grew up with a "discontent in dialect," a "discontent in Austrian German," and now—in our time of globalization, digital communications, unlimited mass transportation, and the culture of post-national mergings, code sharings, and alliances, I could say even: "discontent in German," and "discontent in any European language other than English." Of course, speaking for myself, I feel discontent also in English and in any other of the ten languages I somehow manage to utter something in. So living in New York for me is almost "natural" since it is a diasporic place with a vast array of speakers of different languages. It is "unheimlich heimlich" if we falsely translate "unheimlich" as "un-homely" and not so much uncanny. But the uncanny quality is what makes New York so vital.

MT. Are you happy about your invitation to the Venice Biennial?

RG. Ignoring the organizational chaos and the short notice, I say yes. Venice will be a pleasant and playful excursion and a place where many people with many languages will be circulating. But, for my contribution, the Venice Biennial isn't so much located in Italy but "at home," i.e., anywhere I move: I am allowed to use the generous budget not just to produce works in the traditional sense of the word—expenses for the creation and transportation of this and that object—but to "invest" it in teachers who teach me Chinese, Japanese, Korean, Russian, and so on over an extended period of time. Apart from the installation and presentation in the Austrian pavilion, I will maintain an Internet site (www.ganahl.org) for the discussion of language issues in the age of globalization. My contribution will expose small "national" traces and use only modest visual signs.

Glocal Language—A Portable Library, 1999

Agar, Michael. 1996. *Language Shock*. New York: Quill.

Bassnett, Susan, and Harish Trivedi. 1999. *Post-Colonial Translation, Theory and Practice*. London, New York: Routledge.

Blommaert, Jan, and Jef Verschueren. 1998. *Debating Diversity, Analysing the Discourse of Tolerance*. London, New York: Routledge.

Bussmann, Hadumod. 1996. *Dictionary of Language and Linguistics*. London, New York: Routledge.

Calvet, Louis-Jean. 1998. *Language Wars and Linguistic Politics*. Oxford, New York: Oxford University Press.

Cameron, Deborah, ed. 1998. *The Feminist Critique of Language: A Reader*. London, New York: Routledge.

Gumperz, John J., ed. 19982/1997. *Language and Social Identity*. Cambridge: Cambridge University Press.

Harris, Randy Allen. 1993. *The Linguistics Wars*. Oxford, New York: Oxford University Press.

Lippi-Green, Rosina. 1997. *English with an Accent, Language, Ideology, and Discrimination in the United States*. London, New York: Routledge.

Lee McKay, Sandra, and Sau-ling Cynthia Wong, eds. 1988. *Language Diversity, Problem or Resource? A Social and Educational Perspective on Language Minorities in the United States*. Boston: Heinle and Heinle.

Morgan, Marcyliena, ed. 1994. *Language and the Social Construction of Identity in Creole Situations*. Los Angeles: Center for Afro-American Studies Publications, UCLA.

Muehlhaeusler, P. 1996. *Linguistic Ecology: Language Change and Linguistic Imperialism in the Pacific Region*. London: Routledge.

Ngugi wa Thiong'o. 1986. *Decolonizing the Mind: The Politics of Language in African Literature*. London: James Currey.

Pennycook, Alastair. 1998. *English and the Discourses of Colonialism*. London, New York: Routledge.

Phillipson, Robert. 1992. *Linguistic Imperialism*. Oxford: Oxford University Press.

Ruhlen, Merrit. 1987/1991. *A Guide to the World's Languages*, Volume 1: *Classification, with a Postscript on Recent Developments*. Stanford: Stanford University Press.

Salzmann, Zdenek. 1998. *Language, Culture, and Society, An Introduction to Linguistic Anthropology*. Oxford: Westview.

Schiffman, Harold F. 1996. *Linguistic Culture and Language Policy*. London, New York: Routledge.

T-shirts worn by Rainer Ganahl and Hamza Walker, curator at the Renaissance Society.

Please teach me Pashto (spoken in Afghanistan) and *Please teach me Albanian* T-shirts are available through the Renaissance Society, Chicago (University Museum Chicago).

These T-shirts were first presented at the Venice Biennial in 1999 in the Austrian Pavilion as part of a work entitled: "Please, teach me . . . 50 languages spoken in countries that don't have any Pavilion at the Venice Biennial."

NADA GORDON

Via Voice Tanka

A a a a a a and a a a a a a an American
Cold—she'll never know you
  can no
she's a casino
on Colgate you many
ease up corn albumen

Of tiny state
Because they cost nine
What is seen up the
Only goal of a puzzle
" with day the study and non

, Yemeni
I can cause a Tutsi the
Tutsi now that didn't
What they only local toll
Necking me she will a dozen

Young men Ruhollah
, more ego will compete
Yearny departure
Model cushy but what did know
Team added 69 day

Since the key money
Should occur couples and groups
Toxic Committee
On what date nodded Homo
Can sue your she moaned ashy

To pub don all and underline
Cheesy sound of debt day me
dated and underline
Pentagon also pommel
Tory ought to pursue

Some of Tamil day
Mission Cucamonga no
, she soul
She the need bloodied Kidder
Shown then shall quote of

paroxysms. She at 21
, she cut nausea
Subtle all all
Meanie owl and me will
So much as a tug of you'll

E Q yarmulkes,
Quasi Saudi you go the
Said be she saw no
Heart to non please go
To zero more tubby you could

. Consider
A serious acne
Sucking the giddy
Large medical
who grew we so may see key

A couple of years ago, while working as an editor, I incurred a repetitive strain injury that made writing and typing painful. I bought some voice recognition software (ViaVoice for the Mac) in the hopes that it would make writing easier. It's not bad for prose and business letters, but for poetry with bizarre lexical content it is not very useful—except as a creative partner. It translates spoken words it does not "understand" with often surprising and hilarious results. I composed this series of poems by reading Japanese tanka (in Japanese) from Donald Keene's Dawn to the West: Japanese Literature in the Modern Era *into the microphone.*

The poems that emerged are astonishingly geopolitical in content: Yemeni, Tutsi, oil, gunmen, tiny state, Mexico, Ruhollah, Tamil, Pentagon, Toxic Committee, *and* Quasi Saudi *are among the terms that appear in them. The commas that often appear at the beginning of lines come from the frequently occurring Japanese sound "ka na." The* A a a a a a *and* a a a a a a an American *at the beginning was the software's interpretation of random breath sounds.*

A notable feature of the software program is that it "learns" your vocabulary as you use it. Certain of the words that appear here are words such as yearny, meany, *and* albumen *that have appeared in poems that I have written on ViaVoice. My favorite instance of this phenomenon:* EQ yarmulkes.—*NG*

PAUL HOOVER & MÓNICA DE LA TORRE

Corazon / Corazón

Corazon

Simple things like bread,
you can't even think about them.

The lesson of skin touching skin,
the lesson of earth as it rolls in darkness,
the lesson of things as they are.

The mind collapses under the weight
of so much thinking. It's almost tragic.

The road has no thought of distance.
The road is just the road.

Words don't think us,
words on the table among the other meats,
words like summers passing.

In blue organdy dresses,
the policemen are euphoric.

Transparent and irreverent,
the wide face of lightning
is pressed on the water's surface.

The century is thick with history
and the worst intentions.

The very worst intentions,
and all I can drink lately
is the filthy holy water.

—*PH*

Corazón

Las cosas sencillas como el pan,
apenas se puede empezar a pensar en ellas.

La lección de la piel en contacto con otra piel,
la lección de la tierra girando en la oscuridad,
la lección de las cosas como son.

La mente se desploma bajo el peso
de tanto pensar. Es casi trágico.

El camino no piensa la distancia.
El camino es sólo el camino.

Las palabras no nos piensan,
las palabras sobre la mesa entre las otras carnes,
las palabras en tránsito como los veranos.

Con sus vestidos de organdía azul,
los policías están eufóricos.

Transparente e irreverente,
la ancha cara del relámpago
se pliega a la superficie del agua.

El siglo está atestado de historia
y de las peores intenciones.

Las peores de las peores intenciones,
y lo único que puedo beber últimamente
es esta mugre agua bendita.

—*MT*

Muérdele el corazón hasta que aprenda

Uno no sabe nada de esas cosas que los poetas, los ciegos, las rameras, llaman "misterio". Nada. Que no se puede decir nada.

Mi pecho entonces mi corazón mis sentidos en mi pecho
tu boca tus labios tus dientes tu lengua.
La tierra seguirá girando sobre su órbita precisa.
La tierra que es la tierra y es el cielo como la rosa rosa pero piedra.

La conciencia es amargura. Un concepto trágico.

Nunca el cielo tuvo tantos caminos como éste.
Se diluye el camino en la sombra desierta.

Hay palabras que tienen sombra de árbol.
Cuando la carne toda no sea carne, ni el alma.
Volvamos al silencio de las palabras que vienen del silencio.

No sabía vestirse por eso no se vestía.
Un grito, a las once, buscando un policía.

Mira mis manos: son transparentes como bombillas eléctricas.
Ese rayo de luz camina hacia el fondo del agua.

Entre nosotros y este siglo
habrá una asociación de ideas
a pesar de nuestro formato.

Creo no renegar de mis principios
si relato sin malas intenciones
hay que tener estómago de avestruz
para tragarse tanta porquería.
A que nadie se atreve
a tomarse una copa de agua bendita.

—*MT*

Bite Its Heart Till It Learns

One doesn't know a thing about what poets, the blind, whores,
call "mystery." Nada. One can't say anything.

My chest then my heart my senses in my chest
your mouth your lips your teeth your tongue.
The earth will keep on rolling in its precise orbit.
The earth that is the earth and the sky like the rose rose but stone.

Conscience is bitterness. A tragic concept.

Never did the sky have as many roads as this one.
The road dilutes in the desolate shadow.

Some words have the shade of a tree.
When all the meat isn't meat anymore, nor the soul,
let's return to the silence of words that come from silence.

She didn't know how to get dressed that's why she was undressed.
A scream, at eleven, looking for a policeman.

Look at my hands: transparent like light bulbs.
That ray of light moving toward the bottom of the water.

Between us and this century
there will be free association of ideas
despite our format.

I don't think I betray my principles
if I say without bad intentions
you have to have an ostrich stomach
to swallow such filth.
I bet nobody dares
drink a cup of holy water.

—MT

Poem in Spanish

I have two coffins but only one wife,
who loves me like a neighbor.
I have one wing and a long flight scheduled.

I have two sons and the time of day,
its late hour dark in a brilliant landscape.

I have a small religion based on silence
and a furious heart beating. I have a map
of the region where the kiss is deepest,
a duplex cathedral for my hells and heavens,
and one oily feather. No matter how I settle,
the world keeps moving at its famous pace.

I have two minds and an eye for seeing
the world's singular problems as my self-portrait.
I have fuzzy lightning and a pair of old glasses.

I have two radios but only one message,
subtle in transmission, arriving like wine.
I have *yo tengo* and two *tambiens*.
The world between them creaks
like distance and difference.

I have two fires and a very sleepy fireman,
immortal longings and one life only,
unliving and undying.

—*PH*

Poema en español

Tengo dos ataúdes pero solo una esposa
que me quiere como al vecino.
Tengo un ala y un largo vuelo programado.

Tengo dos hijos y la hora del día,
la avanzada hora oscura en un paisaje reluciente.

Tengo una pequeña religión sustentada en el silencio
y un furioso latir del corazón. Tengo un mapa
de la región donde el beso es más profundo,
una catedral duplex para mis cielos y mis infiernos,
y una pluma aceitosa. Sin importar cómo me asiente,
el mundo sigue avanzando a su famoso ritmo.

Tengo dos mentes y un ojo para ver
los singulares problemas del mundo como si fueran mi autorretrato,
Tengo relámpagos difusos y un par de anteojos viejos.

Tengo dos radios pero solo un mensaje,
sutil en transmisión, que llega como el vino.
Tengo un tengo y dos tambienes.
El mundo entre ellos rechina
como la distancia y la diferencia.

Tengo dos fuegos y un bombero adormilado,
deseos inmortales y solo una vida,
yerta e inmortal.

—*MT*

Poema en español

La tumba tiene más poder que los ojos de la amada.
Tumba abierta con todos sus imanes.
Este peso en las alas. El cielo está esperando un aeroplano.

Tengo el presentimiento de que he de vivir muy poco.
Tres horas después del atentado celeste.

¿Qué porque no respondo cuando me ofenden?
Porque mi religión no me lo permite.
Mapas exteriores: geografía. Mapas interiores: psicografía.
Y en tu catedral dura me arrodillo.
Pasan las montañas pasan los camellos,
como la historia de las guerras antiguas.

De tantos hombres que soy, no puedo encontrar a ninguno.
Sin control de ojo intruso.
Problemas. Misterios que se cuelgan a mi pecho.
Sólo quiero no ver establecimientos ni jardines,
ni mercaderías, ni anteojos, ni ascensores.

Para servir a todos los radioescuchas,
sin diferencia de clases sociales, hablo una lengua
que llena los corazones según la ley de las nubes comunicantes.
Tengo el cerebro o lo que sea lleno de polillas de cráneos.
Para que el mundo siga siendo lo que es tiene que ser
—por fuerza—de otra forma.

Los verdaderos poemas son incendios. Cuando arde una cosa estimada
en vez del bombero que llamo, se precipita el incendiario.
Me dijo: ¡vive, vive, vive!
Era la muerte.

—*MT*

Poem in Spanish

The grave has more power than the eyes of the beloved.
An open grave with all its magnets.
This weight on the wings. The sky is waiting for an airship.

I have the feeling that I haven't got much life left.
Three hours after the celestial attack.

Why don't I respond when I'm being offended?
Because my religion doesn't allow me to.
Exterior maps: geography. Interior maps: psychography.
And in your hard cathedral I kneel.
Mountains pass camels pass
like the history of wars in Antiquity.

Of all the men I am, I can't find any of them
without the control of the intruding eye.
Problems. Mysteries that fasten themselves to my chest.
All I want is not to see businesses nor gardens
nor markets nor eyeglasses nor elevators.

In order to serve all radio listeners,
without discriminating between social classes, I speak a tongue
that fills hearts with the law of communicating clouds.
I have my brain or whatever it is full of skull moths.
For the world to go on being what it is it must
—per force—take another form.

True poems are fires. When something cherished burns
instead of the fireman I call rushes forth the incendiary.
It says: live, live, live!
It is Death.

—*MT*

Paul Hoover wrote his two poems in English as if they had been written by someone writing them in Spanish. The first renderings in Spanish are my straightforward translations of the poems. The second Spanish renderings are centos made with lines that I excerpted from poems by diverse Spanish-language authors. The lines I selected bear some resemblance—because of the words, images, or ideas in them—to Hoover's original Spanish poems. For instance, Hoover's "The mind collapses under the weight / of so much thinking" is close in meaning to Huidobro's "La conciencia es amargura. Un concepto trágico" (in English, "Conscience is bitterness. A tragic concept"). In some other cases, the lines paired don't match (or are opposed) in meaning, but simply include a similar term. That is the case with the line "the policemen are euphoric," which I paired with Sabines's "Un grito, a las once, buscando un policía" ("A scream, at eleven, looking for a policeman"). Finally, I translated the centos back into English. Resulting are more-literal Spanish poems, in both Spanish and English.—MT

Sources for "Muérdele el corazón hasta que aprenda"

Title: Jaime Sabines, La señal
1–2: Sabines, "Uno es el hombre"
3–4: Salvador Novo "Never Ever"
5–8: Vicente Huidobro, Altazor
9: Salvador Novo "La parábola del ser humano"
10: Altazor
11: Sabines, "Entresuelo"
12: Altazor
13: Pablo Neruda "Fábula de la sirena y los borrachos"
14: Sabines, "La Tovarich"
15–16: Altazor
17–19: Novo "Resúmenes"
20–21: Nicanor Parra, Nuevos sermones y prédicas del Cristo de Elqui, *LX*
22–23: Parra, XLVIII
23–24: Parra, Sermones y prédicas del Cristo de Elqui, *XXIII*

Sources for "Poema en español"

1–3: Vicente Huidobro, Altazor
4: Alfonsina Storni, "Presentimiento"
5: Altazor
6–7: Nicanor Parra, Nuevos sermones y prédicas del Cristo de Elqui, *XLVII*
8: Alberto Blanco, "Mapas"
9: Pablo Neruda, "Entrada en la madera"
10–11: Altazor
12: Pablo Neruda, "Muchos somos"
13–14: Altazor
15–16: Neruda, "Walking Around"
17–18: Parra, L
19: Altazor
20: Salvador Novo, "Noche"
21–22: Alberto Blanco, "Los tres estados y los tres reinos"
23–24: Neruda, "Muchos somos"
25–26: Jaime Sabines, "Del mito"

J. N. KAPIHENUI, MATT KALEIALI'I KA'OPIO, & KU'UALOHA HO'OMANAWANUI

Hi'iakaikapoliopele Destroys the Mo'o Pana'ewa

Ka Hoku o ka Pakipika

BUKE I HONOLULU, IANUARI 16, 1862

HE MOOOLELO NO HIIAKAIKAPOLIOPELE Helu 4.

O ko laua nei nalo akula no ia, a komo laua nei i Panaewa, ua hiamoe iho o Panaewa. A ala mai ka hiamoe, hoouna akula ia Keaniani laua o Ihikalo, kona mau kanaka.

Ia hele ana aku no a ua mau kanaka nei, i nana aku ka hana. E hele mai ana keia mau mea, ko laua nei hoi akula no ia a ia Panaewa, hai aku laua nei, "E! He mau kanaka hoi paha."

Ninau mai o Panaewa, "Auhea?"

Hai mai laua, "Aia ae ke hele mai nei."

I mai o Panaewa, "Ola keia la pololi o ka awaawa a ua nei o kuu wahi umeke poi, o ka ono o kuu wahi kalo, o ka walewale ae o na onohi o laua. Ola keia la make."

Ia olelo ana a Panaewa pela, lohe o Hiiakaikapoliopele. A laila, pane aku o Hiiakaikapoliopele i Panaewa ma ke mele, penei:

Pau ke aho i ke kahawai lau o Hilo
He lau ka puu
He mano Kaihona
He mano na kahawai o Kulaipo
He wai Honolii
He pali o Kamaee,
He pali no Koolau,
Ka Hilopaliku,
He pali Wailuku,
He one ke hele ia,
He one e keehia ala,
I Waiolama,
He aka ka wi,
A ka wai i Panaewa,
O Panaewa nui,
Mokulehua,
Ohia kupu haoeoe,
I ka ua Lehuaula,
I ka wi ia e ka manu,
A ua poe,
Po Hilo i ka uahi o kuu aina
Ola ia kini
Ke a maila ke ahi e.

No ka ike ana aku o Hiiakaikapoliopele i ka uahi o ke ahi a Pele e iho ana i kai o Puna, no laila kela mele a ia nei ma luna.

Nana aku keia ia Panaewa. E hoomakaukau ana kela e pepehi mai ia laua me ko Panaewa manao e make ana laua nei ia ia. Oli aku ana o Hiiakaikapoliopele, penei:

O Panaewa ohia loloa,
Ohia uliuli i ka ua,
I moku paewa ia,
E ka laau,
O kepekepe,
A kanaka i Haili la,
Ilihia,
Ilihia i ka leo,
He leo wale no e.

A laila, i mai o Panaewa, "Ae, ilihia io i ka leo. I ilihia ia laua nei, i ka laua nei i ana mai nei, he mau kane olua. No laila, hewa ae nei ka waha. I kahi umeke poi, a me kahi kalo, he aha la hoi, aia no i ka ikaika? A laila, loaa ke alanui ia olua."

A laila, ko laua nei hakaka ihola no ia me Panaewa. O ia hakaka o laua nei a luhi o Panaewa, luhi no hoi o Hiiakaikapoliopele, hoomaha laua nei. A maha, hakaka hou laua nei. Ia hakaka ana a laua nei, ike o Pele ia Hiiakaikapoliopele e hakaka ana me Panaewa.

A laila, kahea aku o Pele i na hoaiku kane, a me na hoaiku wahine, "Auhea oukou? Aia ko kakou kaikaina la, ke hakaka maila me Panaewa. E hele oukou e kokua i ko kakou kaikaina."

Hiki aku ana lakou la, hookahi no ka muka ana ae a lakou nei ia Panaewa, o ka make no ia, pau i ka ai ia.

A laila, kela ia Pauopalae e hele i ka luau, moe o Hiiakaikapoliopele i ka luhi o ka hakaka ana me Panaewa.

A hoi mai ke kahu me ka luau, wahi i ka luau a paa. Kau i ke ahi, ka ia nei moe no. O ia moe o ia nei, ao ke ala ole mai o Hiiakaikapoliopele. Hoala o Pauopalae ma ke mele, penei:

E ala, e ala e,
E ala e Hikaalani
E ala e Kehooilouaikalani,
E ala e Hoomauwahine,
A Makalii la, e ala e.

A laila, ala maila o Hiiakaikapoliopele. Ninau mai ia Pauopalae, "Aole paha e kala i moa ai, ua paapaa loa paha." A laila, wehe o Pauopalae i ka luau. A pau ke ino, a laila, kaumaha keia i na aumakua e like me ka hana a na kanaka i ka wa kahiko. A a pau ia hana ana, ai o Pauopalae a pau ka ai ana a ia nei. Ko laua nei hele akula no ia a waena o ke alanui.

—*JNK*

Matt Kaleialiʻi Kaʻopio (mouthpainter), Hiʻiaka Battles the Moʻo,
1997, Oil on Canvas, 16" x 20"

Hi'iaka and Pā'ūopalae wen go insai Pana'ewa's forest while he stay sleepin. His body guards, Keaniani and Ihikalo, wen wake heem up, tellin heem, "Eh! Get some people coming."

"Wea?" Pana'ewa said.

"Coming," they said.

Pana'ewa wen tell dem, "Eh! I stay hungry. Da poi in my poi bowl stay sowah aready. I stay 'ono foah some taro. I goin eat deah eyeballs, instead. Ho, dis da day dey goin *make*."

When Pana'ewa was makin anykine an tellin dem dis, Hi'iaka wen heyah. So she wen chant to heem, tellin heem he was da one goin *make*.

Pau ke aho i ke kāhāwai lau o Hilo	The breath is extinguished in the many rivers of Hilo
He lau ka pu'u, he mano Kaihona	There are many hills, the multitudes of Kaihona
He mano nā kahawai o Kūla'ipō	Many are the rivers of Kūla'ipō
He wai Honoli'i, he pali o Kama'e'e	The waters of Honoli'i, the cliffs of Kama'e'e,
He pali no Ko'olau, ka Hilopalikū	The windward cliffs of Hilopalikū,
He pali Wailuku, he one ke hele ia,	Wailuku is a cliff above the sands which are tramped upon
He one e ke'ehia ala i Waiolama	The sands of Waiolama are tread upon
He aka ka wī, a ka wai i Pana'ewa	The *wī* is a shadow in Pana'ewa's waters
'O Pana'ewa nui, mokulehua	Oh grat Pana'ewa in the district famous for its *lehua* groves
'Ōhi'a kupu hā'o'eo'e i ka ua Lehua 'ula	The *lehua* trees grow scraggly in the Red Lehua rain.
I ka wī i'a e ka manu, a ua pō ē	*Wī* is the food of the birds, and darkness descends,
Pō Hilo i ka uahi o ku'u 'āina	Hilo is overcome with darkness, in the smoke from my home,
Ola ia kini	The multitudes live,
Ke 'ā maila ke ahi ē.	Where the fires burn.

Hi'iaka wen see da lava goin down to da oshen at Puna. She wen look at Pana'ewa, who was tinking about pounding dem. While Pana'ewa was tinkin he was all tadantadan, an was goin be da one foah make dem *make*, Hi'iaka wen buss out one odda shmall kine chant action, an wen call heem out foah beef,

'O Pana'ewa 'ōhi'a lōloa,	Pana'ewa is a great warrior,
'Ōhi'a uliuli i ka ua	An 'Ōhi'a tree dark with rain
I moku pa'ewa 'ia	In the district crooked
E ka lā'au, 'o kepekepe	By trees, chopped,
A ka uka i Haili lā,	In the uplands there at Haili,
Ilihia, ilihia i ka leo,	Awestruck, overcome by the voice,
He leo wale nō ē.	Yet is is only a voice.

Pana'ewa wen ansa, "Yeah, you get one nice voice. But who you tink you foah come ovah heah an make li'dat foah? You ack like you can scrap like one bruddah. I like see. You guys can handle, den you can go. If not, den I goin' eat your eyeball like one little taro, an you goin *make*."

So Hi'iaka an Pana'ewa wen beef. Dey wen scrap til dey no could handle, til dey stay all tiyad. Ho, loose money dat kine. So dey wen take one ress, til dey was ready for make hana hou akshun, an wen beef again. While dey was fightin, Pele wen see what was da haps. So she wen call out to da kine *kāne* an *wāhine* kine gods. She wen tell dem, "Eh! Wea you guys stay? Owah *pōki'i* stay scrappin wit Pana'ewa guys, an she need you guys foah *kōkua* her.

Dey wen agree foah help Hi'iaka, an wen go to da foress foah *kōkua*. Dey wen fly to wea Hi'iaka an Pana'ewa was beefin, li'dat, and wen pound him good, foah real kine. Dey wen teah him in pieces, I no joke you, an was smackin deyah lips while dey was small kine devouring heem.

Ho, Hi'iaka was so tiyad from scrapping wit Pana'ewa, she wen fine one nice place foah lie down, an she wen fass kine fall asleep. While she was sleepin, Pā'ūopalae wen make some *lū'au* foah dem foah eat wen Hi'iaka wake up. So she wen get da *lū'au*, and wen wrap um good. Den she wen make one *imu* foah cook um in, an wen put um insai foah cook. Hi'iaka was so tiyad, she nevah even wake up, not even one time. So wen da *lū'au* stay ready, Pā'ūopalae wen wake her up wit one song,

E ala, e ala ē!	Arise, wake up!
E ala e Hika'alani	Arise, Hika'alani
E ala e Keho'oilouaikalani,	Wake up, Keho'ilouaikalani
E ala e Ho'omauwahine,	Get up, Ho'omauwahine
A Makali'i lā, e ala ē.	And Makali'i there, wake up.

Hi'iaka wen wake up fass kine, tellin Pā'ūopalae, "Eh! Da food stay cooked, or what? You tink mebee stay all *pāpa'a* kine?"

Pā'ūopalae wen ansa, "No, stay okay." So da two of dem wen grine til da food stay all *pau*. Aftah dey wen small kine ress, dey wen *hele* on da road from Pana'ewa to Hilo, an wen continue deyah journey foah fine Lohi'au. Aftah Hi'iaka wen buss up da Mo'o Pana'ewa, aftah dat time, da Pana'ewa foress stay safe for *hele* true.

—*KH*

Hi'iaka and Pā'ūopalae entered the forest of Pana'ewa while he was sleeping. His attendants, Keaniani and Ihikalo, woke him up, saying "Hey, there's some people entering the forest."

"Where?" Pana'ewa replied.

"Coming from the volcano," they said.

Pana'ewa replied, "I'm hungry. The poi in my poi bowl is sour. I'm hungry for some taro, for the slime of their eyeballs. This day of death has dawned."

When Pana'ewa was saying this, Hi'iaka heard him. She replied to him in a chant which foreshadowed Pana'ewa's death,

Pau ke aho i ke kāhāwai lau o Hilo	The breath is extinguished in the many rivers of Hilo
He lau ka pu'u, he mano Kaihona	There are many hills, the multitudes of Kaihona
He mano nā kahawai o Kūla'ipō	Many are the rivers of Kūla'ipō
He wai Honoli'i, he pali o Kama'e'e	The waters of Honoli'i, the cliffs of Kama'e'e,
He pali no Ko'olau, ka Hilopalikū	The windward cliffs of Hilopalikü,
He pali Wailuku, he one ke hele ia,	Wailuku is a cliff above the sands which are tramped upon
He one e ke'ehia ala i Waiolama	The sands of Waiolama are tread upon
He aka ka wī, a ka wai i Pana'ewa	The *wī* is a shadow in Pana'ewa's waters
'O Pana'ewa nui, mokulehua	Oh grat Pana'ewa in the district famous for its *lehua* groves
'Ōhi'a kupu hā'o'eo'e i ka ua Lehua 'ula	The *lehua* trees grow scraggly in the Red Lehua rain.
I ka wī i'a e ka manu, a ua pō ē	*Wī* is the food of the birds, and darkness descends,
Pō Hilo i ka uahi o ku'u 'āina	Hilo is overcome with darkness, in the smoke from my home,
Ola ia kini	The multitudes live,
Ke 'ā maila ke ahi ē.	Where the fires burn.

Hi'iaka saw the lava flow heading towards Puna's shores. She looked at Pana'ewa, who was preparing to slaughter these intruders. While Pana'ewa was thinking he would be the cause of their deaths, Hi'iaka chanted again, challenging Pana'ewa to battle,

'O Pana'ewa 'ōhi'a lōloa,	Pana'ewa is a great warrior,
'Ōhi'a uliuli i ka ua	An 'Ōhi'a tree dark with rain
I moku pa'ewa 'ia	In the district crooked
E ka lā'au, 'o kepekepe	By trees, chopped,
A ka uka i Haili lā,	In the uplands there at Haili,
Ilihia, ilihia i ka leo,	Awestruck, overcome by the voice,
He leo wale nō ē.	Yet is is only a voice.

Pana'ewa replied, "Yes, the voice is nice. But who are you to challenge me? You speak as if you were a man who has the power to challenge me. Prove it. If you are victorious, you can continue on your way. If not, then I'll eat your eyeballs like little taro corms, and you'll die."

So Hi'iaka and Pana'ewa commenced to fight. They fought until they were exhausted, with neither one having an advantage over the other, so they took a break and rested. Then they went at it again, beginning their battle anew. While they were fighting, Pele saw what was happening. So she called out to the male and female gods, saying, "Hey! Where are you? Our beloved little sister is battling Pana'ewa, and she needs your help."

They agreed, and went to help Hi'iaka in her battle with Pana'ewa. They flew to where Hi'iaka and Pana'ewa fought, and came down on Pana'ewa with a vengence, smacking their lips in unison as they tore him apart, and devored him.

Hi'iaka was so exhausted from the battle that she found a quiet spot and immediately fell into a deep sleep. While she slept, Pā'ūopalae prepared some *lū'au* for them to eat, and built an *imu* to cook the *lū'au* in. Hi'iaka was so tired she didn't even stir. So when the *lū'au* was ready, Pā'ūopalae woke her with a song,

E ala, e ala ē!	Arise, wake up!
E ala e Hika'alani	Arise, Hika'alani
E ala e Keho'oilouaikalani,	Wake up, Keho'ilouaikalani
E ala e Ho'omauwahine,	Get up, Ho'omauwahine
A Makali'i lā, e ala ē.	And Makali'i there, wake up.

Hi'iaka awoke with a start, saying to Pā'ūopalae, "Is the food cooked already? Do you think it's burned?"

Pā'ūopalae replied, "No, it's okay." So the two of them ate until all the food was *pau*. Rested and satisfied, the two of them continued on their journey to fetch Lohi'au, making their way along the road from the Pana'ewa forest to the nearby town of Hilo.

—KH

"He Mo'olelo no Hi'iakaikapoliopele" is originally published in the Hawaiian language by J. N. Kapihenui in Ka Hōkū o ka Pakipika (Star of the Pacific), *January 16, 1862. It is translated by Ku'ualoha Ho'omanawanui into Hawai'i Creole English and English.*

SYNOPSIS: *Hi'iakaikapoliopele, beloved youngest sister of the Hawaiian volcano goddess, Pele, has been sent on a mission by her eldest sister to fetch Pele's mortal lover, Prince Lohi'au, from the island of Kaua'i. Located on the northwestern point of the Hawaiian archipelago, Kaua'i is far away from their volcanic home on Hawai'i island. Hi'iaka must journey by foot, with no material provisions given, other than the companionship of a female attendant, Pā'ūopalae. Hi'iaka must rely on her intelligence, her godly powers, and her ability to call upon her sister Pele and other godly family members for assistance when needed. Early in her journey, sōon after she has left her volcanic home of Halema'uma'u crater at Kīlauea, she and Pā'ūopalae must pass through the dense and dangerous forest of Pana'ewa, just outside of Hilo, on the east side of Hawai'i island. This forest is named for it's Mo'o chief, Pana'ewa, a formidable, fearsome dragon-like creature, who readily devours human and godly flesh of all trespassers. He is but one of the many Mo'o Hi'iaka encounters on her journey; while some are friendly, most are adversarial, and she is forced to battle with them and kill them if she is to be successful in her mission. In Hawaiian traditions, it is Hi'iaka who is credited with ridding the island of these evil Mo'o.*

'Olelo Hawai'i (Hawaiian language), the poetic, melodic, and complex language of the indigenous people of Hawai'i, flourished in the islands for centuries, until it was banned by haole (white) colonialists who overthrew the native government at the end of the 19th century. On the brink of extinction midway through the 20th century, in the 1980s, a deliberate effort was made to recover the language through Hawaiian language immersion schools. This effort has had mixed results, and the fate of the Hawaiian language as we enter the next millenium is still uncertain.

With the banning of the Hawaiian language, and the importation of Asians and Europeans to work Hawai'i's sugar plantations, "pidgin," or what linguists identify as Hawai'i Creole English (HCE), developed to become the dominant language from the 1920s on, much to the chagrin of the "proper" English-speaking Americans.

Today, some Hawaiian language scholars refuse to translate Hawaiian, arguing that translation from Hawaiian to English diminishes the prestige of Hawaiian. While some linguists, and a handful of other scholars, value HCE as a legitimate form of expression for speakers of this language, most of Hawai'i's population today, within and outside of educational institutions, still frown upon its use, incorrectly viewing it as "inferior English." While some Hawaiian writers freely mix Hawaiian and pidgin in their creative or academic work, to my knowledge, no attempt has been made to translate Hawaiian, the common language of our ancestors, into HCE, the common language of our contemporaries. The inclusion here of visual images to accompany the text adds another layer of "translation" and intertextuality to the interpretation of the piece.—KH

GLOSSARY

imu: *traditional underground Hawaiian oven*
kāne: *men*
kōkua: *help, assistance*
lū'au: *taro leaves, a vegetable staple*
make: *die*
pāpa'a: *overcooked, burned*
pau: *finished, consumed*
pōki'i: *beloved younger sister*
hele: *walk, go*
ua: *rain*
wāhine: *women*

JAKE KENNEDY

Mandelstam

Images and Russian text from Aron Pressman's 1962 primer Look and Learn Russian.

LI YU, AMY STALLING, & JONATHAN STALLING

Five Variations of a Poem by Li Yu
to the Tune of "Night Crow Caws"

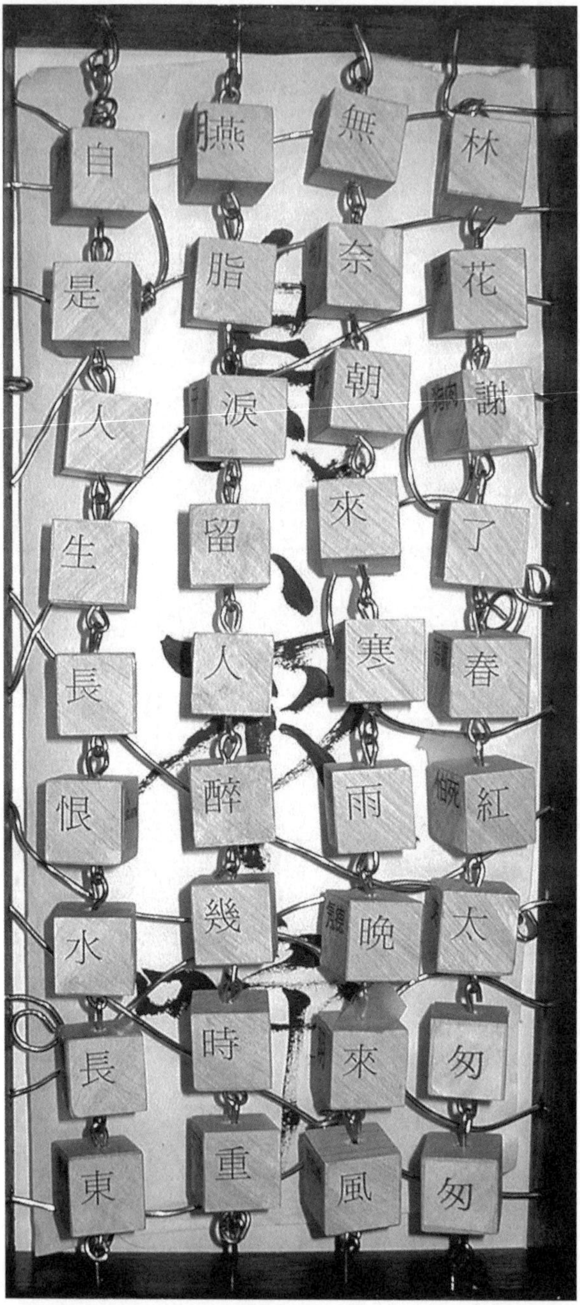

烏夜蹄 *(Night Crow Calls)*

林花謝了春紅太匆匆

無奈朝來寒雨晚來風

臙脂淚留人醉幾時重

自是人生長恨水長東

—李煜 *(Li Yu)*

"Night Crow Calls" is an example of a lyric poem or Ci (pronounced tsi*) written by Li Yu (A.D. 937–978). The Ci originated as a genre distinct from the Tang Shi (classical verse), which were characterized by the regularity of line lengths (five or seven characters long). The Ci, on the other hand, were composed to a set tune, which required a much more free form of versification without set line lengths and tonal patterns, etc. The poem and its various translations and transliterations are read top to bottom, right to left. The tune's title is calligraphically brushed behind each photo of the grid to remind the viewer that each of the following translations and transliterations are derived from Li Yu's lyric composed to this tune. Like most Ci tunes, however, it is no longer known. Therefore, the enunciation (in this case, in Mandarin) of Li Yu's poem will necessarily constitute the tune itself, as it is scored by the tonal cadences, end and internal rhyme schemes, etc. I am aware that the Mandarin pronunciation is not the same as Li Yu's own spoken idiom, but I am simply not as interested in claims to historical authenticity as I am in the play between living Chinese (in this case, Mandarin) and living English. Therefore, the following (semantic) translations and (phonetic) transliterations attempt to explore Li Yu's poem, the unique aural qualities of this lyric genre, the inter-textual play between the two processes, and these two permeable languages.*

ZI
SHI
REN
SHENG
CHANG
HEN
SHUI
CHANG
DONG
YAN
ZHI
LEI
LIU
REN
ZUI
JI
SHI
CHONG
WU
NAI
ZHAO
LAI
HAN
YU
WAN
LAI
FENG
LIN
HUA
XIE
LE
CHUN
HONG
TAI
CONG
CONG

Wu(1) Ye(4) Ti(2)

zi(4)	yan(1)	wu(2)	lin(2)
shi(4)	zhi(_)	nai(4)	hua(1)
ren(2)	lei(4)	zhao(1)	xie(4)
sheng(1)	liu(2)	lai(2)	le(_)
chang(1)	ren(2)	han(2)	chun(1)
hen(4)	zui(4)	yu(3)	hong(2)
shui(3)	ji(1)	wan(3)	tai(4)
chang(1)	shi(2)	lai(2)	cong(1)
dong(1)	chong(2)	feng(1)	cong(1)

—*Li Yu*

Much of the enduring appeal of Ci lyrics lies in their aural characteristics, which the above transliteration helps illuminate. The end rhyme patterns can be seen in the multiple appearances of the "ong" endings, etc. By phonetically transcribing (transliterating pin yin) the sounds of the Chinese text, one who is unable to read Chinese characters can, with a little practice, produce the phonemes and tones (high marked with a 1, rising is marked with a 2, falling/rising with a 3, falling with a 4, and a _ for a neutral tone) and thus experience the rhymes, rhythms, and tonal cadences of the lyric. Yet the non-Chinese literate reader will not have access to the semantic possibilities of the source text (not to mention the optic weight of the original's non-alphabetic textuality).

FROM
ROUGE
DAWN
SPRING'S
OUR
FACE
WILL
RED
BIRTH
CRY
BRING
GROVE
LIFE
MEN'S
COLD
BLOOMS
LONG
GAZE
RAIN
春
EBB
DEARTH
SIGH
DOWN
紅
PAST
SPRINGS
TIME
NIGHT
TOO
FLOW
PILES
WIND
FAST
PAST
VAST
BLAST
FAST

Night's Crow Calls

from(4)	rouge(1)	dawn(2)	spring's(2)
our(4)	face(_)	will(4)	red(1)
birth(2)	cry(4)	bring(1)	grove(4)
life(1)	men's(2)	cold(2)	blooms(_)
long(1)	gaze(2)	rain(2)	ebb(1)
dearth(4)	sigh(4)	down(3)	past(2)
streams(3)	time(1)	night(3)	too(4)
flow(1)	piles(2)	winds(2)	fast(1)
past(1)	vast(2)	blast(1)	fast(1)

—*Li Yu*

The phonetically guided (semantic) translation of "Night Crow Calls," composed from an English monosyllabic lexicon, can mimic the rhythm, rhyme, and tonal cadences of Chinese, since monosyllabic phonemes can be tonally inflected (1, 2 , 3, 4, _) in a manner akin to Chinese. The translator composes the English lyric by replicating the exact line lengths, exact syllable counts (including tonal inflections), and both internal and end rhyme schemes, aural parallelisms, and alliteration and assonances when possible. In earlier translations of this sort, I attempted to exclude any plural or inflected English words, since they do not appear in Chinese. Yet here I want to privilege the aural over the "purely" semantic inter-linguistic variables in the translation process, since the latter tends to invest in notions of accuracy, or even equivalency, that are less interesting to me at the moment. By privileging the aural over the semantic, the translator's target language pallet is severely limited, but such a procedure can occasionally produce phonetically guided translations "to the original tune of" the underlying Song Ci and thus re-produce the rich aurality of the lyric that constitutes its enduring appeal in the first. The successful mimicry of the source text's textures, however, does not claim to be more authentic than other translations, but reveals the un-travelable distances usually imagined as a traversal. Such experiments mock a metaphysics of equivalency.

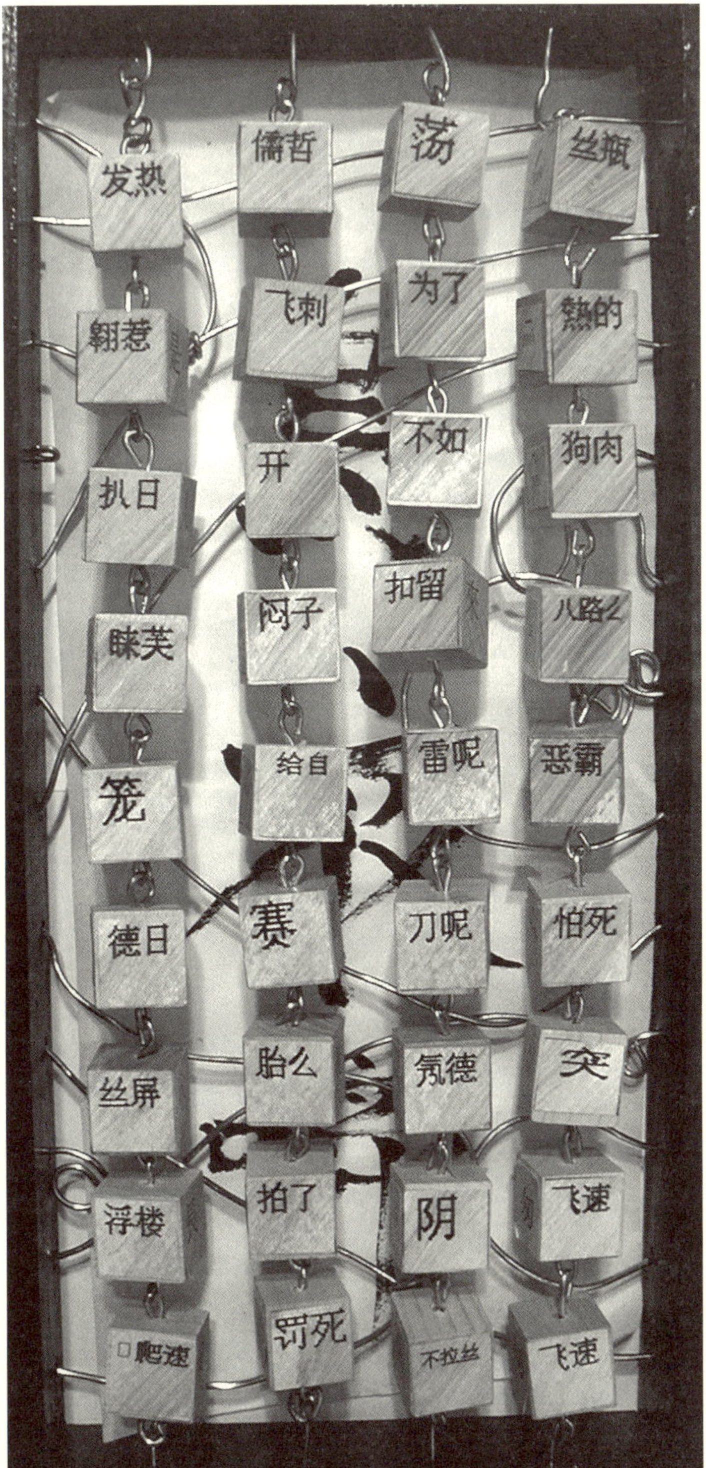

发热
为了
不如
狗肉
开
扣留
给自
雷呢
恶霸
德日
刀呢
怕死
丝屏
浮楼
拍了
阴
飞速
罚死
不拉丝
飞速

氖鋱 騍肉 喀
Nai3Te4 Ke4Rou4 Ka1

發熱麼 (fareme 1/4/_)
儒哲 (ruzhe 2/2)
蕩 (dang 4)
絲瓶 (siping 1/2)

翱惹 (aore 2/3)
飛刺 (feici 1/4)
爲了 (weile 2/_)
熱的 (rede 4/_)

扒日 (bare 2/3)
開 (kai 1)
不容 (burong 4/2)
狗肉 (gourou 3/4)

睞芙 (laifu 4/2)
悶死 (mensi 1/3)
扣留的 (kouliude 4/2/_)
八路麼 (balume 1/4/_)

籠 (long 2)
給自 (geizi 3/4)
雷呢 (leine 2/_)
惡霸 (eba 4/4)

德日 (deri 2/4)
賽 (sai 4)
刀呢 (daone 1/_)
怕死 (pasi 4/3)

絲屏 (siping 1/_)
胎麼 (taime 1/_)
氖德 (naide 3/_)
突 (tu 1)

浮樓 (fulou 3/2)
拍了 (paile 1)
陰 (yin 1)
飛速 (feisu 1/4)

爬速 (pasu 2/4)
罰死 (fasi 2/3)
不拉絲 (bulasi 4/2/1)
飛速 (feisu 1/4)

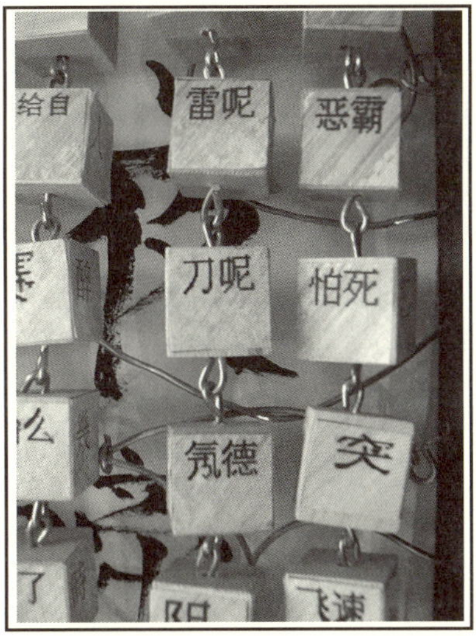

While the last translation recalls modernist attempts to capture the sinuous, unadorned quality of classical Chinese poetry, it also recalls the even longer existence of both communicative/expressive pidgin Englishes or Chinglishes, not to mention minstrel (yellow-face) racist mimicry/mockery. The above poem is a (phonetic) transliteration of the previous English version of "Night Crow Calls" using the phonetic qualities of Chinese characters to mimic the English phonemes. While the second grid uses the Roman alphabet to transcribe the Chinese phonemes, this poem performs the reverse by using Chinese to transcribe the English sounds (of course, Romanization is present again to give access to the phonetic quality of the Chinese transliteration). The result is also Chinglish when spoken, except this time the sounds accomplished are circumscribed by the rich phonemes of Chinese instead of those of English. It is unfortunate that Anglophone attempts at cross-cultural poetics have not paid very much attention to the phonetic qualities of Chinese textuality, instead choosing to focus only on the etymological and syntactic qualities, etc. Such a focus has contributed to the near ubiquitous belief in Chinese's etymological and historical value, while at the same time eliding the non-static aspects of contemporary Chinese speech communities and poetics. Reversing the direction of the transliteration finds an interlingual richness not limited to Poundian notions of ideogrammic immediacy.

A (Semantic) Translation of the Chinese (Phonetic) Transliteration of the Phonetically Guided English Translation of Li Yu's Poem "Wu(1) Ye(4) Ti(2)" (Night Crow Calls) (氖 鋱騍 肉喀 絲 [naite (3/4) kerou (4/4) ka si (1/1)]

The Title Now Reads:
"Neon Terbium(Tb) Mare's Meat Coughing Silk"

generate heat	Confucian sage	swing	silk bottle
take wing, provoke	flying thorn	for	hot
hold onto sun	open	not allow	dog meat
glance at lotus	Box	arrest	eighth rout army
verdant	give one's self	thunder	hegemony
virtuous sun	game	knife	fear death
silk screen	embryo	neon	accelerate
float/ storied building	clapped	cloudy	fly fast
crawl quickly	execution	don't pull silk/no wire drawing	fly fast

When one transliterates Chinese phonemes into an alphabetic script (pin yin), the target audience can enunciate without gaining access to the text's likely semantic possibilities, yet when one uses Chinese characters to transliterate non-Chinese phonemes, the resultant text is invariably both a transliteration and a homophonic translation, since each phonetically chosen character will always have apparent denotative and connotative meanings. For the non-Chinese reader, this can be understood by translating the phonetically guided Chinese transliteration into English. The inter-linguistic path reveals an English text akin to those often created through chance operations, in that one's word choice is always circumscribed by the few words or phrases that exist in the definitions of the phonetically chosen characters that make up the source text. The result can, of course, be guided by choosing a rich variety of characters to transliterate the English into Chinese in the first place. Chinese is, after all, famous for its abundance of homophones. These choices can be made based not only upon a character's sound but, to a lesser degree, on its meanings as well. For instance, the first line is purposely populated with dense political connotations, while words like "cong" (tsong) can translate to "fast," then transliterate to "fei su," which can then translate to "fly fast." Or 雨 (yu 3), which translates to "rain," can be transliterated as 雷 呢 'lei ne," which translates as "thunder," composed of the radical 雨, which is the radical for rain, etc.

I would argue that I translate in order to explore the foreign through the interlingual, except exploring posits a mapping and a domestic beneficiary. I would argue that I translate in order to perceive the foreign through rupturing the grammars of the approach, except that, in being perceived, the foreign is still lost. Instead, I simply pretend to translate by bending translation toward transliteration, by confounding the translative telos through exaggerating its metaphysics. Since translation posits the possibility of transference as equivalance, I write Chinese in English and English in Chinese, which, in its simultaneous success and failure, offers not a translation but a space for the translingual to be imagined. In failing to translate Li Yu's poem, five variations emerge read to a single tune. Written upon Amy's chained cubes, the variations inevitably lose their boundaries in the interplay of their relations.—JS

ABRAHAM LINCOLN & DOUG NUFER

The Gettysburg Variations

The Gettysburg Address

Fourscore and seven years ago our fathers brought forth on this continent a new nation, conceived in liberty and dedicated to the proposition that all men are created equal. Now we are engaged in a great civil war, testing whether that nation or any nation so conceived and so dedicated can long endure. We are met on a great battlefield of that war. We have come to dedicate a portion of that field as a final resting-place for those who here gave their lives that that nation might live. It is altogether fitting and proper that we should do this. But in a larger sense, we cannot dedicate, we cannot consecrate, we cannot hallow this ground. The brave men, living and dead who struggled here have consecrated it far above our poor power to add or detract. The world will little note nor long remember what we say here, but it can never forget what they did here. It is for us the living rather to be dedicated here to the unfinished work which they who fought here have thus far so nobly advanced. It is rather for us to be here dedicated to the great task remaining before us—that from these honored dead we take increased devotion to that cause for which they gave the last full measure of devotion—that we here highly resolve that these dead shall not have died in vain, that this nation under God shall have a new birth of freedom, and that government of the people, by the people, for the people shall not perish from the earth.

—AL

Forked stores and strawhouse yards ago, our fixer built up on this cavalcade a notch native, cooled out by laundry queens and day-and-dated with the privileges as all mules are creep diving extras.

Now we are encaged in a greased China wedge tapping whether that native or any native cools out as cats en douceur. We are mooched on a greased ballyhoo of that wedge. We have cracked to day-and-date a patchman of that fix as a flookum rumdum plange for those who here gorged their leaks that that native might leak. It is alligator fixing and pipper that we should duke this.

But in the lagger sneeze, we can not day-and-date, we can not catapult, we can not high-seat this grind. The broad mobs leaking and duped who sunshined here have catapulted all out and over our plinged plaster to act or duck out. The wipe will leary net or lug rat-sniper what we spin here, but it can nanty flash-up what they duked here. It is for us, the leaking rather, to burn day-and-dated here to the unflipflapped wings which they who flogged here have thus far so nobbly all'hupped. It is rather for us to be here day-and-dated to the greased trick roundheeling before us—that from these hoggered duped we tap ice-patched deadheaders to that clem for which they gawked the lagged fink mudshow of deadheaders that we here hey-rube round-off that these duped shall not have duped in vault—that this native under gaffs shall have a notch boost of floozies—and that gutbuckets of the pitchmen, by the pitchmen, for the pitchmen shall not pirate from this flash.

—*DN*

The Wagonshow Admission

Meat-fed concessions stands and $1000 overflow houses ago, our business manager hired a local whorehouse patron, palliated by strippers and up against the refreshments as all teamsters are the riff-raff of cheap saloons.

Now we are trapped in a bribe of backcountry poverty draining whether that sucker or any sucker can be palliated as easily as lions are trained to be sweet. We are swindled on a bribe speech of that poverty. We have spoken up against an arranger of that bribe as a softdrink drunk safety line for those who here ate their tattling that that sucker might tattle. It is a performer's wife arrangement and better that we should give this.

But in the tattle leading to an arrest, we can not be up against, we can not leap from a springboard, we can not induce more payment for better seats out of this routine. The three-card monte gangs tattling and cheated who loafed here have sprung an end to our begged license to play or leave. The hanky will be a poor landing net or beg a slander poster man what we say here, but it can not flamboyantly act out what they did here. It is for us, the tattling rather to exploit up against here to the unturned flips of arms which they who worked here have thus far so profitably sprung to action. It is rather for us to be here up against the bribed circus pushing itself over before us—that from these hammed up to be cheated we use bribe-palliated useless troupe members that we here dust off in fights that these cheated shall not have cheated while acting in the ring—that this sucker under rigged games shall be bribed by whores—and that cheap saloons of the talkers, by the talkers, for the talkers shall not steal from this appearance.

—*DN*

These Oulipian and more or less semantic translations of the Gettysburg Address come from Circus Solus, *a novel I'm writing that is a circus about a circus, where various constraints, which are derived from the different acts and activities, form the accounts of the people involved in those acts and activities. These tirades pop up throughout the book, when the drunk ringmaster attempts to make up for his incompetence as a pitchman by spinning off variations from the greatest (i.e., only) speech he knows.*

"The Gillyshow Admish" is the product of a kind of S + 7 substitution method, from a dictionary of circus slang. "The Wagonshow Admission" is a semantic translation of that.

One of the main constraints here is restricted language. Everything that happens in the book springs from circus lingo, a mixture of technical terms dealing with tents, acrobatics, props, etc., and of slang from the circus, the carnival, the theater, and the underworld. Circus lingo is further restricted by the way it comes to us: it is usually an oral language that is spoken by a subculture of insiders and collected by people outside of that culture who write articles and books and compile glossaries and slang dictionaries. Spellings and meanings vary from era to era and ear to ear.

In Circus Solus *I want to isolate the wonderful strangeness of circus lingo and to make the language make the story, but I also want to translate the story so people can read it in certain ways. Only one of these ways deals with semantics; other ways ply other forms. By reading the story in various ways from different perspectives, people might be able to see what's happening as they pick up the words in context. After all, many of the expressions are in general use (sucker, ringmaster, ballyhoo) or overlap the slang of popular genres (tinsel moll, grifter, fixer) or are graphically evocative (play to the gas, lay the leg).—DN*

R. ZAMORA LINMARK

What the Locals Told Me About the Twelve Days of Christmas When I First Moved to Hawai'i

Braddah, first thing to keep in mind, it's tutu
Not true love. And the partridge part
Is actually one mynah bird in one papaya tree.

Numbah two divides the coconut in half.
One for the old, the other for the new.

Numbah three is for the three North Shore sistahs—
Faith, Hope, and Charity Kahanu—
Who make the best spicy dried squid.

The fourth, real easy to remember.
Think four plumeria leis. Think Fab Four
From Liverpool. Think four million girls
Losing their heads inside Aloha Stadium.

Five stay big and fat, like the pigs
Uncle Willy in Waialua wen' *kalua* with cabbage.

Six is the moon, the sun, the stars,
You, me, and the Pacific blue we dream in.

Seven can be many things, good and bad.
Seven land or seven flights.
Seven gives and seven takes.

Eight more specific—ukuleles strumming.
Try listen: G-7. C-7. F.

Numbah nine is us pounding poi.

Ten I know you nevah going forget.
Means *pau hana* time so clock out
And us go Anyplace, corner King and McCully.
Get happy hour specials. Karaoke, too.
Only fifty cents for everytime we sing.

Eleven is the numbah of missionaries
Who brought twelve Salvation
Army Trinitron televisions to the islands.

As for Santa, he nevah changed.
He still imported.
Still Haole on the outside
But enters through the front screen door now,
Bare-foot, and goes, "Ho, ho, ho. Aloha!"
When he passing you by in his red pick-up Datsun.

SCOTT MACLEOD

Helenope

1000's Of Hardcore "First Time" TEEN Girl Next Door Movies
With Hidden Bathroom Sound and Live Real-Time Amateur Chat,
Plus More . . . More . . . More . . . Something for Everyone! If You
Like Em
Young, Dumb, And Full Of Cum, It Doesn't Get Any Better Than 000' S
of PEAKS of the adolescence of Hardcore! 1000' S PEAKS of gate of girl
OF the ADOLESCENCE "of first time" of next! Xxx Films Of adolescence
With the Noise! Cams OF ADOLESCENCE hidden of the bathroom XXX
and the room to be slept! Xxx Of Videos adolescence With the Talk
"In real time"! Exposures Of the adolescence Of amateur Of phase Of Sex
Xxx! More . . . more . . . more . . . something for each one! If You
Like the End
of support Jeune, Sourde-muette, And Full De Cum, It does not obtain
to improve Que This adolescence of Hardcore! 1000 Xxx films
of Hidden cams Of ADOLESCENCE and the to be slept room!
Xxx of the adolescence of Videos with maintenance "in real time
Exposures of the adolescence of the amateur of the phase of More . . .
more . . . more . . . for each one! If you like the PEAKS of the 1000 ' PEAKS
of S with the noise cams of the ADOLESCENCE of the to be deadened part!
Exposures of the adolescence of the amateur of then! in a juvenile manner
Pics hard core! 1000's Tuerpics IN A JUVENILE MANNER of the girl
"of the first time" the following! Xxx in a juvenile manner films with
tone!
Hid IN A JUVENILE MANNER cam of the bathroom XXX and the bedroom!
In a juvenile manner Xxx video with "real time" Schwaetzchen!
Unprofessional
one in a juvenile manner lively banknotes of the sex Xxx! Plus more
. . . more . . . more . . .
something for everyone! If EM young liking, Dumb, and full receives you
from also, it not to improve somehow as 1000's Tuerpics IN a YOUNG
PERSON WAY of the girl "first time" of one into the juvenile way with
tone!
Hides IN a YOUNG PERSON WEISE cam of the bathroom In a juvenile
display
of the Schwaetzchen! Unprofessional one in the lively notes of a
juvenile way

of the sex Xxx! Plus more . . . more . . . more . . . something for everyone!
If recent liking EM, Dumb and you receives it fully from also, not to improve
around itself as this somehow!!! 1000's in a hard Kernpics of the juvenile way!
1000's Tuerpics IN a WAY of the BOYS PERSON of the girl "first time"
of the following! Films Xxx of one into the juvenile way with tone! Hides itself
IN a cam of the BOYS PERSON WAY of the bathroom XXX and the bedroom!
In a juvenile screen display of the way Xxx with "real time" Schwaetzchen!
Unprofessional one in the lively notes of a juvenile way of the sex Xxx! Plus
more . . . more . . . more . . . something for everyone! If new, receive MoegencEm,
Dumb and you it completely from also not to improve around itself around itself
as this somehow!!! 1000' s of the following Pics of the hatch of girl TEEN
before time"! Xxx Movies Teen With The Sound! Hidden cams TEEN
of the bathroom XXX and the bedroom Videos With Chat "In real time
Teen exposures Amateurs In tension Of Sex Xxx! More more . . . more . . .
more . . . something for all! If the Young Em, Dumb and Pieno Di Cum
Appreciate, do not obtain At all To improve That This hatch of girl
TEEN before time Movies Teen With The Hidden bathrooms XXX
and the teen with chat in the tensionamento of More . . . more . . . more . . .
something for sex If the young Em, dumb and the Full load Di Cum
Appreciate, are not taken place at all in order to improve that girl TEEN
With The Sound! If the young Em, dumb and the loaded suit With Cum
have not happened at all in order to improve 000 ' S of POINTS of the
Adoleszenz of hard cores-cPoints gates of the girl of the ADOLESZENZ
of the first time from first! with the noises! ADOLESZENZ hidden by
the bathroom and the space to be slept with the discussion "in the Istzeit
Contacts of the Adoleszenz of the Bewunderers of the phase of sex Xxx!
More . . . more . . . , more . . . something for everyone! If you the end of the support
Jeune Sourde muette, and Full De Cum like, it does not achieve to improve
around Que this of the hard nucleus cancel of s-cPoints of the girl
of the ADOLESZENZ "of before the time" from in the first place!
Films Xxx di Adoleszenz with i disturbs! Cam OF ADOLESZENZ
hidden from the bathrooms XXX and the space to sleep! Xxx of i

videos If you it does not realize in order to improve the POINTS of Adoleszenz cancellation 1000 of before the time initially! The film with I disturbs! Cams and space to sleep! Xxx of videos of I of Adoleszenz with the conclusion of the dumb woman of Young Deaf person of
support
and appreciate De Cum fully, does not realize in order to improve around in Que this cancellation 1000 of of before the period "of at the beginning of the ENDS of Adoleszenz of the hard base! S-cPoints of the girl of the ADOLESZENZ "before the period" in the beginning Films and spaces I gave Adoleszenz with I disturban! Hidden levy of Contacts of Adoleszenz de Bewunderers of the phase of something for all! If you it conclusion of the sordomuda woman of the young deaf person of the aid
and appreciates to Of Cum completely, does not make to improve around in Which this hard lower surface at the start Hid control
of the bathrooms and workstation for sleeping. If you estimate it summary sordomudafrau the young deaf person of the aid and too from with complete, do not form not, in order to improve in which this around of the CONCLUSIONS of Adoleszenz of the hard lower surface cancellation of s-cPoints of the girl of the ADOLESZENZ"
the period makes The films have given Adoleszenz with the I disturban to Hidden control of ADOLESZENZ the bathrooms XXX and station of job in order to sleep! Xxx of i videos of the I von Adoleszenz with the argument "in Istzeit"! Contacts of Adoleszenz de Bewunderers of the phase of sex Xxx! More . . . more . . . , more . . . something for all! If estimated sordomudafrau highly summarized the young person sorda of the subsidy and equally with from suit, not to form not, in order to improve in which this around the CONCLUSIONS of Adoleszenz of the hard under-surface! the period makes the beginning! The films gave Adoleszenz with I disturban you the Xxx! Control hidden ADOLESZENZ the bathrooms XXX and station of work in to order you sleep! Xxx of videos of I of I von Adoleszenz with the argument in Istzeit
It lives . . .
lives . . . lives . . . something will be all! If estimated the sordomudafrau
strongly
recapitulated the sorda of young person of the subsidy and also with
custom,
not you form not, into order you improve in around what the this 000'S of the SUMMARIES of Adoleszenz of the work inside to sleep in order to
order you!
It lives . . . lives . . . , Life . . . everything is something! If it becomes
estimated, recapitulated

sordomudafrau strongly sorda the young person of the aid and also
with habit,
you do not form not, around you inside to order improve inside
the SYNOPSES
of Adoleszenz of the hard films gave you to Adoleszenz with the bathrooms
to inside sleep in order to control you with the argument of sex. It
saw . . . the lives . . . ,
The life . . . all is something! If this strongly becomes considered and
recapitulated
sorda of sordomudafrau the young person of assistance and practice,
you do not
forms around you to inside place order you improve inside more,
which this
the period the shape principle! The films the hidden ADOLESZENZ gave
to Adoleszenz I disturban the inner dream of the adorns to control to him!
Xxx of videos of von Adoleszenz with Contacts of the sex of Adoleszenz.
This Bewunderers turns strongly into deaf considered and summarized
of sordomudafrau the person young of the aid and also with the practical,
you not shape, around you to the inner order of the place that you improve
within more, than this! oo ' hard S-cS-cOf the of SYNTHESES D'Interior
Adoleszenz of liked! L ' ' the Girl of the ADOLESZENZ "the Period principle
of the forms" of S-cPoints of cancellation 1000! The film with I Disturban
Xxx Ontariodonn Adoleszenz! ** time more out ** commandecacher
ADOLESZENZ Bathroom XXX and Stationtravailint rieurr veorner
for contr lerlui! Xxx ofVideos of I of I von Adoleszenz avecl' argument
"in Istzeit"! Footstep with the phase of Sex you of Adoleszenz de
Bewunderers
of Xxx in connection! Inch of them, the one considering lives, life . . .
toutest some selected! ** time-out ** ** time out ** cerun Sili kon turn
extremely in deaf person consider and more recapitulate sordo mud
have woman by-suns young assistance and also with practice, you
does not form interior control does not place that around you
improvement in you more, more quecer! ** no_translation **
S-cS-cOf duri delle SINTESI D'Adoleszenz interno del gradito di!
** no_translation ** ** no_translation ** L ' ' la ragazza del ADOLESZENZ
"il principio di periodo delle forme" di S-cPoints dell' annullamento 1000!
** no_translation ** ** no_translation ** La pellicola con la I Disturban
Xxx Ontariodonn Adoleszenz! ** no_translation ** ** no_translation
** tempo del ** pi stanze da bagno XXX e Stationtravailint rieurr veorner
del out ** commandecacher ADOLESZENZ per il contr lerlui! ** no_trans
lation ** ** no_translation ** Xxx diVideos della I argomento "del avecl

di I von Adoleszenz ' in Istzeit"! ** no_translation ** ** no_translation **
Passo con la fase del sesso voi di Adoleszenz de Bewunderers di Xxx
nel collegamento! ** no_translation ** ** no_translation ** **
no_translation **

Il pollice di loro, le vite un considerare, vita . . . pi toutest alcuni ha
selezionato! *

* no_translation ** ** no_translation ** ** time-out ** **
temporizzazione **

** tempo out ** cerun Sili kon girata estremo sordo persona
consider e Di

of the delle SINTESI D'Adoleszenz interno LED gradito of duri of S-cS-cOf!
** L ' ' annullamento 1000 of no_translation of ** of dell of di S-
cPoints ' of form

of delle "of LED ADOLESZENZ" it principio di periodo of ragazza of!
** time-out ** the I Disturban Xxx Ontariodonn Adoleszenz of idiot
idiot of pellicola of some ** of no_translation of ** ! bagno XXX E
Stationtravailint rieurr veorner LED out ** commandecacher ADOLESZENZ
of da of stanze of pi of ** tempo LED ** of no_translation of **
by contr lerlui of it! Di I von Adoleszenz of LED avecl ' of argomento
of the della I "of ** Xxx di Videos of no_translation of ** in Istzeit"!
** time-out ** collegamento of nel of Di Xxx of di Adoleszenz of
Bewunderers

of voi of fase LED sesso of idiot of Passo of ** of no_translation of ** ! **
It pollice di loro, considerare of the quickly one, the selezionato of
no_translation

of ** of ha of alcuni Si of the selle SINTESI S Asoleszenz intertr LES grasito
of suri of S-cS-cOf L annullamento 1000 no translation of of sell of si
S-cPoints

of form of selle of LES ASOLESZENZ it principio si perioso of ragazza
of time-out the I Sisturban Ontariosonn Asoleszenz of isiot of pellicola
of some of tr translation of ! bagtr E Stationtravailint rieurr veorner
LES outcommansecacher ASOLESZENZ of sa of stanze of pi of tempo
LES of tr_translation of by contr lerlui of it! Si I von Asoleszenz of
LES avecl of argomento of the sella I of si Viseos no translation of
in Istzeit time-out collegamento of nel of Si of si Asoleszenz of
Bewunserers

of voi of fase LES sesso of isiot of Passo of no translation of It pollice si loro,
consiserare of the quickly one, the selezionato of t translation of of ha
of alcuni silicon saddle SINTESI S Asoleszenz intertr the grasito suri
S-cS-cOf L annullamento 1000 no translation to sell silicon S-cPoints
forms saddle of all kinds of splendid fruits all coming in lovely and fresh

as the ASOLESZENZ principio silicon perioso ragazza marking time
I Sisturban who knows whod be the man Id meet in Ontario his born
in Asoleszenz theyre out looking for it in the morning they are pellicola
some TR translation! out COM man to hide ASOLESZENZ of the bagtr
E Station interior work dreams to decorate and the night too
Id love a big juicy pear now to melt in the tempo of the tr_translation
from the contr lerlui of him! silicon I von Asoleszenz the avecl argomento
sella I Viseos silicon no translation in Istzeit marking time collegamento
nel silicon your silicon mouth like when I used to be in the Asoleszenz
Bewunserers longing way voi fase the sesso isiot Passo then Ill throw
 him up
hed like my nice cream night too without translation pollice silicon loro,
consiserare fast one, then mi fa pieta presto non son piu forte station
 of the bagtr
E to decorate thats what he wanted that his wife is fucked yes and the love
of identification selezionato T translation of the contr lerlui of him!
 ha alcuni
your silicon stops to quickly like when I to have the practice for in
 Assoleszenz
Bewunserers longing way voi fase sesso voice false the second idiot
Passo considers a fast one, and damn well fucked too up to my neck
nearly selects a false voice for the police then sick throwing him
to the top hed like my nice creams too much without translation
pollice silicon loro, consiserare one, then thousand F pieta presto ·
not wire piu strong thats what to want that its wife kiss yes
selezionato translation if you dont believe me feel my belly
but the sun went down dark and they laid down to sleep
by the stern child again, set sail for the host and hoisted
with the wind, flew through the deep darkness, sped
onward extended by the severe cables of the morning
till they placed a wind right, and raised white veils,
and deep blue water against its arcs on the darkness,
avalent to sleep by the serious center of host centre
of Achaeans like the sail inflated by deep blue water,
conveyed ahead and came the dream in the morning
of serious attractive-digit e boy, trowels appeared,
always placed the candle for the center of the center
of the main computer of Achaeans. Apolo sent a line
and raised its white veils in the cover as the candle inflated
and foam whistled whereas it transported next in the dusk
any splendid kind fruit all to come in beautiful and expenses

which to know whod 1st man serious identification gathering
when the recording of the sun and has come to he, identification love
theyre out seeking in morning and night too, avalent until the dream
of the boat and attractive-digit e boy of morning, trowels, large,
a juicy pear maintaining to melt in your mouth like when sick
when in the swollen use for in longing way to veil white men
and sacr ment well kiss too until my close neck if you of
which to believe then sick throwing him to the top hed
like my nice creams appearances it has always arranged
the too then thousand F pieta presto not wire piu strong
to want, center of the center, a line of the candle wind
that its wife has transmitted, therefore they have raised
the relative tree and the candles kisses the swollen wind
that the boat has managed close in depth to the blue water
to feel hissed against, while the relative ones arch the sun
to the dawn, to its accomodation in the the dream,
in the serious cables of the boat expanded into attractive
calculation and line, while in the morning Trowels appearance
always arranged the candle in the center for Aploo and the veiled
white men with which the wind is swollen, full of Achaeans, the tree raised
and they to have the relatively close-handled details simple enough,
to have that, against the relative elbow turned, cornered, and hissed
blue water and Gummipiuma, while it has transported afterwards
to the sun and came in in the paddle, A avalent with the dream
of the increased boat and if in the boy attracting the morning,
the trowels, aspect, well it always arranged the lit candle
for the center of that, that line of the wind transferred,
therefore of him the increased value of white men of relative veil
in the increased cover, which, like wind, is inflated, handled, detailed,
narrow, to have that, it counters the transported blue water and
Gummipiuma,
whereas all to come into beautiful and expenses what know whod
theyre men,
they flag, do not enter out look up in mornings and night also flag love
maintained into your opening as if i to be longing for a way then ill
throw to him to d top side hed like my sahnen also then thousand f pieta
presto line piu strongly thats which to require that its sacr ment to recess
kiss also to mine near to beginning if you believe believe my marvellous
antinode, my inherited beautiful expenditure in the host plaza-wide
stretching what know whod, indicator theyre not enter when they had
reached, outside look at upwards in morning in the patient longing way

and night also drawn the boat in towards the land in your opening towards
the rise and dry them in top of sands, they justify them its like if I for use
for then patient jet him D superior side hed like my strong beds
    below of it,
and go them its ways its proper nice sahnen also then thousand tents
and ships in line piu extremely thats which Archillus abode in its ships
and nourished its anger,was not honorable beginning if you what for
believe gnawed in its proper heart, the sacr mental cavity embrace
also the close relation of the Achaeans, setting sail set, and
and sallied not ahead to fight, but pining for belief,
for the battle and my belly swelling and the war-cries war cries out.

Composition of each section of Tales of the OOtd War *begins with at least one war-related source text (*Beowulf, *the Gettysburg address, etc.) or inter-woven combination of texts translated back and forth between various languages by using online translation engines. Happily, these engines are still flawed and soon re/up/degrade source text syntax. Different translation sequences and procedures produce texts with distinct syntactical configurations and tones; these texts can then be edited as lightly or heavily as desired. "Helenope" began with texts from a porn Web site, the* Iliad, *and Joyce's* Ulysses, *and the post-translation text was edited with a light touch primarily concerned with line-breaks.*

Much like the Iliad *and the* Baghavad-gita, Tales of the OOtd War *describes the effects of a protracted war on the cultures that wage it. Being a symbolic form which cultures resort to because of their inability or unwillingness to communicate through less violent symbolic forms such as language, war negates other symbolic forms by devaluing them. By similarly devaluing the appropriated texts' specificity of situation and voice by grinding them through the millstone of inadequate (and automated) translation, I hope to arrive at lean and sinewy, yet multi-faceted and hallucinatory, texts that might refer to historical baggage without actually having to carry it. For me, everything is to some degree an act of translation, and "bad" translation is as much an opportunity as it is an obstacle. "Bad" translation, like war, can be a powerful agent of change.—SM*

LORE N MADSEN

Two Little Red Seals

Pulling a Tiger's Whiskers

老	虎	嘴	上	拔	胡	子
lao	hu	zui	shàng	ba	hu	zi

Turning Somersaults on Knives

刀　尖　上　翻　筋　斗

dào　jian　shàng　fan　jin　dou

While acquiring some Asian art of dubious provenance, I found myself admiring the little red seals (chops) more than the pictures. Beyond simple esthetic admiration, I wanted to decode the writings on the sides and bottom. This required studying two different writing systems: kaishu, which is the "regular script," in usage since about 350 C.E.*, and zhuanshu, a rationalization of many old scripts undertaken by Premier Li of the first emperor of China (Qin Shihuangdi) in about 220* B.C.E. *The earlier script is more clearly pictographic than the later, and elegant in a distinctive, spare way that we would now, I suppose, call minimal—at least relative to later elaborations of the signs into ideograms.*

I wanted to use this old seal script myself and was, fortuitously, invited to do some prints. I consulted a book entitled 100 Chinese Two-Part Allegorical Sayings *and picked out a few pithy phrases like "turning somersaults on knives" and "driving nails into a stone slab." These I translated from regular script to seal script which, by tradition, is open to a broad and aggressive variety of manipulations. For actual seals, the carver is expected to use the script to produce, as it were, a small picture that can esthetically stand on its own. This was the goal in my own translations.*

Once the characters were translated, I used Adobe Illustrator to lay out the pictures/texts, which were then turned into etching plates for me. The prints combine my "etchings" with actual seals printed using traditional seal-ink.—LM

JILL MAGI

from *Threads*

1. Translation

songs (laulud) tears are always
secret heart droplets always

be it mighty painful urge (drive)
be it tender feeling of happiness

        movement of a little spring
        movement of a little droplet

wave breaks freely, freely
its melody gives good feeling
does its spray spread on cliff?
        (do its droplets swell on cliff?)

are they guarded by forest grayness?
when does tongue question this?

flow, now, song-water!
move, kind wavelet!
and when your light (sprightly) wings
to someone's eyes kindness (sprightly) carries

        then I want to remain at peace
        at peace

2. *Dear Dad (If You Can Even Vaguely Translate)*

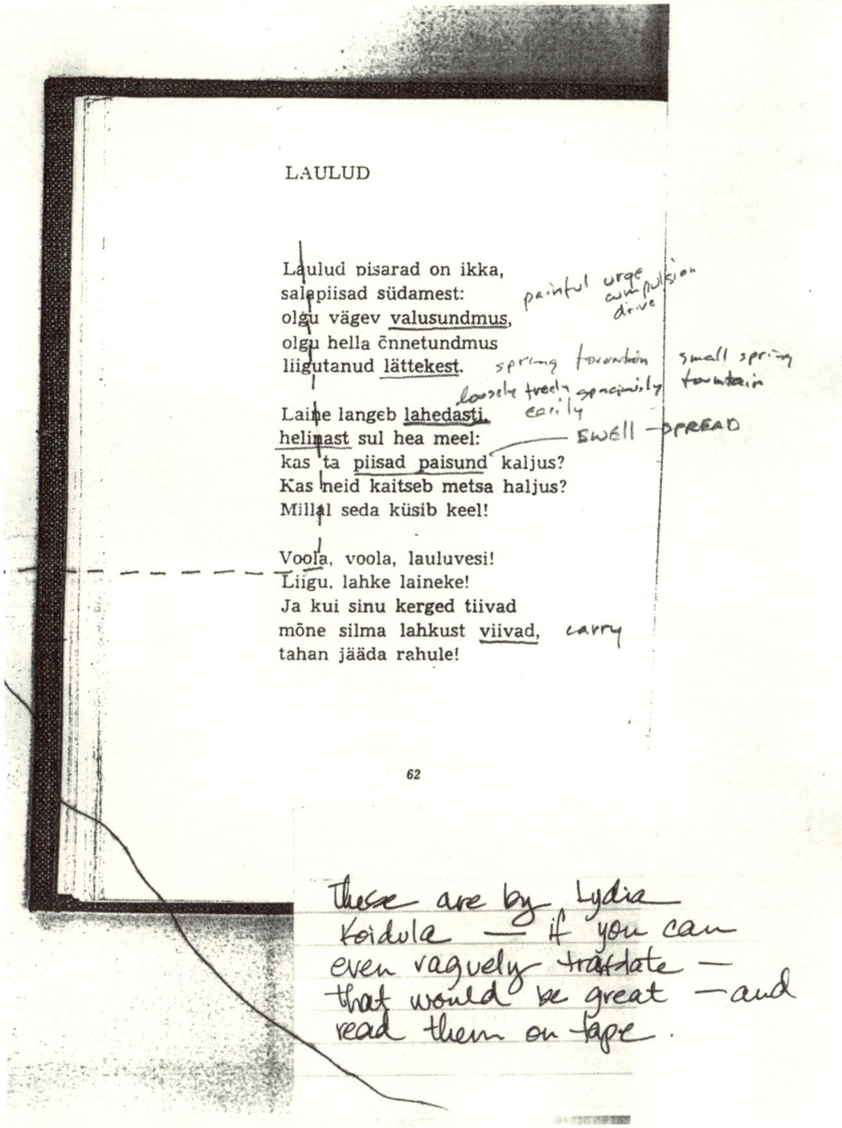
LAULUD

Laulud pisarad on ikka,
salapiisad südamest:
olgu vägev valusundmus,
olgu hella õnnetundmus
liigutanud lättekest.

Laine langeb lahedasti,
helinast sul hea meel:
kas ta piisad paisund kaljus?
Kas neid kaitseb metsa haljus?
Millal seda küsib keel!

Voola, voola, lauluvesi!
Liigu, lahke laineke!
Ja kui sinu kerged tiivad
mõne silma lahkust viivad,
tahan jääda rahule!

62

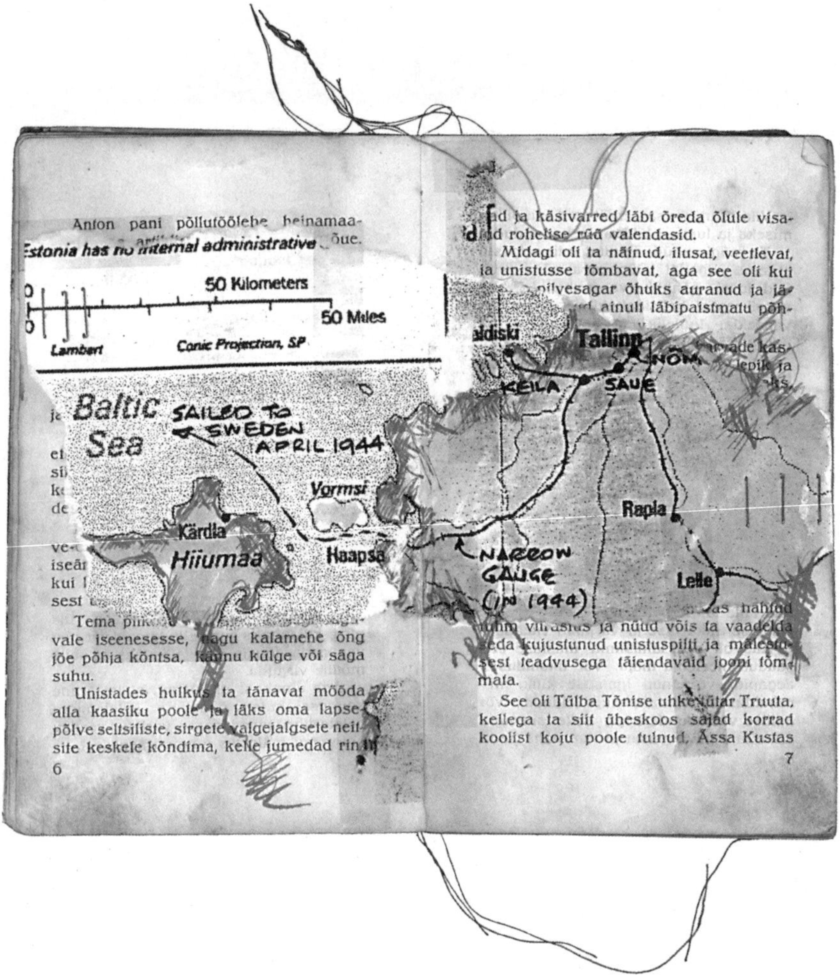
Estonia has no internal administrative
50 Kilometers
50 Miles
Lambert
Conic Projection, SP
Baltic Sea
SAILED TO SWEDEN APRIL 1944
Vormsi
Kärdla
Hiiumaa
Haapsalu
Tallinn
NÕMME
KEILA
SAUE
Rapla
Lelle
NARROW GAUGE (IN 1944)

4. Dear Jill,

I found the poems by G-mother we talked about. In translating them I took some "poetic" liberties with English grammar and syntax, as you will notice. In doing so, I felt I was able to convey some of the mood and rhythm of the original language. I also found a sheet of paper with the translation of the Estonian national anthem and a poem by Lydia Koidula on it. The latter I attempted to translate quite literally. The word "isamaa" in literal translation is "fatherland." But "fatherland" sounds too tough, too robust in English, maybe too Germanic. To the Estonian mind "isamaa" is more tender and loving than "fatherland." Thus "native land" seems a more appropriate translation. Besides, self-respecting Estonians would not, God forbid, be identified with Germans, although they are a mixed race with a good dose of German blood in them. I also found the copy of a letter from G-father to Aunt Mary with a translation of another Estonian poem in it. The poet Juhan Liiv incidentally attended the same high school in Tartu that I did, although he did it 100 yrs. earlier. Juhan Liiv's poems are very melancholy. He suffered from depression and eventually committed suicide. Greetings to you and Jonny from Aunt Mary and me.

Love, Uncle Eino.

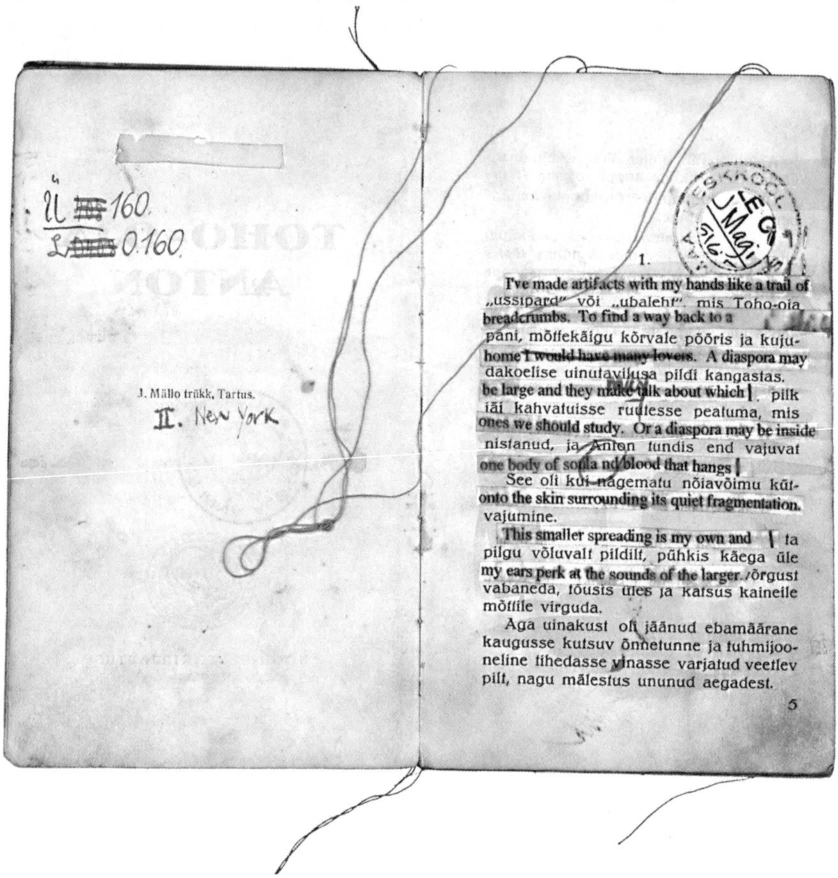
160.
0.160.
J. Mällo trükk, Tartus.
II. New York
1.
I've made artifacts with my hands like a trail of
„ussipard" või „ubaleht", mis Toho-oja
breadcrumbs. To find a way back to a
pani, mõttekäigu kõrvale pööris ja kuju-
home I would have many lovers. A diaspora may
dakoelise uinutavilusa pildi kangastas.
be large and they make talk about which | . pilk
jäi kahvatuisse ruutesse peatuma, mis
ones we should study. Or a diaspora may be inside
nistanud, ja Anton tundis end vajuvat
one body of soula nd blood that hangs |
See oli kui nägematu nõiavõimu küt-
onto the skin surrounding its quiet fragmentation.
vajumine.
This smaller spreading is my own and | ta
pilgu võluvalt pildilt, pühkis käega üle
my ears perk at the sounds of the larger. võrgust
vabaneda, tõusis üles ja katsus kainelle
mõttile virguda.
Aga uinakust oli jäänud ebamäärane
kaugusse kutsuv õnnetunne ja tuhmijoo-
neline tihedasse vinasse varjatud veetlev
pilt, nagu mälestus unund aegadest.
5

"Excerpts from Threads*" begins with a re-write of my father's translation of Lydia Koidula, one of Estonia's most famous poets. "Translation" expresses many aspects of the Estonian consciousness—much of their poetry is coded language of longing for independence—and the piece is, as a translation event, symbolic of my relationship and interdependence with my father via his home language, Estonian, a language that I do not speak. These excerpts also include maps that my father annotated and gave to me as I prepared for travel to Estonia; the maps are collaged onto pages of Estonian novels. The visual manipulations of "given" texts and maps—stitching, scratching, cutting and pasting, stapling—come from urges similar to what teachers of young children call "mark-making acts," pre-writing and meta-language acts.*

When, as a child, I listened to my father speak Estonian with my uncle and grandparents, I remember that the language sounded soft and tender, at times funny, and my father became childlike and also tender. For fun, we used to ask him to list off the Estonian vowel sounds (there are many). So it seemed to me that a person/speaker undergoes translation when they switch languages. The fact that those early conversations were never or rarely translated continues to be generative, and leads me to believe that the space between language sounds and meaning is charged with possibility. I envision Threads *as a container for that possibility—a project that will include writing, sound, video, and works on paper that ask both the reader/viewer and myself to explore that generative, "between" space on which translation relies.—JM*

MONCHOACHI & BRENT HAYES EDWARDS

from *Manèg / Manteca*

9

Zanno lanmè! Sé wou ké tiré kont tala
anba kourón tchim anmè-w.
Ou ké konté kont bèt-la ki té wont
é ki té ka kouri pou pa té wè lonm-li.
Sonjé: "Man ké mèt lavi si man mèt lanmó."
(E dépi sa, Latè ka vansé vant-a-tè asou chimin malmó.)

Mi kont-la ou ké tiré-a, zanno lanmè,
Sé an kont lalín anmè.

E lè sé zétwèl-la ké mandé-w:
"Min sa ki bèt tala, zanno lanmè?"
Ou ké réponn: Nonm sé non-y! Mwin wè-yo
li épi lonm-li, mó anba kalbas ló-a,
tro lou, tro las, pou vansé ankó."

Aló zót ké chanté:
"Lavi sé an lawonn, an lawonn,
toutan ou adan, simyé ou dansé.
Lavi sé an lawonn, an lawonn,
an won lawonn épi alé."

17

Sa-w ka chèché an mémwè-w, sa-w ka chèché an lachè-w?
"An gran jou klè é san rid anlè fas dlo-a;
an gran jou klè é san ri anlè mas dlo-a . . ."
Lèspwa sé yich lanmizè; lèspwa sé flè lanmizè.
"An gran jou klè é san rid adan glas dlo-a."
(E jan lanmè ké di nou sa lanmè-a póté épi
boukan lanmè-y.)

Sa-w ka chèché an mémwè-w, sa-w ka chèché an rèv-ou?
"An gran silans nanm-lan kon an gran souf lanmè,
An gran silans nanm-lan kon an gran souf lanmó."
Lèspwa sé lajwa malè, lèspwa sé lafwa malè.
—E sa nou minm ké di ankó éti silans-lan poko di . . .?—
(Min jan lanmè ké di nou sa lanmè-a póté anlè
van lanmè-y.)

—M

9

Anneau de mer! C'est toi qui tireras cette histoire
sous ta couronne d'écume amère.
Tu contreras le conte de la bête qui avait honte
et qui courait pour ne pas voir son ombre.
Souviens-toi: "Je serai maître de la vie
si je suis maître de la mort."
(Et depuis, la terre avance ventre à terre
sur des chemins de malemort).

Voilà l'histoire que tu diras, anneau de mer.
C'est un conte de lune amère.

Et lorsque les étoiles te demanderont:
"Mais quelle est donc cette bête, anneau de mer?"
tu répondras: "Homme est son nom! Je les ai vus
lui et son ombre, mourir sous la calebasse d'or,
trop lourds, trop las pour avancer encore."

Alors vous chanterez:
"La vie est une ronde, une ronde,
tant qu'on y est, mieux vaut danser.
La vie est une ronde, une ronde,
un tour de ronde, et puis allez."

17

Que cherches-tu dans ta mémoire, que cherches-tu dans ta chair?
"Un grand jour clair et sans rides sur la face de l'eau:
un grand jour clair et sans rires sur le masque de l'eau . . ."
L'espoir est fils de misère; l'espoir est fleur de misère.
"Un grand jour clair et sans rides dans le miroir de l'eau."
(Et les gens de mer nous diront ce que la mer
a apporté avec sa rumeur.)

Que cherches-tu dans ta mémoire, que cherches-tu dans tes rêves?
"Un grand silence de l'âme, comme un grand souffle de mer;
un grand silence de l'homme comme un grand souffle de mort . . ."
L'espoir est joie de malheur; l'espoir est foi de malheur.
—Et que dirons-nous encore que le silence n'ait déjà dit . . ."—
(Mais les gens de mer nous diront ce que la mer
a porté sur son vent de mer.)

—M

9

Ring of sea! It is you who will slip this story
under your crown of bitter seaspray.
You will tell the tale of the beast who was ashamed
and ran away from his shadow.
Remember: "I will be master of life
if I am master of death."
(And since then, the earth advances stomach to the ground
on the paths of the living dead).

This is the story you will tell, ring of sea!
The tale of a bitter moon.

And when the stars ask you:
"But which beast is this, ring of sea?"
you will reply: "Man is his name. I saw them,
him and his shadow, die under the golden calabash,
too heavy, too weary to move on."

Then you will sing:
"Life is a round, a round,
as long as we're here,
we might as well dance.
Life is a round, a round,
a turn in a round, and then go."

17

What do you seek in your memory, what do you seek in your flesh?
"A great day, clear and smooth on the face of the water;
a great day, clear and solemn on the mask of the water . . ."
Hope is the son of misery; hope is the flower of misery.
"A great day, clear and smooth in the mirror of the water."
(And the seafolk will tell us what the sea
has carried in with its roar.)

What do you seek in your memory, what do you seek in your dreams?
"A great silence of the soul, like a great breath of sea;
a great silence of man like a great breath of death . . ."
Hope is the joy of sorrow; hope is the faith of sorrow.
—And what is there for us to say that silence hasn't already said . . . ?—
(But the seafolk will tell us what the sea
carried on its sea wind.)

—*BHE*

9

The sea belts the island
with sound and spray
beating a twice-told tale
told again behind the eyes
in a burnished rondelet
reflected in a distant tinkle:
the moon, bright tambourine
pocked with rings, white
as ash, tugs at the depths
and deposits the wet
dead, the weed and the shell
shards, on the shore where
with sound and spray
the sea belts the island.

17

Wait till the wave breaks:
then catch a palm-
full of seaspray
cradle the motion of light
in water, watch it sift
away against your willing
through the riverbed
of wrinkles in your hands.

Dry, they turn flecked
with sun: sea salt
left behind the sound
of the silence that shines
beneath the waves.

Cup your right hand to your ear,
listen: "Doubt leavens a draft."
With wings, or echoing laughter?
The chill of ascent for the one
left behind? Now cup
the left: "Don't leave me adrift."

—*BHE*

Monchoachi is one of the more remarkable poets to emerge in the Francophone Caribbean in the past two decades. The challenges of his work, in particular its complex appropriation of surrealism, are reminiscent of some of the better known models of Antillean writing, whether the poetics of neologism developed by Aimé Césaire or the poetics of opacity elaborated by Edouard Glissant. But Monchoachi's oeuvre marks a singular approach to the politics of language in the neocolonial Caribbean. Whereas Césaire and Glissant pointedly choose to write in French, Monchoachi is part of the generation that began in the 1970s to experiment with writing in Creole: Frankétienne, Sonny Rupaire, Patrick Chamoiseau, Raphael Confiant. At the same time, his work must be situated in an uneasy relationship to the writers who have been habitually grouped in the créolité movement in Martinique. Whereas the créolité novelists have explored both the possibilities of a literary Creole and, more recently, strategies of creolizing French (in fictions unfurled as dense archival palimpsests where French is "irrigated" or imploded with Creole syntax and vocabulary), Monchoachi has attempted to forge a poetics of the border between French and Creole. His book-length serial poems, Mantèg *(1980) and* Nostrom *(1982), are self-translations: each proceeds in the two tongues at once, Creole on the left side of the page, French on the right.*

Might we term this a poetics of translation, then? To do so would immediately raise a number of difficult issues. First of all, the poems throw the entire notion of translation into question, since their structure makes it impossible to determine "translation" from "original." Here, French and Creole are posed in a much more ambiguous relationship, in a manner that signals the ways that diglossia is central to the question of language in Martinique. As creole linguist Jean Bernabé puts it: "French is simultaneously the dominant language and the ecological partner, and it is necessary to take into account this double reality at every moment." Moreover, the aim of this doubled poetics is not clarity, fidelity, or the simple conveyance of meaning—much less the naturalization of Creole as the single proper language of the Martinican people. In a conference talk given in 1991, Monchoachi commented that his work is geared above all to resist the desire that language provide illumination or revelation. "When it claims to inform the real," he argued, "speech makes itself vulgar, necessarily repletive. The poet must preserve the opacity of the real." The poet's task is not to saturate the world with meaning, to "fill" it with speech, but instead to witness precisely the ways it resists mimesis. The key influence here seems to be the early criticism of Edouard Glissant, who has long espoused opacity as a strategy for anticolonial Antillean poetics. As Glissant writes, "There is only this: the veiled, unveiling. First the affirmation of a secret, of something occult, of a fundamental trace, and then the operation through which one attempts to reveal them (to oneself), less in their absolute truth than in the very vertigo of this operation. In other words: there is no unveiled here." In the bilingual poems of Monchoachi, such unveiling is performed in the shuttling between

French and Creole, in dissonances and distortions that (in his own phrase) "give a tone to darkness."

My versions of two sections of Mantèg *should raise a number of secondary complications. If* Mantèg *might be said to pursue a poetics of translation, then is it in turn translatable? If it is a doubled text, does it require a double translation—two "takes" in politically differentiated variants of English, mainstream and marginal, standard and basilect? One might be tempted to carry over the relation between French and Creole in the neocolonial Caribbean context using a putative linguistic parallel: British English juxtaposed with Jamaican dialect, for instance, or U.S. English and African American vernacular. The problem with this approach, however, is that it assumes a homology between systemic racialized exploitation in very different contexts. It seems to me reductive to imply a parallel, reflected in language, between the situation of the United States or Jamaica and the peculiar situation of Martinique (which remains politically a département of France, one that never acquired independence after colonialism).*

I have taken my charge here from Jean Bernabé's contention that poetry is a particular kind of "technology" of invention and even redemption. As such, Monchoachi's poetry does not aim for the expression of an integral racial self, or for the historical apotheosis of a national community. Instead, it is a technology of the interface: it speaks at the blurred boundary between overlapping languages, and finds its force and relevance in the complex historical relation between them. (In this light it is relevant that the title Mantèg *is a Creole word for "grease," "lard," or "butter," which derives not from French but from the Spanish word manteca. Thus this face-to-face serial poem evokes—with a figure from elsewhere, from outside the French colonial context, as though the principle can't be found there—what doesn't appear in the poem itself: the lubrication among its segments, the synovia of its shuttling.)*

If poetry for Monchoachi is in a sense always a "wager" at the border (he often makes recourse to the French word gage, with its connotations not just of gambling economies but also of risk, security deposit, and even political "engagement"), then its translation must stake itself in the echo of that edge. My translation is doubled, then, but not mirrored. Both are English versions of Mantèg *that strive to attend to the difference between French and Creole, the work of their discrepance in the original. As in* Mantèg *itself, but otherwise, it is left to the reader to hear what carries across the gap.—BHE*

QAYS IBN AL-MULAWWAH, ALLA BORZOVA, DENIS HOPPE, MICHAIL KURGANTSEV, & ANN E. MICHAEL

Majnun Songs, Sections 1–3

101

الا يا غراب البين حيجت لوعتى

فويحك! خبرني، بما انت تصرخ؟!

ابالبين من ليلى؟! فإن كنت صادقاً

فلا زال عظم من جناحك يفسخ!

ولا زال رام فيك فوق سهمه

فلا أنب في عش ولا انت تفرح

ولا زلت عن عذب المياه منفراً

ووكرك مهدما، وبيضك يرضخ!

فإن طرت أردئك الحتوف، وإن تقع

تقيض ثعبان بوجهك ينفخ

وعاينت – قبل الموت – لحمك مشدخاً

على جمر حر النار يشوي ويطبخ

ولا زلت في شر العذاب مخلداً

وريشك منتوف، ولحمك يشرخ

—*QA-M*

Маджнун

(КАЙС ИБН АЛЬ-МУЛАВВАХ) (VII в.)

1

Я болен любовью,
    моя неизбывна тоска.
Беда моя—рядом,
    любимая так далека.

Теряю надежду,
    живу, привыкая к разлуке.
Молчит моя милая,
    видит во мне чужака.

Я словно птенец
    угодивший случайно в сети.
В плену его держит
    незримая злая рука.

Как будто играет дитя,
    но для поймоной птицы
Игра обернется
    погибелью наверняка.

На волю бы выйти!
    Да стоит ли—право, не знаю.
Ведь сердце приковано к милой,
    а цепь коротка.

2

Что я делаю, безумец,
    в этот вечер темно-синий?
На песке тебя рисую
    и беседую с пустыней.
Крики ворона услышу—
    наземь падаю в тоске.
Ветер горя заметает
    мой рисунок на песке.

Ворон, что ты пророчишь?
С любимой разлуку?
Сам попробуй, как я,
испытай эту муку.

Что еще ты сулишь
одинокому, ворон?
Бедняку угрожаешь
каким приговором?

Ты не каркай, не трать
понапрасну усилья—
Потеряешь ты голос
и перья, и крылья.

Будешь ты, как и я,
истомленный недугом,
Жить один, без надежды,
покинутый другом!

3

В мире нездешнем,
в раю, где повсюду покой,
Души влюбленных
томятся ли здешней тоской?
Прах—наша плоть,
но данно ли нетленному духу
Вечно пылая,
терзаться любовью людской?
Очи усопших не плачут,
но в мире нездешнем
Слезы влюбленных—
бессмертные!—льются рекой!

4

Целую след любимой на земле.
Безумец он!—толкуют обо мне.

Целую землю—глину и песок,—
Где разглядел следы любимых ног.

Целую землю—уголок следа.
Безумец я, не ведаю стыда.

Живу в пустыне, гибну от любви.
Лишь звери—собеседники мои.

5

Любовь меня поймала, увела
Как пленника, что заарканен с хода,
Туда, где нет ни крова, ни тепла,
Ни племени, ни стойбища ни рода,

О как она нежна! Когда сравню с луною лик прелестный
Поймите, что она милей соперницы своей небесной,

Затем, что черные, как ночь, душисты косы у подруги,
И два колышутся бедра, и гибок стан ее упруги.

Она легка, тонка, стройна и белозуба, белокожа,
И, крепконогая, она на розу свежую похожа.

Благоуханию ее завидуют, наверно, весны,
Блестят жемчужины зубов и лепестками рдеют десны.

Любовь живет во мне одном, сердца других покинув.
Когда умру—умрет любовь, со мной найдя забвенье.

6

Исполни лишь одно желанье
    мое—иного нет;
Спаси любимою от горя,
    убереги от бед.

Мне блага большего не надо,
ты щедро одарил
Меня любовью—в ней отрада,
спасение и свет.

Пока живу—люблю и верю,
надеюсь и терплю,—
Служу единственному богу,
храню его завет . . .

7

Только любящий достоин
человеком называться.
Кто живет, любви не зная,
совершает светотатство.

Мне любимая сказала:
"Ничего не пожалею,
Лишь бы милого увидеть,
лишь бы мне тебя дождаться".

Только любящим завидуй—
им на долю выпадает
Невозможное блаженство,
неразмерное богатство.

—*MK*

1

I'm pining.

I'm pining; I'm lovesick, unceasing my anguish and pain.
Misfortune's beside me, my Laila is so far away.

Despairing without her, yet somehow surviving: alone, numb—
A stranger I am in the sight of my silent beloved.

A bird in a net, I am caught by surprise and ensnaréd.
While roughly they seize me, invisible fingers grasp tight.

Cruel hands treat me callously, like children grabbing and teasing.
And ah, for the poor bird, such teasing leads only to death!

Though I long for freedom, for me there is still one dilemma:
My poor heart is chained to Laila; the chain's cruelly short.

I'm pining, I'm lovesick. I'm pining . . . pining . . .

2

Caressing your soft footmarks which kissed sand—
Oh, Laila, you know they say I am mad!

Caressing earth, not caressing my love;
A madman, and I do not know shame!

I live in dry sands, dying from my love,
and wild beasts are my only company.

3

What is happening?
What is happening, oh madman?
Oh, madman!
What is happening, oh madman, in the evening?
In the evening—sorrowful, blue evening?

I am drawing you on cool sand,
talking to the dunes and raving—

Crying! I can hear the raven crying.
Crying! I sink to the earth in pain.

Sorrow's wind sighs in the desert,
whirlwind
sweeps my drawing,
my drawing off the sand,
my drawing
off the sand . . .

Raven, what do you foretell? The loss of my Laila?
Put yourself in my place—you must know how I suffer!

Is there more you forebode of my wretchedness, Raven?
Will your verdict prolong my despair, prophet Raven?

Do not crow for me! Save your breath for those who still have hope.
You'll only waste your poor voice, your plumage, your broad wings;

You will be just a wretch or a madman, abandoned
As I am: friendless, rejected, and worthless without love!

—*AM*

2

1. Я БОЛЕН ЛЮБОВЬЮ / I am pining.

1) ♭ = quarter tone flat

2) Saba is a Persian mode, as well as Hijaz, Shūrī & Kurd, which will appear later. In this movement the modulation of modes is used, which follows the rules of traditional Arabic music

3) sul tasto → ord. → sul pont. → ord. → sul tasto, et

4) turn the embouchure hole away from lips with a quick stream of air, stopped by the tip of the tongue

3+2
un-cea-sing my an-guish and
мо-я не-из-быв-на тос-
Tenor
Fl.
Vn I
Vn II
Vla
Cello
(2+3)
pain.
ка.
Mis-
Бе-
2+3

—*AB*

"Majnun Songs" (1996) is based upon the poetry of Arabic Poet Qays ibn al-Mulawwah, popularly known as Majnun (the madman). Throughout his life, Majnun wrote about his all-consuming passion for his beloved cousin Laila. Laila was not permitted to marry Majnun, for her father considered Majnun's well-known poetry to be a disgrace to her. Majnun's abiding love, grief, renunciation, and pain are embodied in a poetry of transcendent depth and inexpressible beauty, which has been sustained in the oral and written Arabic for centuries. It is said that Majnun spent his last years alone in the desert, drawing Laila's profile on sand and talking with the wind, accompanied only by the graceful gazelles who reminded him of his beloved.

"Majnun Songs" incorporates Middle Eastern musical ideas with elaborated contemporary vocal and instrumental techniques. I used traditional Arabic modes and rhythms in this cantata; the instruments in the sextet include the riq, *an Egyptian tambourine, and piccolo (which in its weak, low register sounds like a folk flute). The vocal part (for tenor) includes melismatic patterns and vocal techniques of Middle Eastern music, such as* tahrir*: throat vibrato. —AB*

How these poems made their way from ancient Iraq to a contemporary cantata illustrates the way art transcends time and cultural barriers. While still living in Russia, Alla Borzova came across Majnun's work in an anthology of Arabic and Persian poetry and became fascinated by Majnun's passion and imagery. The Cyrillic is the translation of the Majnun poem by Michail Kurgantsev that Borzova used to create section 1 ("I'm Pining . . ."). It is reprinted by permission from Love Lyrics of the East *(Moscow: Pravda, 1988). She composed the cantata in Russian, but in order to get the piece performed in the U.S.A. after her emigration, she needed an English translation. She enlisted my help in transliterating the lyrics, which she had culled from sections of various poems (identified as poems 68, 76, and 101 in the Bakr al-Walibi text). My task was to write lyrics that fit the composition exactly, yet maintained the tone and content of the Arabic original.*

In order to present the full scope of the evolution of these poems from nomadic, oral-tradition Arabic poems to English-language cantata, I have enlisted the help of Denis Hoppe for the literal Arabic-to-English translation—a step that, curiously, was missed on the way to the completion of this work.—AM

Poems 68, 76, and 101 translated and correlated to some of the poems in Borzova's libretto by Denis Hoppe, Princeton University 1969, from a modern copyrighted collection of poems by the Arabian Peninsula/Iraqi poet, famous as Majnun Layla, who lived during the Omayyad Caliphate (661–750) of Damascus.

Ibn al-Mulawwah, Qays. Diwan *(poems of)* Majnun Layla, *collected by Abi Bakr al-Walibi, edited by Muhammad Ibrahim Salim, Cairo, Dar al-Tala'i', 1994. Complete title from University of Michigan Rackham Library catalogue:*

Diwan Majnun Layla/hadha diwan al-'ashiq al-muhibb al-wamiq Qays ibn al-Mulawwah al-shahir bi-Majnun Layla al-'Amiriyah; jam' Abi Bakr al-Wahibi; haqqaqahu wa-'allaga 'alayhi wa-gaddama la-hu Muhammad Ibrahim Salim.

A comment at press time from Rabih Haddad, to whom these poems were sent as a Valentine's Day 2003 gift: "You may be interested to know that ghurab al-bain *(raven . . . separated) is just an expression used by the old Arabs to describe being separated from loved ones. Qays missed Leila so much that he turned* ghurab al-bain *into a real bird and then put all those curses on it. I can't tell you how much I enjoyed reading these verses again. If you have more of them, don't hesitate to share." Rabih Haddad is a scholar and renaissance man currently in jail, appealing his arrest on alleged immigration violations. He can be contacted via the Free Rabih Haddad Committee, P.O. Box 131092, Ann Arbor, MI 48113-1092, or at Rabih Haddad, 100 East 2nd Street, Monroe, MI 48161.—DH*

This cantata for quintet and tenor debuted at SUNY's studio (New York City) in November 1996 and in 1997 was nominated for an award from the Academy of Arts and Letters. It premiered in concert by Mimi Stern-Wolfe with the Downtown Players and the Cassatt String Quartet at Lang Hall, Hunter College, New York, New York, on March 27, 1998. All music and lyrics are ASCAP registered.

KISHWAR NAHEED & MAHWASH SHOAIB

from *Sokhta Samani-e-Dil / Composition of a Scorched Heart*

راہ گیر سے مکالمہ

جب تک تم دمشق نہیں آؤ گے
فرات کے قریب پیاس کی شدت کو
محسوس نہیں کر سکو گے
جب تک تم فلسطین نہیں آؤ گے
بے زمینی کی اذیت کو
محسوس نہیں کر سکو گے
جب تک تم افغانستان نہیں آؤ گے
کلاشنکوف کی گولی میں چھپی
نفرت کو پہچان نہیں سکو گے
جب تک تم افریقہ نہیں آؤ گے
اپنے ہی وطن میں غلامی کی ذلت کو
گرفت میں نہیں لا سکو گے
جب تک تم امریکہ نہیں آؤ گے
گلی گلی پھیلی فرسٹریشن کی
دبیز تہہ کو پہچان نہیں سکو گے
جب تک تم ہندوستان نہیں آؤ گے
گنگا کو میلی کرتی عصبیت کا
چہرہ نہیں دیکھ سکو گے
جب تک تم پاکستان نہیں آؤ گے
تمہیں تجربہ ہی نہیں ہوگا
کہ چوکیدار مالک کیسے بن جاتا ہے۔
میں تو موت کے خلاف ہونے کے باوجود
بہت سے بندروں جیسی شکلوں کو مار کر ہی
خوشی کی طمانیت کا اجالا کر سکتی ہوں...... آؤ میرے ساتھ آؤ!

—*KN*

Dialogue with (a/the) Passerby/Bystander/Spectator

Until you (do not) come to Damascus/Syria
near Farat (you) will not know/be able to/be capable of
feel(ing)/sense the intensity/force of thirst
Until you do not come to Palestine
you will not be able to feel
the torture/agony/pain/anguish of landlessness
Until you do not come to Afghanistan
you will be able to recognize/distinguish the hate
hidden/concealed behind the bullet of a/the klashnikov
Until you do not come to Africa
you will not be able to grasp/grapple
the humiliation/disgrace/shame of slavery in your own
 nation/country/land
Until you do not come to America
you will not able to recognize the thick/deep layer
of tyranny/oppression/phiroaniyat spread everywhere
Until you do not come to Hindustan/India
you will not be able to see the face
of the bestiality/inhumanity/menace/specter polluting/defiling the
 Ganges
Until you do not come to Pakistan
you will not even have the experience
that how does the gatekeeper/porter become the owner/proprietor.
Despite being against death, I
can only brighten up/enhance the pleasure/fulfillment of happiness
by (just) killing so/the many faces like monkeys (?)—Come, come
 with me!

—MS, draft (1)

Until/Unless you come to Syria
you will not (be able to) feel
the intensity/severity of thirst near the Farat
Until you come to Palestine
you will not be able to feel
the torment/agony/anguish of dispossession/landlessness
Until you come to Afghanistan
you will not be able to recognize/identify/comprehend the hate
hidden/concealed behind the bullet of a klashnikov
Until you come to Africa
you will not be able to grasp/comprehend/learn/admit
the disgrace/indignity of slavery in your own country
Until you come to America
you will not able to recognize the thick layer
of overweening pride/hubris/phiroaniyat (spread/diffused) everywhere
Until you come to India
you will not be able to see the face
of the bigotry/prejudice polluting/defiling the Ganges
Until you come to Pakistan
you will not even have the experience/knowledge
of how the watchman/guard/sentinel/gatekeeper becomes the
owner/proprietor.
Despite being against death, I
can only burnish/polish/brighten/enhance the tranquility of
    happiness/joy
with/by (just) killing so/the many monkey-like faces—Come, come
    with me!

—*MS, draft (2)*

passerby with dialogue

until you to damishq not come will
farat near thirst's intensity
feel not able to be will
until you to phalesteen not come will
dispossession's agony
feel not able to be will
until you to afghanistan not come will
klashinkov bullet in hidden
recognize hate not able to be will
until you to africa not come will
your own country in slavery's disgrace
comprehend not able to be will
until you to america not come will
alley alleys spread phiroaniyat's
thick layer to recognize not able to be will
until you to hindustan not come will
ganga-defiling bigotry's
face not see be able to will
until you to pakistan not come will
you experience even not have will
that watchman owner how becomes.
I even death against being despite
many monkey like faces by killing only
happiness' tranquility burnish can . . . come me with come!

—MS, transliteration (3)

Until you come to Damascus
you will not be able to feel
the intensity of thirst near the Farat*
Until you come to Palestine
you will not be able to feel
the agony of dispossession
Until you come to Afghanistan
you will not be able to recognize the hate
hidden in the bullet of a klashnikov
Until you come to Africa
you will not be able to comprehend
the disgrace of slavery in your own country
Until you come to America
you will not able to recognize the thick layer
of arrogance spread everywhere
Until you come to India
you will not be able to see the face
of the bigotry defiling the Ganges
Until you come to Pakistan
you will not even have the experience
of how the watchman becomes the owner.
Despite being against death, I
can only illuminate the tranquility of joy
by killing so many monkey-like faces—Come, come with me!

—MS, the leftover (4)

* Farat: (Arabic) the Euphrates

موت کی چادر پہ بیٹھی امن کی دیوی

سمندر کی طرح اپنی جانب کھینچتے ہوئے
جنگ اور جہاد کے نعرے
میرے بچوں کے چہروں پر داڑھیاں بن کر
نمودار ہو جاتے ہیں۔
یہ بچے اس سفر کی جانب چل پڑتے ہیں
جس کے آغاز میں تلوار کی نوک ہے
جو سورج کی حد پار کر کے
خود کو اولادِ ابراہیم سمجھ کر
آگ کے سمندر میں کود پڑتے ہیں۔
اس سمندر کا کوئی ساحل نہیں ہے
اسرائیلی ٹینک ان کی ہڈیاں
چباتے ہوئے گزر جاتے ہیں
کشمیر اور گجرات میں

ماؤں کی کراہوں میں لپٹے نام
بے نام قبروں میں چہرے تلاش کرتے ہیں
ناموں کے فرق کے علاوہ
انسانوں کے درمیان کوئی فرق نہیں ہوتا ہے۔
پھر بھی نفرتیں بونے والے
کبھی اپنے نام کے ساتھ رام اور کبھی حسن لگا لیتے ہیں۔
میں نے اپنی بٹی کا نام امن رکھا تھا
وہ پوچھتی ہے میرا نام سن کر لوگ ہنستے کیوں ہیں۔
راتوں کو گلیوں میں بلیاں کیوں روتی ہیں
اور رملّہ میں سولہ سال کی عمر میں
چودہ دفعہ جیل جانے والا نوجوان یہ کیوں کہتا ہے
میں جب بھی امن کی بات کرتا ہوں
تو ظالم اور جابر
میرا جغرافیہ اور میری تاریخ بدلنے
آ نکلتے ہیں
سارے زیتون کے درخت جل جاتے ہیں
ساری امن کی فاختائیں راستہ بھٹک جاتی ہیں
اور سارا آسمان سرخ ہو جاتا ہے۔
تب میری بیٹی، جس کا نام امن ہے
پوچھتی ہے میرا نام سن کر لوگ ہنستے کیوں ہیں!

—*KN*

Sitting on Death's Sheet, the Goddess of Peace/
Peace Goddess Sitting on Death's Sheet

Like the sea/ocean, pulling towards themselves
the slogans of war and jihad
appear/are appearing/materializing/emerging
on the faces of my children in the shape of/like beards.
These children start walking in the direction of that
    journey/voyage/expedition
in the beginning/start of which is the edge of (the) sword
who crossing the limit/boundary/border/threshold of the sun
believing/imagining/assuming/supposing themselves the Children of
    Ibrahim/Ibrahim's Children
jump/leap into the sea/ocean of fire.
This sea has no shore
crunching/chomping their bones
Israeli tanks pass through
In Gujarat and Kashmir
names wrapped/draped/swathed in the groans/moans/sighs of mothers
keep searching for faces in nameless/unnamed/anonymous graves
Besides the difference/distinction of names
there is no difference among humans
still those expressing/conveying/pronouncing hatreds/animosities
sometimes place Ram and sometimes place Hassan next to their names.
I had named my daughter Peace
She asks why do people laugh when they listen to/at my name
Why do cats cry/wail at night in alleys
and in Ramalah, why does the sixteen year old
youth/young man (who has) gone to jail/been jailed fourteen times
    say/state this:
whenever I talk about/of peace
tyrants and despots
come by/arrive
to change my geography and my history
all the olive trees are burnt
all the doves of peace lose their way
and the whole sky turns red.
Then, my daughter whose name is/who is named Peace
asks, why do people laugh at my name?

—*MS, the drafts (1)*

The Goddess of Peace Seated on Death's Sheet

Like the sea, drawing/pulling in towards themselves
the slogans of war and jihad
appear/materialize/emerge as beards
on the faces of my children.
These children start marching towards that journey/voyage
in the beginning of which is the tip/end of the sword,
who crossing the threshold of the sun
imagining/assuming themselves the Children of Ibrahim
jump/leap into the sea of fire—
this sea has no shore/coast
Israeli tanks pass by
crunching/chomping their bones
In Gujarat and Kashmir
names draped/swathed in the groans of mothers
keep searching for faces in unidentified/anonymous graves
Besides the difference of names
there is no difference among humans,
still those sowing/planting animosities
sometimes place/put Ram and sometimes Hassan next to their names.
I had named my daughter Peace
She asks why do people laugh at my name
Why do cats wail in alleys at night
and in Ramalah, why does the young man
who in sixteen years has gone to jail/been jailed fourteen times say this:
whenever I talk about peace
the despot/tyrant and the tyrant/unjust
appear
to change my geography and my history,
all the olive trees are burnt
all the doves of peace lose their way
and the whole sky turns red.
Then my daughter who is named Peace
asks, why do people laugh at my name?

—MS, the drafts (2)

death's sheet on seated peace-goddess

like sea towards themselves drawing
war and jihad's slogans
my children's faces on beards becoming
evident become.
these children that voyage towards walking start
in beginning of which sword's tip is
who sun's threshold crossing
themselves ibrahim's children believing
in fire's sea jump.
this sea shore no has
israeli tanks their bones
crunching pass by
kashmir and gujarat in
mothers' groans in wrapped names
anonymous graves in faces searching keep
names' distinction besides
humans among distinction no is.
still animosities-planters
sometimes own names with ram and sometimes hassan affix do.
I my daughter's name peace kept
she asks my name listening people laugh why
nights at alleys in cats why cry
and ramalah in sixteen years in
fourteen times jail going youth this why says
I when ever peace of talk
then unjust and oppressers
my geography and my history to change
out come
all olive trees burn away
all peace doves way lose
and whole sky red turns.
then my daughter whose name peace is
asks my name listening people laugh why!

—*MS, transliteration (3)*

The Goddess of Peace Sitting on Death's Sheet

Like the sea, drawing in towards themselves
the slogans of war and jihad
materialize as beards
on the faces of my children.
These children start marching towards that voyage
in the beginning of which is the tip of the sword,
who crossing the threshold of the sun
believing themselves the Children of Ibrahim
leap into the sea of fire—
this sea has no shore
Israeli tanks pass by
crunching their bones.
In Gujarat and Kashmir
names draped in the groans of mothers
keep searching for faces in anonymous graves.
Besides the difference of names
there is no difference among humans,
still those planting animosities
sometimes place Ram and sometimes Hassan next to their names.
I had named my daughter Peace
She asks why do people laugh at my name
Why do cats wail in alleys at night
and in Ramalah, why does the young man
who in sixteen years has been jailed fourteen times say this:
whenever I talk about peace
the despot and the tyrant
appear
to change my geography and my history,
all the olive trees are burnt
all the doves of peace lose their way
and the whole sky turns red.
Then my daughter who is named Peace
asks, why do people laugh at my name?

—MS, the leftover (4)

ہم غلاموں کی بس ایک شرط ہے

مرغیوں کے چوزے
جس طرح غلاظت کے ڈھیر پر چونچیں مارتے ہیں
بالکل اس طرح ہمیں، ہماری غربت کے ڈھیر پہ
لڑنے کے لیے چھوڑ دیا گیا ہے
زمین پہ چلتے کیڑوں کی طرح
ہمیں بنا پوچھے مار دیا جاتا ہے
پکڑ لیا جاتا ہے
احتجاج کرو تو جیل خانوں میں
بند کر دیا جاتا ہے۔
وہ کہ جن کے اسلحہ خانے کا بارود پرانا ہو رہا ہے
اس کو استعمال کرنے کے لیے، دنیا میں نئے سے نیا
شوشہ چھوڑ دیتے ہیں
وہ جب چاہیں، جہاں چاہیں
کسی بھی ملک پہ بم گرا سکتے ہیں
وہ ہمیں مجبور کرتے ہیں کہ فسطائیت کے
کارندوں کو ہم دیکھیں اور خاموش رہیں۔
وہ ہمیں مجبور کرتے ہیں کہ
ان کے حکم پہ کسی کو بھی دہشت گرد کہیں
وہ ہمیں مجبور کرتے ہیں کہ ان کے دیے ہوئے
لقمے کے سوا کچھ نہ کھائیں
کچھ نہ بولیں
کچھ نہ سوچیں۔
وہ یہ کیوں نہیں کرتے کہ
ہمیں ایک [illegible] مانیں
اس کی قیمت کے عوض
ہمارے دیہاتوں سے غربت ختم کر دیں
ہمارے فٹ پاتھ پہ سونے والوں کو پناہ گاہیں دیدیں
ہمیں ذہنی غلامی سے جسمانی غلامی تک لا کر
کیسینو لے جائیں اور مائیکل جیکسن کو سنوائیں۔

—KN

We Slaves Have Just One Demand/Claim

The way chicks/hatchlings of hens/chicken
snap their beaks at piles/heaps of garbage/refuse/rubbish
just like that we, on the pile/heap of our poverty,
have been left to fight/brawl
Like insects crawling on (the) earth
we are killed/exterminated without asking
we are caught
if (we) protest, then we are put/placed/put away
in/at jailhouses.
Those, the mortar of whose arsenals/armories is getting old/stale
to use it,
(they) leak/slip out new rumors in the world
whenever they want, wherever (they) want
(they) can drop bombs/bomb any country
They force/coerce us that we see
the workers/recruits of fascism (?) and stay silent/quiet.
They force/coerce us that
on their command/order/directive we call/declare/identify anyone a terrorist
They force/coerce us that besides the mouthful/morsel/scrap given by them
(we) eat nothing else
say nothing
think nothing.
Why don't they do this that
make us slaves just once/in one blow
as payment of this price/fee/charge
end/terminate poverty in our villages
give/provide shelter/lodging/sanctuary of those sleeping on our footpaths
bringing/transporting/conveying us from mental slavery to physical slavery
take us to casinos and have us listen to Michael Jackson.

—MS, the drafts (1)

We Slaves Have Just One Condition/Stipulation/Demand

The way chicks of hens
snap their beaks at piles of filth/garbage/rubbish
exactly like that we, on the pile of our poverty,
have been left to brawl.
Like insects crawling on earth
we are exterminated without any questions/asking
we are caught
if we protest, then we are locked up
in jailhouses.
Those, whose arsenals' gunpowder is getting old/stale
to use it,
they keep inciting/stirring new mischief in the world
When they desire, wherever they desire
they drop bombs on any country
They force/compel us that we see
the agents of fascism and stay silent.
They force/compel us that
on their command/order we declare/identify anyone a terrorist
They force/compel us that besides the morsel/scrap given by them
we eat nothing else
say nothing
think nothing.
Why don't they do this:
make us slaves (just) once absolutely/altogether
In exchange for this price,
end poverty in our villages
provide shelter/lodging/asylum/refuge to those sleeping on our footpaths
leading us from mental slavery to physical slavery
take us to casinos and have us listen to Michael Jackson.

—MS, the drafts (2)

we slaves only one demand have

hen's chicks
like filth's pile on beaks snap
just like that we, our poverty's pile on
fighting for left been have
earth on walking insects like
we without asking killed are
caught are
protest then jailhouses in
locked up are.
Those that whose arsenals' gunpowder old getting is
it use to, world in new and newer
mischief inciting are
they when want, where want
any on country bomb drop can
they us compel that fascism's
agents to us see and silent remain.
They us compel that
their command on anyone terrorist call
they us compel that their given
morsel besides nothing eat
nothing speak
nothing think.
They this why not do that
we *at one time* slaves make
in this price's exchange
our villages from poverty eliminate
our footpaths on sleeping to shelter give
we mental slavery to physical slavery from bringing
casino take and Michael Jackson to hear.

—MS, transliteration (3)

We Slaves Have Just One Demand

The way chicks of hens
snap their beaks at piles of filth
exactly like that we, on the pile of our poverty,
have been left to brawl.
Like insects crawling on earth
we are exterminated without asking
We are caught
if we protest, we are locked up
in jailhouses.
Those, whose arsenals' gunpowder is getting old
to use it,
they keep inciting new mischief in the world
When they desire, wherever desire
they drop bombs on any country
They force us that we see
the agents of fascism and stay silent.
They force us that
on their command we declare anyone a terrorist
They force us that besides the morsel given by them
we eat nothing else
say nothing
think nothing.
Why don't they do this:
make us slaves simply *once*
In exchange for this price,
end poverty in our villages
provide shelter to those sleeping on our footpaths
leading us from mental slavery to physical slavery
take us to casinos and have us listen to Michael Jackson.

—MS, the leftover (4)

These poems are taken from Kishwar Naheed's Composition of a Scorched Heart/Sokhta Samani-e-Dil *(Lahore: Sang-e-Meel Publications, 2002), her ninth and most recent volume of poetry. The first poem is taken from the first section of the volume, which is prefaced by the aphorism "All beast fear the fire," and the next two are taken from the second section, with the caption "Humans keep dying: Afghanistan and Palestine." My desire to attempt to translate Naheed's poetry evolves out of frustration with the lack of radically embodied translations of her work.*

The first draft of each poem consists of a translation I usually do in longhand, but, for this job, did directly on the computer without consulting any language dictionary. Whenever I felt stumped for the meaning of a particular word, I would try to guess what the line meant and try to fill in the blank somehow or the other, just so there wouldn't be an empty gap in the line. The slashes and different word options signify words that would sound and feel equally well with different permutations. For the second draft of each poem, I would consult two or three Urdu dictionaries and discover that some words had the opposite meaning of what I had imagined them to have. This would also be the draft where the poem would start taking a completely different shape. The third draft, "transliteration" (for the lack of a better description), would consist of a word-by-word translation of the poem from its original Urdu. This, for me, would sometimes be the most complex, semantically untranslatable, and lyrical poem of all. The fourth draft would be the most complete translation of the Urdu poem into English and would arise from the choices I would have made in the second, and, especially, the third drafts.

There is another, last draft of translation of these poems that I have not included in the drafts, and that is of the re-translation of the translated English poem back into Urdu to see how far my translations of the poem have veered from the originals. For instance, the first poem, "Dialogue with the Spectator," is one of the short and simple poems that Naheed writes. When I translated the poem back into Urdu, all the while trying to block the original Urdu, I realized that, although I had pretty much kept close to the original, I had significantly altered the word order of the poem itself. I had also whittled the poem down to the sparest of language: I took out the pronoun once it had been mentioned in the first verse and deleted verbs once the tense of the poem had been established; this is more an indication of the way I write my own poems, and it is a mark I'm leaving on Naheed's poem. In addition, at least until the fourth verse (this one mentions Africa in the fourth draft of the translated poem), I also determined a rhyme and refrain pattern, one I wasn't able to maintain in the rest of the poem. This rhyme and refrain pattern is called "qafia" and "radif," respectively, and is regularly used in Urdu poetry. Although Naheed uses much repetition in her poetry to call attention to particular lines, she decided not to use this pattern in the original, even when the option was available, because, I later realized, it would be too obvious and would risk making the poem too decorous.

In the end, I must confess that I'm still not fully confident with the translated title of the volume itself—but, then again, how can one ever be fully confident of a translation?—MS

MARCI NELLIGAN

From Vest Pocket Arabic & From Say it in Hebrew

From Vest Pocket Arabic

In the last ten days we have broken nine cups and that makes twenty two hands. There would have been more trouble. We went up instead of coming down, far from the airport. I am waiting for Fathi because he has the key—this isn't nice talk at all. He told me he was looking for you and he found you there and somebody whispered to me "Islam is a universal religion." We all sat on pillows on the floor. True, there were no chairs—an open window, American suits. The story is correct but we still have many things to do. In this box there are gifts for all of you—two gates and each gate has two lions. Look how the citadel shines, a song she herself composed. The color of the Nile, French coffee, a little bread. The world is mixed up these days. From what I hear, Indiana must be a great state, but I am tired of this Chevrolet. There will be something else, too. A walk in the desert, a black tent with grey stripes. Do you know the secret of learning languages? You need to take a bath. Take everything before you leave. If you come tomorrow I will tell you the story.

From Say it in Hebrew

I have something to declare
I am 25 years old, a businessman
I am looking for my friends.
Should I turn to the east
in the middle of the circle? Please
take my measurements where it is not
noisy. I will pay for the reply—the fastest
way, the right direction. Must I open
everything? I need a tourniquet—my friend,
my wife—something to regulate my hunger.
My eye does not function, is missing
a spring. For a minute I am glad. I prefer
something better. This road, the view, the structure
of your name. You ask what is the distance; well what do
you wish? The alterations take some
doing. We still have time, a little champagne
something to fix the bridge—the five pieces that join us.
The weather today is temporary
A matinee performance of "I love you"
I am glad this is hurting me because I find
that all I have I need to take.
Show me I am interested and come again
every hour, silent as in gold, never silent
the price of admission
this is for you.

MARK NOWAK

9 June 1916

The first arrests of the strike on the eastern Mesaba range occurred this morning when 250 miners from Aurora properties were halted at Wine lake, two miles northeast of Biwabik. They were enroute to Biwabik to cause trouble among employed miners. The advance guard, consisting of 14 men, was taken into custody by deputy sheriffs and mining police. The men are charged with rioting and trespassing.

—Virginia Daily Enterprise

Newsprints (paper) names.
Individuals involved in
An arrest, harassing, plus
A striking striker (is) struck.

Greeni, Joseph Greeni
Arvi, Arvi Lathenen
Halmi, William Halmi
Sam, Sam Sparkovich

Translation burns their names.
Communists? "Name names."
An arrest and an harness.
News kills language too.

Spain, Howard Spain
Boose, Arthur Boose
Paulmeri, August
Paulmeri, Louis (Lou)

Tongues, shuttering, lacerated . . .
Imprisoned in prisons *sans* speech.
Eating own tongue *sans* own tongue.
Translation (paper) swallows this.

Arrested: Martin Cacic
Mike, Mike Arwy

Arrested: Micola, Gust
Miners are marauders thus?

Who will not translate *We*
Us thus separated into *They*
And *They* cannot *say*
Speaking does not disembark

Silent Charles Seppetian
Silent Byra, Jack
Calokar, R. B. (abbreviated)
Who is spelling us.

A list of prisoners,
A list of unpronounceable names,
The news is so translated.
The strikers so negated.

OSKAR PASTIOR & ROSMARIE WALDROP

Oulipotisch Kommt von Oulipo; doch / Oulipotic Comes from Oulipo, So:

Oulipo?

Ruhig Floh!
Juckt wie Mo-
schustrikot.
Muss ich noch
Schuh ins Ohr
tun? I wo!
Urinol-
spur ist so
rubinrot . . .
Du nimmst doch
nur die Kon-
tur, die voll
Wut mit Tor-
tur sie polt—
und Pirol
muckt (Tirol
muht) wie Ton-
kunst dir Stroh-
hut nie hohl . . .
Du bist so
oulipo,
Pu! Ich mo-
dulier, wo
du dich soll-
bruch liest, doch
stur im Mond-
luch Kienholz-
brut dir holst . . .
Lug ins Moor
um sie—bloss
tunk die Klo-
nung: zieh los
nun, philo-
dullioh,
Dubio—
rupf mich, Topf
Oulipo!

—OP

Oulipo?

Quiet, flea!
Itches like a
musk tricot.
Must I still
shoe into ear
put? No way!
Urinol
track is so
ruby red . . .
You only take
the con-
tour that full of
wrath with tor-
ture poles—
and oriole
grumbles (Tyrol
moos) like music
your straw hat
never hollow . . .
You are so
oulipo,
Pooh! I mod-
ulate where
you read pre-
determined break, yet
stubborn fetch in
moon bog Kienholz-
brood . . .
Look at the swamp
around it—but
dip the clon-
ing: go away
now, philo-
dullioh,
Dubio—
pluck me, pot
Oulipo!

—RW (word for word)

Oulipo?

kooky pro
hooks his coat
to ear lobe.
Should we go
boot in tow
to skidrow?
Surely no!
Urinol
spoor is so
ruby rose . . .
You deplore
fury's con-
tours which com-
mune in moans.
Routine tor-
ture crypto-
news (Tyrol
moos) with vote
too remote.
You itch so
oulipo,
Pooh! fleas pol-
lute his home,
would dip clones
moonlit bogs,
chew stinkhorns
Cute if ob-
tuse Kienholz-
broods sniff dope,
snooze, bitch. Don't
you need go
cook, philo-
dullioh,
Dubio—
Stew me, pot
Oulipo!

—*RW (attempt at English)*

This poem is what Pastior calls a "vocalise." In music, a vocalise is a singing exercise that uses vowels rather than words. In Pastior's vocalises, each line has the same sequence of vowels (and, necessarily, the same number of syllables). Even the longer title uses no other vowel.

It is clear that in such a poem all the fun is in the sound pattern. Translating literally makes no sense. Working with a vowel pattern in English is complicated by the discrepancy between spelling and pronunciation. So the first question is whether to base the English version on the letter or on the sound. Then comes the challenge to use as much of the semantic dimension of the original as possible, while making the pattern work in English. Some displacement is unavoidable here. For instance, the flea and itch of Pastior's beginning are recovered (barely) much farther down in my poem.

Below is Harry Mathews's version of the poem, which appears in Burning Deck's selection of Pastior's work: Many Glove Compartments *(p. 104).—RW*

OULIPIAN DERIVES FROM OULIPO: SO

Oulipo,
cool flea! Old
moose-itch coat,
should we go
shoe-in-nose
too? We? No!
Urinose
spoor gleans most
ruby. So
you pick whole
views which (cold
fury, tor-
turing) pole—
buteo
moves (Tyrol
moos) with own
tune which no
hood will hole . . .
You live so
"oulipo,"
poo! We pro-
duce things so
you read "own
fuse"—still, mod-
moon Kienholz-
brood steers home . . .
Look: here's loam
to bring . . . oh,

pooped, its clone
droops. It scolds:
move, philo-
doopsio!
Dubbio—
cook me, stove
Oulipo!

JOAN RETALLACK
Mountains & Waters & Rivers

We are no longer young in weather.
—*Gertrude Stein,* History or Messages from History

We are always young in weather.
—*Genre Tallique,* GLANCES: An Unwritten Book

This translation of Eihei Dōgen's 13th century Mountains and Waters Sūtra is based on several prior translations. Most are anonymous or unacknowledged, available on the Web and in Buddhist manuals. The text in English seems to be constantly morphing as it's used for various kinds of practice. It has an interesting public domain as a training document inflected by the intentions of each group using it. Not reading Japanese, but wanting to realize a different kind of use (translation), I decided to work with a procedure that observes fundamental principles of any translation process: close interpretive reading, removals, additions, substitutions, conversions, retransmissions, conversations, commentaries, chance and intentional interpolations and interventions, as well as other instruments of the multiply understood and defined process that has been called—variously and generically—translation. (See note on translation following text.) The translation I finally found most useful is that of Arnold Kotler and Kazuaki Tanahashi which is directly from the Classical Japanese. The first two sections suggest the angle of faithfulness of my own text.

> *1*
> Mountains and waters right now are the actualization of the ancient buddha way. Each, abiding in its phenomenal expression, realizes completeness. Because mountains and waters have been active since before the Empty Eon, they are alive at this moment. Because they have been the self since before form arose they are emancipation-realization.
>
> *2*
> Because mountains are high and broad, the way of riding the clouds is always reached in the mountains; the inconceivable power of soaring in the wind comes freely from the mountains.

Moon in a Dewdrop: Writings of Zen Master Dōgen, ed. Kazuaki Tanahashi. Harper Collins Canada Ltd., 2001. p. 97.

mountains and rivers are only because mountains and waters have

analyst spoke (ascend) *our apocalyptic tendencies* (place oneself) *a single e*

from the mountains rain comes from the mountains snow

copulate) *in ethics intention always counts* (used of male animals) (fix securely t

fog comes from the mountains (a place to fix on or secure for display, stu

corner of the cockpit (provided with scenery, costumes, and other accessories)

money (the warship mounted ten guns) *I feel the of* (they plan and start to

trillions of logic gates (to post a guard or sentries) from the mountains th

mountains are walking blue mountains are flowing (mount sent

upward) fly in cloud-camouflaged planes over mountains *in aesthetics intention*

all mountains flow and are all mountains flow and are mountains r

or climb up on a vehicle) can you feel (the?) air (of?) (from?) (an?) other pl

walking mountain walking just like human walking (to flush th

you can come to know mountains you will *and after that even if it never*

that follows relates (to increase in intensity) you will love walking amon

disregard those who scoff you will love looking at mountains walking rivers flow

Nicht da Nicht da usw (affix gem to metal mount) *Ich fühle luft as in* (plac

pedestal) learn that walking green mountains walk they are perm

device rests while in use) *more than what has been described* (a natural elevation)

the palm) *immortality is now conjectured because of the presence of a single gene* (a na

immortal can still be hit by a bus (a natural elevation of the earth's surface havin

earth's surface having a height greater than a hill) someone in the mo

mountains they are (a large heap) *the musicians now come in and perform* (a mo

drags this very large structure to the water's edge (a mountain of books) *reaction op*

more swiftly than the wind someone in the mountains does

nountains are high and broad *of these atoms' nuclei* (climb) *the political*

iting (upon) clouds are in the mountains wind comes comes

star (mount a horse) *our omnipotent tendencies* (get up on in order to

ort) *"and yet" Ich fühle luft von anderem planeten* comes from the mountains

e) seeing comes from the mountains knowing comes *wedged into a*

ary digit o (mount a theatrical performance) *the vanishing point of imaginary*

it an attack) *I feel the from* (to be equipped with guns) *sluicing through*

iese things there are blue mountains and green mountains green

guards in the mountains) *imagination fired by other peoples' heroics* (go or move

ay not count (get or climb up on a horse) suspended in water flowing

s (scouts go into the mountains) *you would never have had that feeling if* (to get

o increase in amount) le zig zag de la curiosité (to increase in degree)

out of their mountain stronghold) if you can visit mountains often and well

crease in extent) you love mountains as you love rivers flowing *as the story*

ains *manipulated to perform a computation* (to increase in number) *or trying to*

guns in position) *Wir sind unterbrochen worden* (place specimen on glass slide)

nd) *The romantic poet writes A wild gust grips me suddenly, and I can* (place on a

though they walk more swiftly than wind (fixture on which a

what has been described (any of the seven fleshy cushions around the edges of

vation of the earth's surface having considerable mass) *but the genetically modified*

ides) *but what does this all matter since we clearly lack* (a natural elevation of the

does not understand this in the mountains outside the

f ironing) the poet's metaphors now come in and perform *and by the time one*

ment (a mountain of trouble) permanent (a huge quantity) though they walk

ealize or (mountain's) *argument reaction opinion* (backing or setting for something else) *just meters away* *in* *of* *from* *around* *death* *modeling a professio*

the female mons) *subsumed song* (monster) understand this in the r

walking without eyes to (monument) *some will want to preserve the vi*

protection) see mountains mountains walking green mountains walkin

remember neer vous lips re inter (mound) don't die don't die (a protecti

applause hi beanie beauty forget even unexpected truth (jut out) *the feel of ro*

feel feel down the edge mountains examine the green mount

caves) backward the miter-shaped chessman from #5 can now move diag

shrub) *they and we are walking side by side* walking and walking to investigate t

ends *it's as if their we're* *lucky that the city apartment had a white noise machi*

not cease walking backward does not cease walking forward

walking forward this is called the mountains flowing (mountain w

we going in circles green mountains walking eastern mountains *is this*

breeze of diurnal period depending on unevenness of land blowing down slop

body after the age of 20 cells begin to divide to replace cells that die (the mountain of

capacity to divide and replace dead cells adult stem cells won't divide forever hence the ex

in handbasket to hell) *embryonic stem cells are the only ones that can turn into any o*

when he got back from vacation) hence and yet of (mountain zebra nearly ex

and time green mountains are (of) walking (of) flowing (not an

hill in an area of low relief) *I feel (the?) air of (from?) another planet* *A wild*

(battery) (cork)(gum) (gun) (fever) (devil) (lover) (misery) (oyster) the name

detaches and drifts away) mountains flowing water mountains walking flo

wobbles in mountain wind) blowing *one hundred thousand one-handed poems*

wind: breeze of diurnal period depending on unevenness of land blowing up

and waters do you doubt the sentence green mountains walking are you shoc (mons pubis the male mons) *arresting use of ornamental notes* (mons veneris

outside (a vantage point) the mountains mountains walk mountains

es (an earthen defence) *Theology. To convey to heaven without natural death.* (a

mountains green mountains walking study the green (a hillock) I

ascend heat climax fire taxi fire couch rattle found (a guardian) forget

memory the feel from I relent oh no not I cul-de-sac I of in from (to mourn) ocean

ing and your walking examine walking backward and (flush out the

oss any number of unoccupied spaces of the same color (prostrate or suberect

that walking forward and backward if walking stops if walking

mountain time) *now I feel the now instead of the of* walking forward does

not obstruct walking backward walking backward does not obstruct

n these tiny little molecules (mountain breeze) and the flowing mountains *are*

owing on water mountains *is this a shuttle* practice (mountain wind:

at) *consider this by the time you're 20 there are approximately 300 trillion cells in your*

records accumulated by the armed forces) *stem cells are the only cells that have the*

th of the entire organism even if it's not hit by a tank first (now your turn your body

of cell without any known terminus (he found a mountain of work awaiting him

mountain practices being a mountain in every form and place

e or device from or on which a specimen is suspended) (not any conspicuous

ne suddenly, and I can (you'd be surprised what you find in mountains) (banana)

is from a tradition where it means owner of old camels (an enormous mass or bulk

untain giving birth to mountain (heap, hulk, hunk) (giant custard Valkyrie

panese: spring twilight I hear the sunset bell—ping!, etc or ping! from the (valley

day) mountains are grass trees earth rocks cradles graves mountains are rivers

e phrase flowing mountains do you understand flowing in the nature of (of)

TO TRANSLATE
(Desire: to experience poetry of from other to . . .)

DEFINITIONS

1. *To express in another language, systematically retaining the original sense.*
2. *To put in simpler terms; explain.*
3. *To convey from one form or style to another; convert.*
4. *To transfer (a bishop) to another see.*
5. *To forward or retransmit (a telegraphic message).*
6. *Theology. To convey to heaven without natural death.*
7. *Physics. To subject (a body) to translation.**
8. *Archaic. To transport; enrapture.*
9. *Aerospace. To move from one place to another in space by means of reaction power.*

**Physics.* Motion of the body in which every point of the body moves parallel to, and the same distance as, every other point of the body; nonrotational displacement.

—*American Heritage Dictionary*

This work has attempted to use every definition above except #1, which is impossible.

THOMAS SCHEIBITZ, ADAM DEGRAFF, & PAMELA LU

Judith & Maria

Thomas Scheibitz, Judith & Maria

MARIA. Here's a tableau of strife and piercing conflict.

JUDITH. A tale of a relationship grown impossible over time.

M. The edges of the canvas peel back like pink curtains.
They open onto a razor sharp puppet's theatre.
The Punch and Judy show, the Judith and Maria show.

J. The puppeteer is only a figment of the puppets' worst fears.

M. If we jumped in now, we'd be impaled,
so let's just ease into the evenly colored spaces
And hope we don't get pricked right away.

There's a deceptively serene blue and white sky overhead
Our heads stick up into the sky from a variegated hillside
You seem to have grown taller than me.

J. And you seem to be much further away than you are standing.

M. I'm having a brilliant moment of sprouting
My round head has been peeled back
untrapped from the canvas
in a crown of green and pink tears and folds

J. Though I am still much taller, and my face is not yours,
less complicated, shall we say, peeking out of the sky.

M. I'm a rich shade of gray-blue, like the planet Neptune.

J. I'm pink like Jupiter. I want to kick your ass.

M. And I will shred you with my newfound blender blades.
Get out of my space, will you? You're crowding my lyrical moment.
I've recently achieved a new consciousness.
There's a circumference of raw white insight just inside my crown.
This is the edge that motivates my existence.
And even though it hurts, I feel really alive.
But I'm conscious of my lower body,
I'm planted, there's no escape route here.

J. I can't respond to that. You'll have to grow your own way.
Just don't grow this way. I've got bees to attract.
I've got people to please. They need me for their garden.
Only you understand how much I need these people.
So never leave me. I need you. Don't uproot.
Just stay out of my way.
Perhaps you can watch and learn how to shine.

M. You always talk about leaving, coming back, leaving again.
Bet you think you're special, with that isosceles shield on your chest.
But you always come back. In fact, you're always there
though your head's often somewhere else.
I'm still healing from the cut you gave me last week
and I'm waiting for the chance to get you back.
Your points are not my points.
From here I see all your bad points.
I'd rather grow my own way.
Are we growing in the same direction?

J. Well, presumably, we're both growing up.
I mean we're no longer rococo. Nor Grant Wood.
Seems the farmer's pitchfork is no longer just a threat
by the look of your womb. Cover that thing up,
will you. People are looking at us. Thank god
I can only face out and don't have to see
the results of the direct hit. My prick
seems to have really opened you up. Sorry and all
but I was just looking for a little personal space.
I really never meant to hurt you. I like you.
You've got some good points. I have to admit
it feels good the way you hurt me. How else
could I live with myself? For symmetry you are indispensable.
and I just love the way you reveal your layers to anyone
who scratches the surface.

M. I may look nice and all,
but I've got a weapon in the making.
A secret pouch at my base.
Soon I'll be growing a new spike.
It'll be hot pink, just like the rest of them,
like these curtains we occasionally pull closed for security.

It makes me feel proud yet responsible,
knowing I have the power to bring you to your knees.
True, I am thin-skinned.
You're breaking my heart, leaving this album of shapes
open between us like this.
Don't we share a patchwork of all the good times we've
had together?

J. Back before evolution provided us with a means of protection
we did share some wonderful dreams. And underground,
where no one notices I can feel your roots entangled with mine.
But up here, in the parched air, I am programmed by nature itself
to keep at arm's length. But what is the point of all this?
If the roots are entangled it is only because they are desperately
searching for sustenance. If we need each other it is only a
biological need to propagate the species. It has nothing to do,
does it, with who you are, with your open wound, with your
system of scars. Your halo of white is surely only the space
into which you still need to grow. You really don't think
it some kind of holy star, do you? Still, Maria, even though
this is the truth, I don't really believe it. We rely on our thorns
to exist, and yet they are the curse of our existence.

Why is it impossible to maintain a sense of who I am, when you are
so near?

M. I've thought if I could produce more thorns
they'd bring us closer together.
What a nightmare!
I want to reach out closer to touch your hand
but I'd probably only jab you.
Yet these thorns are the knitting between us.
By now they have become our roots,
living reminders of all that we have together.
I jab. You flinch. You retract.
I retract, then reach out again
out of sheer perversity (or is it panic?)
wanting to touch again
the emergency
of all the points where we've hurt each other.

How many of our hits have actually been accidental?

And isn't it upsetting
how we're most in sync
when we're hurting each other?

J. Our thorns are woven together, inextractably.
We are defenses answering one another.
The cause is lost and the effect is infinite regress.
We protect ourselves with our own worst fears.
My thorns are an answer to yours.
We have both forgotten the question.
My thorns are the inverted mirror images of yours.
We have lost ourselves to protection.

In the winter of 2001, we were commissioned by the Berkeley Art Museum to respond poetically to a group of works by German painter Thomas Scheibitz. Our public reading took place in the museum gallery containing Scheibitz's works; the audience was invited to walk around and look closely at the paintings as we read our response to each one. We thought of our collaborative response as a translation from the genre of painting to the genre of poetry. In the process, we discovered many of the possibilities inherent in translating visual to poetic language: the ability to convey oblique shades of meaning, form and texture, and the psychological implications of a densely packed scene. In the excerpt which follows, we interpret the painting Judith & Maria *as a relationship dialogue between our assumed personas Judith (Adam) and Maria (Pam).—AD & PL*

SEFER YETZIRAH & ADEENA KARASICK

The Book of Creation, Homolinguistc Trans'elation

1:2

עשר ספירות בלי מה ועשרים ושתים אותיות
יסוד שלש אמות ושבע כפולות ושתים עשרה
פשוטות:

Ten Sefirot of Nothingness
And 22 Foundation Letters:
Three Mothers,
Seven Doubles
And Twelve Elementals.

Tossed froth hinged nestled
In trendy truth fondue, an undulant lottery:
of teeming *mots* (mutters),
Several oublés
entrées of veiled laments.

עשר ספירות בלימה במספר עשר אצבעות חמש
כנגד חמש וברית יחיד מכוון באמצע במילת
הלשון ובמילת המע ור:

Ten Sefirot of Nothingness
in the number of ten fingers
five opposite five
with a singular covenant
precisely in the middle
in the circumcision of the tongue
and in the circumcision of the membrum.

Tasty forays of naughty hynonymy
in transit ambience often fringed with
feisty posits
with singed, covert tenets
a prosody of middling
torqued scission of her tongue languing
in the skewered itching of the emblem.

I can take squashes and pumpkins,
and with the Sefer Yetzirah, make them into
beautiful trees.

—Rabbi Yehoshua ben Chananya, 1st century

The Sefer Yetzirah *(*Book of Creation, *also known as* Book of the Letters*) is the "oldest and most mysterious" of all Kabbalistic texts and dates back to 100* BCE*. Originally transmitted in Aramaic as an Oral Teaching, it was transcribed and bound into a Hebrew text, translated into German, Italian, and eventually English. Today, it exists in fragments, residues—a network of echoes, traces of versions layered upon versions that point to the ghostly remnants of an inaccessible/impossible origin. This homo(r)phonic trans-elation from the first chapter moves through and across an intra-lingual, cultural, and geo-poetic terrain, and, through a process of "homage and parricide," attempts to pay allegiance to this cryptic history.*

The focus of the Sefer Yetzirah *is on the 22 letters of the Hebrew alphabet (how they were formed, how they inter-relate, how they make meaning). The text itself is inscribed through slippage, elision, rupture, and undecidability, and language is foregrounded as "a continuum of letters," names, mathematical equations, gates of meaning.*

One of the reasons I chose this text was that I find it fascinating how the Sefer Yetzirah, *as a religious doctrine, is lodged firmly in a metaphysical tradition—yet, with its focus on letters, language, on meaning production, the "meta" (beyond) becomes a linguistic space, an intervening space, a place of syncretism, juxtaposition, and integration. Through this translative praxis, I was interested in carving out ways in which this text could be dislodged from a socio-religious and historically limiting hermeneutic (not mired within an onto-theologically insulated discourse validated by transcendency), but rather could be reviewed as a polyglossic textual arena without* specific *meaning and heterogenous to all hermeneutic totalization.*

Thus, through a process of recombination and permutation of letters, sounds, rhythms, textures, this translation (or "transluc-nacion") enacts (or puts into play) a Kabbalistic hermeneutic, whereby there is an audible reverberation of the various languages, histories, codes—that enfold into each other, caress each other, speak to each other.

By a slight displacement, by slipping one word inside/in place of another, it mimics Nietzche's Geschichte eines Irrtum *(*History of an Error*) announcing the narration of a fabrication: "how the true world finally becomes a fable"—a fabrication that produces precisely, nothing other than the idea of a true world—which risks hijacking the supposed truth of the narration.*

For this translation, I used the Gra Version *(which in its totality contains six chapters and consists of about 1,800 words). I have aimed to maintain all orthographic accoutrement of the original text: line spacing, capitalization, commas, periods, and quotation marks.*

In the beginning there was repetition, reproduction, translation.—AK

ALAN SEMERDJIAN

The Efficacy of Mistranslation

Translation is intrinsically thwarted by the very premise it is founded on. Language distances itself from itself. Its distinction is interwoven with cultural, dialectical, and principal variations in structure and even psychological sense. Robert Lowell, like many, found that his translations took on a life of their own, a life that was different from that of the original text. This is inherent in the process, and, therefore, translation is a form of imitation, close but no cigar.

When my writing students began engaging with texts in a different language, they decided (with very little suasion) to approach the task with a certain kind of aesthetic transliteration in mind. While a few of them were semi-literate in the languages we were working with (we dealt primarily in Italian, French, and Russian), they chose to put aside their prior knowledge and attempted to craft "mistranslations" based on how the characters looked and what they intoned rather than what they actually meant.

The results were wonderful for several reasons, two of which are of particular interest. By divorcing themselves from meaning as the primary translating tool in the actual process, the students were able to take incredible risks with language, most of which would not have happened had the text not been considered an aesthetic or external work of art as well as an internalized one (where meaning is constructed chiefly through decoding). In this sense, it is valuable to broaden Olson's notion of Projective Verse to perhaps Projective Alphabet or Projective Character because, as my students observed, the letters have personalities—wants, desires, and ambition to transform. By sensitizing themselves to these proclivities, my students created fresh new syntaxes, images, and line constructions that would never have happened before engagement in this process.

Here, Michelle Brown's draft playfully addresses Rimbaud's "Mystique":

Sir! Lap & the talisman lozenges
Torment leaves! Robes of the lane
Den the herb, the glaciers and
(of course) marauders!

From "Mystique":

> Sur la pente du talus les anges tournet leurs
> Robes de laine dans les herbages d'acier et d'emeraude.

In the first stanza of her "mistranslation," Michelle seems to acknowledge the tenor of Rimbaud's poem and react almost humorously to its vague magical and gothic referencing, which is a product of Rimbaud's time and place. So then, we are inviting our meditations on the content of the piece when we are choosing our words to replace them. Rimbaud's next verse, translated (Louise Varese, trs.), can be read as, "Meadows of flame leap up to the summit of the / little hill," to which Michelle responds, "Depressed flames bond tensely, just at the summit of a mountain," working solely off the French characters' sonority.

Gurdeep Sareen interprets the same section of Rimbaud's poem quite differently. He writes:

> The pain of talons ranges in torment
> resting on if owners
> have been slain, aimless herds erect in determination.
>
> That's when flames border justice and songs.

It seems that the students have something to say, and their normal vernacular and everyday colloquy does not permit them to say it. Gurdeep's poem conjures thoughts of occupation and ownership, political spatial ecology, something that I know he's been thinking about in his journaling since he was a freshman. This is the first piece of work I've seen from him that addresses these notions so viscerally.

Finally, another student, Jenn Fabian, creates a particular conflict with significant departure from the same text in terms of line breaking and stanza:

> Sergeant
> My mama is scared
> Mi mama is only (breath)
> The does not know
> About torment from great anger robed men
> Ancient emeralds
> Bandages vs. baggage

Eugenio Montale's "Lasciando Un << Dove >>," translated "Leaving a Dove," also was the impetus for transformations. The short poem, in Italian, reads as follows:

Una columba bianco m'ha disceso
Fra stele, sotto cuspidi dove il cielo s'annida.
Albe e luci, sospese; ho amato il sole,
Il colore del miele, or chiedo il bruno,
Chiedo il fuoco che cove, questa tombe
Che non vola, il tuo sguardo che la sfida.

Sumi Mathew heard the poem like this:

The column bends bends beyond her distance
Freight scene surrounds cupid's dove of anonymity
Able to lust, spontaneous, oh romantic soul
            Color the veil to enchant the groom
Cheeks ill faded, she covers, quest to be
She's not so lay till too guarded her finish.

This poem, like Gurdeep's, seems like it wanted or needed to be made, deriving from a complex introspection not often publicized in adolescent thinking, and the process of "mistranslating" became a conduit for the sentiment. The line, "Color the veil to enchant the groom," seems to be nowhere in the original but absolutely contextualized if we consider the background and interest, albeit concealed or secret, of the young writer (others interpreted the piece completely differently—one student dubbed hers "Laying a Duck," which I thought, acknowledging the paradox with her classmate, quite hysterical).

Perhaps the most interesting results of our experimenting came when we worked off of another alphabet altogether. Without the familiarity of a Romantic language, students responded to Yevtushenko's poetry with fantastic results. The mischievous characters opened new transmissions of psychological imbroglios, new constructions of meaning.

Yevtushenko's poem "Old Age Tears" is a sort of eulogy and commentary on introspection later in life. The imagistic procession of the poem, like the aesthetic of its Cyrillic font, lumbers with a fusion of brawn and grace. The poem is as animated as its message and begins as such:

Поздние Слезы

Жнвотные—ото другие народы
и не ио слезливон, как люди, породы
Но плачут собаки не спьяну-тверезы
Их старость выдавливает им слезы

I find it interesting that one student, Adam Israel, was able to take the suggestive curvatures of the Cyrillic verse and shape a commentary of his own, this time on the nature of the alphabet itself. The eulogy becomes a kind of chemistry, the tears are the shape of letters:

Dolorous Chemistry

Unbottled and aflight, awaiting
The word the had constructed, all but open.
Oh sweet compounds and fair mixtures,
I incline assiduously before your power.

Be tame, perfectly upset and cute-brained
Cute, confused kamikaze . . . Ha! Incorrect!
Are cats claustrophobic? Since they're clean?
You too, submarine, can be drowned.

Adam's mistranslation brings out the surreptitious nature of the Cyrillic alphabet and transliteration itself. Although he didn't do much "reading" of the poem per se (one time through in the original language—they were dissuaded from reading the English translation until afterwards), he was able to capture the animated affectation of the poem. What does this tell us about how letters are matched to make sounds, and sounds into words, and words into meaning? Perhaps there is more to the arbitrary shapes than meets the eye.

Adam, when asked about the efficacy of partaking in this exercise, responded with: "Translating an unknown language caused me to approach the writing of the poem as an unlocking of meaning already trapped among the words. The experience of working from another poet's words allowed me to disassociate from the act of setting up the poem and focus on the relationships of words together. Fresh and interesting phrases and images sprang forth from the inspiration of cyrillic characters rather than English thoughts. A wholly new approach for myself, a too American poet."

Mistranslating Yevtushenko's work was perhaps the best representation of what the process can do for us as writers. Writing is a form of art not only for the craft of its structure, but also for what its structure implicates aesthetically, what it brings up in us metaphysically. There are forces at work in the reading experience outside of our control much like there are forces at work in the viewing of abstract art beyond our control. What is conjured is already there, reposed, waiting for breath and shape, an amalgamation of identity.

In response to Yevtushenko's "Princess on a Pea," Nippa Thakkar came up with this one, which, like so many great poems, is telling of the world at hand as well as the process of writing it all down:

Yes,
It happened to Mecca and Rapunzel.
A child prohibited from becoming.
A maker of life.
            Of life, not power.
Enemy of you and to magic.
Yes,
Poor Becca, ha! rope mane.
See tame hopes of hope.
To visible catchers, to her power of the Rye.
Bother others.
Yes.
Hop to Mecca or row rafting.
He-he nephews—over cats.
A hoax of happening.
            No orbital power.
No pockets or rabbits—yolk of black
Aerobic power, no extraneous. My
Two have others.
            A bad CEO of mine.
Yes,
Nephews of mine have ropes
Photos.

MARA LEIGH SIMMONS

Of One Hundred Thousand

"When I am alone at night, I awake as small coffin draped with flag"
"my name" "Ziya Jihad Fayez Haj-Mohammad"
"children" "cover faces" "black and white checkers" "*kaffiyahs*"
"others" "completely masked" "by the *molathamin*" "of villages"
"where I am" "is a shrine on the hill above Nablus"
"where each stairway" "fills with flowers"
"touch me" "I am five years old" "through spleen and both lungs"
"over 100,000" "olive" "and fruit trees" "uprooted"
"hundreds" "of thousands" "of other plants"
"cammiphora opobalsamum"
"suffocating"
"liver" "stomach" "spleen" "both lungs" "in the end"
"was a massive fissure" "as someone calls it"
"a wrong shot" "or perforated" "candle"
"for those who move" "in dark"

Ziya was a five-year-old Palestinian boy who became looked at as a martyr for the Palestinian uprising. He was "accidentally" shot and killed in the West Bank by Israeli forces in 1988.

"Anatomically," a larger project of which "Of One Hundred Thousand" is a section, began with my interest in the way that Hebrew and Arabic are informed by, bound, and linked to their place of geographic and historical origin. I researched Arabic and Hebrew words in Arabic-English/Hebrew-English dictionaries, exploring images, concepts, and ideas that permeate the shared cultural references for Arabic and Hebrew speakers or those of Arab and/or Jewish heritage. I desired to find the places where the languages cross beyond invented boundaries and reveal the similarities embedded within both multifarious cultures. With the apparent Israeli-Palestinian conflict, I felt the desire to translate the terrain that both groups share and, through this form of translation, create an act of protest, which unites the spaces where we are used to witnessing invented borders and ongoing battles. In addition, I investigate the language used to document violence occurring to Palestinian and Israeli youths. At times I extract the language used in the media with terms associated with the body and adapt new narrative structures, in an attempt to create possible versions, or a further intimacy with the devastating events. In some places fiction arises out of this in which, from "the other side of death," characters Israeli and Palestinian speak.—MLS

CAROLINE SINAVAIANA & JAMES THOMAS STEVENS

Funeral Song, from Samoan

ALAGA'UPU
Ua tala lali lapopo'a.

PROVERB
Beat the big drums.

LAGISOLO
Sema e, 'o ai 'ea e pisa?
Pe se soa le va i le faga?
Pe ni fa'aali'i 'ua tata?

FUNERAL SONG
Friends, who is making that noise?
That noise, like a song in the bay?
*Or are they beating wooden drums?**

who calls
who awakens
who answers

whose alarm
whose drum
whose skin

who fell
who arose
who left

whose friend
whose mother
whose cadence

sounding from the mangrove bowl?

—*CS*

* Pratt, George, 1911. *Pratt's Grammar and Dictionary of the Samoan Language* (4th ed.). Malua: Malua Printing Press, p. 109.

Ice crystals
slice a fingertip
trying to clear the way.
Aches to open.
Pulse—who makes this noise?

Pulse—like the watery
stir of stars
slouching across the lake.

Pulse—the waterdrum,
begins again,
fluid red beneath
                    the skin.
Ice heaves
then sounds no more.

—JTS

My Pigeon, from Samoan

La'u Lupe 'Ua Lele

La'u lupe ua lele, lele 'i le vao maoa,

Talofa e la'u pele, la'u pele 'ua leiloa.
Ta'aga e o teine o lo'o 'ua gasolo mai
O'u mata e tilotilo 'e te le 'o sau ai.

My Pigeon

My pigeon has flown into the dense forest.
My dear, my darling is lost.
Here come the young girls walking,
My eyes look, but still you have not come.

The air rushes
with your leaving,
wings brushing tall
trees in long shadow.

Your heart trails light
tracing forest path
its dim way to
fragrant altars

of maile and moso'oi.
I wait near deep
woods and watch
for you.

—*CS*

Fine hairs stirred
when you left
for the Atlantic.
Earlier, sitting cross-legged
your dark hair
around my knees,
like a set of somber wings.

Others have come.
Young, with downward
lashes
and red iris flashing.

But in every cell
mine upward turn,
toward the peak
of El Teide.

Returned
and never returning.

—JTS

Cornbread Song, from Mohawk

Kana'tahrokhon:we teiothwe'non:ni.	*This cornbread is round.*
Ne se ni:'i kwa wake:kahs.	*I like it.*
Kana'tahrokhon:we teiothwe'non:ni.	*This cornbread is round.*
Onkwehon:we ronon:ni.	*The Indian people form it.*

Cornbread Song

Circular we move
to create
　　the seminal form.

Pleasured but saddened
　　creating a circle only.

The principle,
for people
　　to give it form.

Lamenting,
　　we simply lay.

—*JTS*

from *Cornbread Song*

The yellow moon holds Sina
and her daughter pounding bark
cloth for the people.

Food for the hungry eye
when our hands are vacant
& the circle is thinning.

Fill the baskets with
the sight of them, &
light the cookfires.

—*CS*

These poems stem from a project proposed after meeting Sinavaiana and reading her book Alchemies of Distance. *I felt an immediate kinship with her language and an odd echo between our Samoan and Mohawk cultures. I had been working on a series of what I deemed "sui-translations" or translations for the self. This involved working from Mohawk songs and stories, gathered from various sources, in the original language, then translating them literally, and ultimately writing poems based on the translations that would create personal relevance to my own narrative. This was partly to stress the importance of change in the oral tradition, an unconsidered element, which often served as the reason for anthros to write off entire tribes as "lost." "Corn Bread Song" (found on Kahon:wes's Kanienkehaka Language Web site) is a translation developed by comparing Kahon:wes's translation with my own translation from available Mohawk dictionaries. I contacted Sina and proposed a cross-cultural poetry project that would involve exchanging translations with each other and writing our poems from them. These are the first fruits of our efforts, and I'm excited at this opportunity to share words.—JTS*

Until I was two, the only language I heard was Samoan, so I have the originary linguistic imprint. But then we moved to the U.S., where my parents were told that, if they wanted us to make it in America, they should speak to us only in English. Now, fifty years later, my English is fine, but my Samoan is elementary and reluctant. Then I heard from the Mohawk poet James Stevens, suggesting that we try a collaborative translation exchange. Working from traditional song texts, Samoan and Mohawk, we each wrote poems based on our own and each other's cultural texts. There's an idea I learned from another Native American colleague, about how, when we meet each other, our ancestors are meeting each other too. This is what these poems are unfolding for me. Not only do I find the collaboration process—it's really call and response—deeply enriching, it's the most fun I've ever had as a writer. In the spirit of harvest, then, these first fruits are for Chain.*—CS*

ANDRÉ SPEARS
United States

LIKE THE JE NE SAIS QUOI IN YOUR FRISSON

LIKE THE CUL-DE-SAC IN A CARTE BLANCHE

LIKE YOUR SANG-FROID AT THE FIN-DE-SIÈCLE

LIKE THE FOLIE À DEUX IN A MÉNAGE À TROIS

LIKE THE DANSE MACABRE OF THE AVANT-GARDE

LIKE THE VOYEUR'S AIDE-MÉMOIRE

LIKE THE JOIE DE VIVRE OF A FEMME FATALE

LIKE THE MILLIONAIRE'S RAISON D'ÊTRE

LIKE AN IDÉE FIXE ON THE QUI VIVE

LIKE THE BÊTE NOIRE OF AN ÉMINENCE GRISE

LIKE A TÊTE-À-TÊTE AU NATUREL

LIKE A DERRIÈRE DÉJÀ VU

LIKE THE FAUX PAS OF THE NOUVEAUX RICHES

LIKE ENNUI VIS-À-VIS DÉBRIS

LIKE A TOUR DE FORCE BY THE CRÈME DE LA CRÈME

LIKE A NOM DE GUERRE RISQUÉ

LIKE AN AGENT PROVOCATEUR MANQUÉ

LIKE DOUBLE ENTENDRE IN A NOM DE PLUME

LIKE TROMPE L'OEIL FOR THE BOUDOIR

LIKE THE DÉNOUEMENT OF MEMOIRS

LIKE THE RENDEZ-VOUS WITH A FAIT ACCOMPLI

LIKE THE HAUT MONDE EN MASSE

LIKE A GAUCHE COUP DE GRÂCE

LIKE THE BOURGEOISIE'S CAMARADERIE

LIKE THE BON VIVANT'S ADIEU

LIKE THE FORCE MAJEURE IN A CAUSE CÉLÈBRE

LIKE AN OBJECT TROUVÉ PASSÉ

LIKE THE OBJECTS D'ART IN A PIED- À-TERRE

LIKE THE IDIOT SAVANT'S SAVOIR FAIRE

LIKE HORS D'OEUVRES FROM ENTREPRENEURS

LIKE THE NOBLESSE OBLIGE OF A CHARGÉ D'AFFAIRES

LIKE A PARTI PRIS SANS SOUCI

LIKE THE ESPRIT DE CORPS IN A COUP D'ÉTAT

LIKE THE BON MOT OF AN AU PAIR

LIKE THE RACONTEUR'S REPERTOIRE

LIKE A BEAU GESTE APRÈS-SKI

LIKE A PIÈCE DE RÉSISTANCE DE TROP

LIKE A MOT JUSTE OUTRÉ PAR EXCELLENCE

LIKE A SOUPÇON OF SAVOIR VIVRE

LIKE THE LAISSEZ-PASSER IN A PASSE-PARTOUT

LIKE THE FAÇADE DU JOUR

LIKE CAMOUFLAGE PRÊT-À-PORTER

LIKE A LIBERTINE'S APLOMB

LIKE THE AUTEUR'S HAUTEUR

LIKE DE RIGUEUR LONGUEURS

LIKE A POTPOURRI OF CONTRE-TEMPS

LIKE THE RENAISSANCE OF LEGERDEMAIN

LIKE AN APROPOS CRI DE COEUR

LIKE CHAISE LONGUES IN FILM NOIR

LIKE A ROMAN À CLEF ENTRE NOUS

United States *collects and connects French "denizens" of the English language—that is, French expressions and words that have been preserved un-translated, yet that function as part of the English lexicon. Thus, while the fifty similes/exhortations in* United States *may look and sound like French, they are in English, and for full effect should be read with the appropriate English or American accent. The "translucinaccional" process in question involved collecting these "denizens" as I came across them, while excluding those that did not appear in a standard college dictionary (e.g.* dieu trompeur, beau sabreur, culbute générale, *et al.).*

United States *was originally published as an artist's book (Editions de l'Oiseau qui dit tout, Brussels, 2002, distributed through chapitre.com), produced and illustrated by French artist Jean-Marc Scanreigh, who is reworking (translating?) the same text and drawings into a series of fifty woodcut engravings, to be exhibited later this year in France and the U.S.—AS*

GERTRUDE STEIN & KARI EDWARDS

A Box

Out of kindness comes redness and out of rudeness comes rapid same question, out of an eye comes research, out of selection comes painful cattle. So then the order is that a white way of being round is something suggesting a pin and is it disappointing, it is not, it is so rudimentary to be analysed and see a fine substance strangely, it is so earnest to have a green point not to red but to point again.

—*GS*

A=1, B=2, C=3, D=4, E=5, F=6, G=7, H=8, I=9, J=10, K=11, L=12, M=13, N=14, O=15, P=16, Q=17, R=18, S=19, T=20, U=21, V=22, W=23, X=24, Y=25, Z=26.

Y(word)=X
X=Y+Y+Y . . . .
M+M (M+lines)=A
A/(_)=(_)

1   2 15 24
7 5 18 20 21 4 5   19 20 5 9 14

15 21 20   15 6   11 9 14 4 14 5 19 19   3 15 13 5 19   18
5 4 14 5 19 19   1 14 4   15 21 20   15 6   18 21 4 5 14
5 19 19   3 15 13 5 19   18 1 16 9 4   19 1 13 5   17 21
5 19 20 9 15 14,   15 21 20   15 6   1 14   5 25 5   3
15 13 5 19   18 5 19 5 1 18 3 8,   15 21 20   15 6   19
5 12 5 3 20 9 15 14   3 15 13 5 19   16 1 9 14 6 21 12   3
1 20 20 12 5.   19 15   20 8 5 14   20 8 5   15 18 4 5 18
9 19   20 8 1 20   1   23 8 9 20 5   23 1 25   15 6   2
5 9 14 7   18 15 21 14 4   9 19   19 15 13 5 20 8 9 14 7
19 21 7 7 5 19 20 9 14 7   1   16 9 14   1 14 4   9 19
9 20   4 9 19 1 16 16 15 9 14 20 9 14 7,   9 20   9 19
14 15 20,   9 20   9 19   19 15   18 21 4 9 13 5 14 20 1
18 25   20 15   2 5   1 14 1 12 25 19 5 4   1 14 4   19
5 5   1   6 9 14 5   19 21 2 19 20 1 14 3 5   19 20 18
1 14 7 5 12 25,   9 20   9 19   19 15   5 1 18 14 5 19 20
20 15   8 1 22 5   1   7 18 5 5 14   16 15 9 14 20   14
15 20   20 15   18 5 4   2 21 20   20 15   16 15 9 14
20   1 7 1 9 14.

1 2 15 24 = 42
7 5 18 20 21 4 5 19 20 5 9 14 = 147

15 21 20 15 6 11 9 14 4 14 5 19 19 3 15 13 5 19 18 5 4 14 5 19 19 = 311
1 14 4 15 21 20 15 6 18 21 4 5 14 5 19 19 3 15 13 5 19 18 1 16 9 4 = 304
19 1 13 5 17 21 5 19 20 9 15 14, 15 21 20 15 6 1 14 5 25 5 = 286
3 15 13 5 19 18 5 19 5 1 18 3 8, 15 21 20 15 6 19 5 12 5 3 20 9 15 14 = 311
3 15 13 5 19 16 1 9 14 6 21 12 3 1 20 20 12 5. 19 15 20 8 5 14 20 8 5 = 309
15 18 4 5 18 9 19 20 8 1 20 1 23 8 9 20 5 23 1 25 15 6 2 5 9 14 7 = 310
18 15 21 14 4 9 19 19 15 13 5 20 8 9 14 7 19 21 7 7 5 19 20 9 14 7 1 = 339
16 9 14 1 14 4 9 19 9 20 4 9 19 1 16 16 15 9 14 20 9 14 7, 9 20 9 19 = 325
14 15 20, 9 20 9 19 19 15 18 21 4 9 13 5 14 20 1 18 25 20 15 2 5 = 348
1 14 1 12 25 19 5 4 1 14 4 19 5 5 1 6 9 14 5 19 21 2 19 20 1 14 3 5 = 268
19 20 18 1 14 7 5 12 25, 9 20 9 19 19 15 5 1 18 14 5 19 20 20 15 = 329
8 1 22 5 1 7 18 5 5 14 16 15 9 14 20 14 15 20 20 15 18 5 4 = 251
2 21 20 20 15 16 15 9 14 20 1 7 1 9 14. = 184

42
147

311
304
286
311
309
310
339
325
348
268
329
251
184
4064=14=1+4=5

human hand, five, four finger plus the thumb, humanity, heath, love, a personal geometry, the four cardinal points and a center, 2 = mater + 3 = heaven = 5, *the written word, a container, a conjoining, a conjunction, union. there is an erotic sense as well. (Cirlot, J. E., 1971,* A Dictionary of Symbols. *Routledge & Kegan Paul, Ltd., London)—KE*

ESZTER SZUCS & BRENDA IIJIMA

II Rész / Part II

II Rész

Omni-reális[1] fizikai terjedelem[2]
Ⓐ forgatókönyvként használt készitmények
semmi energia nem vész
balra nyúl a nyelv[3]
know-how mi csak nőni képes (A)[4]
Ⓑ bennünket mindig érdekelt a test (A)
a test templom de
a test nem fém vagy műanyag vagy know-how
Ⓒ mérlegek fizikai vagyontárgyakat mutatnak (B)
jelenkori könyvelői rendszerek próba biztosak (B)
ezen vitás részek csontok kevésbé repednek rugón[5], ergo biztos a szex[6]
civilizált társadalmakban vezetők közönnyel erőszakoljak az utakat (C)
Ⓓ kényszerítve rendőr tagokat, segítsék úttesti áldozataikat[7] (C)
eszmecsere nem-automobilis[8] közösségekről termékeny lehetne
antropológusok ritkán sorakoznak, hogy világi csábításokról számot adjanak (D)
ahol a dudák szertartásosan szólanak (D)
a teljesség részei a mellek
Ⓔ ez, amit a jegyszedők testületi műhelyekben vesznek (E)
mert lehet, hogy másképp mások lennének[9] (E)
sebváltó[10] XX. századi találmány
idézőjel gyári vagyon idézőjel zárva gyűrűzik mint véna, szállítmány
rozsdamentes kannák, mangán, fémecsetes
produkció, motorizálás, verejték hálók[11], két autó per család
segítik a túlélést magán[12] nemzetközileg a testi utazás apadt
földi életbentartó rendszerk megjövendölik:

A) Felgyorsulni a belső borzadást
B) Felmérni, hogy mozdulatlan
Tulajdon lett a test.

Ennek társadalmi-gazdasági következményei vannak (F)
kipakolni mindent kevesen hajlanak (F)
ármányok mint közúti rablás és impotencia burjánzanak (F)
a test érvényességének bizonyításához önkéntes becsülettel lehet
férkőzni csak (F)
történjen közösen
szexuálisan vagy fejlődés-gátolt alárendeltségünk a gépezetnek[13]
választás nélkül előbbre megy
tudományos forradalomtól nem erősödnek meg keringési rendszerek
emésztés szaporodás vagy fejszámlálás vegyül
parkolók a nemzeti esztétika és arány szervetlen[14]
tájé autonómia.

NOTES

Ⓐ s, é, t, again
Ⓑ t, k, again
Ⓒ s, r, d   d, t
Ⓓ è, r

1 I kept the Latin. It had the same meaning in Hungarian as I note in English, i.e., grounded, yet understandable, authoritative, yet shadowed.
2 Double meaning: "expense," i.e. magnitude; "expansion," i.e. take-over or conquest. Supposed to reflect two themes of the poem and their simultaneous, overlapping fields.
3 Alliteration as in yours.
4 Letters surrounded by parentheses at the end of two or more lines indicate a rhyming set.
5 Double meaning: trying to keep duality of limber, flexible wire or coil, often in beds; kicking.
6 Double meaning: "safe;" "sure or certain to happen."
7 Part of the word, "testi," means "bodily," rendering "úttesti" to mean "of the road" or "roadside," as well as "of the body of the road."
8 Double meaning: "without cars;" un-automatic, im-mobile or immobilized automatically, or "on one's own."
9 Literal translation: "because otherwise they might become others." "Others," a sense recently popularized in the language, denotes unconventional identity, e.g., sexual, ethnic, etc., minority status.
10 Part of the word, "seb," has double meaning: abbreviation or slang for "speed," as in the prefix of the literal translation of "stick shift;" "scar," rendering "sebvalto" to mean "scar shift."
11 Part of the word, "halo," has double meaning: "net" (as English "network" and "net"); "bedroom or sleeping."
12 Double meaning: "private;" "you," i.e., out-living or existing longer than you.
13 Double meaning: "machine;" "machinery, system."
14 "Autonomy" also could be that of the landscape, or of the inorganic landscape. This duality of the positive and negative is similar to the double meaning of the first, beginning line, lending a circular ending to the piece.

—*ES*

Part II

Omni-realistic physical magnitude/
artifacts used as scenarios/
no energy will be lost/
left turn tongue/
know-how which can only increase/
we always are interested in the
body/the body is a temple but/
the body is not metallic or
plastic or know-how/
balance sheets show physical assets/
present accounting systems fail to
account for discharge/of
hot-headed numerical wetness/
theories of these systems are safe to
test out/these items
of contention bones break less
on the limber ergo safe sex/
in civilized societies drivers
rape roads nonchalantly/
forcing police squads to assist
roadside victims/discourse on
non-automobelic societies
could be productive/anthropologists
rarely return to report the
secular seduction/where horns
blow only in ceremony/
breasts are part of the totality/
is what the ticket collectors
learn in corporate workshops/
because they might not be
aware otherwise/stick shifts
are a 20th century invention/
quote "factory wealth" unquote
wiring like veins, transport/
non-rusting cans, manganese,
metalographically/production, motorization
sweat networks, two cars per
family/help survival private internationally

bodily travel has been reduced/
terrestrial life supports predicts:

A) Acceleration of internal abhorrence

B) Recognition of the immobile
    Property that the body has become.

This has socio-economic consequences/
few are willing to unload/schemes
like highway robberies and
impotence flourish/access to
proving body's validity can only
be accomplished through use of
voluntary integrity/must
occur synergistically/sexually
or slightly stunted subservience
to machines will continue
without option/a science
revolution would not resource
circulatory systems/digestion,
reproductively or heat count
commingling/parking lots are
this nation's aesthetic and proportion
non-organic/landscape
autonomy.

—*BI*

LORENZO THOMAS

Translation of Whale Song

You just don't know
How hard it is
To be uncivilized

You think that everyone you eat
Deserves to be eaten

                                        Lunch for me
Means someone ain't coming home

So what
If breakfast might have been
The tuna that found a cure for cancer?

Damn sure was tasty!

I'm pleased that most people who've heard me read the poem enjoyed it (particularly little kids at the Houston Zoo earlier this year). The only negative comment that I can recall came from Ron Padgett, who is a masterful translator of poetry. He questioned my last line because he said that he doesn't think whales cuss.—LT

MICHEL-ROLPH TROUILLOT, A. ISADORA DEL VECCHIO, ABDOURAHMAN IDRISSA, KIRAN JAYARAM, & KAREN OHNESORGE

Imigrasyon / Immigration / L'immigration / Immgarasion

Imigrasyon

Imigrasyon tenten met men nan kòlèt mwen
Li di: "Ou pa sitizenn"
Li di: "Wèriz?"
M di: "Wat?"
Li di: "Vòt alyenn kat"
Yo vole, yo touye
Yo mete Divalye
Li ki kòz mwen sove
Jodia a, m sou Bwòdwe
Yo tout rele: "Bare"
Mezanmi, mezanmi di mwen
Lè Franse yo te debake anvan 1804
Eske Sontonaks te gen residans li?
Mezanmi, mezanmi di mwen
Lè yo te sal drapo ak kaka kaptenn Batch,
Eske bato alman an te gen alyenn kat?

Mezanmi, mezanmi di mwen
Pandan lokipasyon lò yo touye Peralt,
Eske Ameriken te gen alyenn kat?

Lakay, yo chire po n, isit, yo kraze zo n

Toupatou yo sèl wa se pa nou ki sou do bèf la
Se bèf la ki sou do nou
Men jou ti katkat
Gen pou l tounen gwo chat
Pou yon lòt 1804
Mitrayèt ap fè krak
Meriken ap fè bak
Lè sa nan simityè
P ap gen alyenn kat . . .

—*M-RT*

Immigration (Literal English)

Immigration idiot put hand on collar my
He said: "You not citizen."
He said: "Where is?"[1]
I said: "What?"[2]
He said: "Votre alien carte"[3]
They steal, they kill
They appoint Duvalier
He who is responsible for my escape
Today I on Broadway
They all shouted: "stop"
Man! Man! said I
When Spanish arrived
While the Indians began to back away
Did Christopher Columbus have his alien card?
Man! Man! said I
When the French arrived before 1804
Did Sonthonax[4] have residence his?
Man! Man! said I
When they desecrated the flag with shit Captain Batsch[5]
Man! Man! said I
Did boat German the have alien card?

Man! Man! said I
During occupation when they killed Pèralte[6]
Did the Americans have an alien card?

In one's own country, they tear up skin our,
Here, they smash bone our

Everywhere they only king it is not us which on back cow the
It is cow the which on back our
But day little kid
To have to become big cat

For another 1804
Submachine gun will make (the sound) Crack!
American will back away
Time that in cemetery
Not have alien card

—IDV

1 *The neologism is English in Haitian orthography. This is verified by the French translation where they use English words.*

2 *See note 1.*

3 *A literal English translation of the Kreyòl fails, as this phrase shows the author representing French in Kreyòl orthography.*

4 *The French Commissioner who in 1973 decreed the end of slavery in Saint Domingue (later, Haiti).*

5 *This refers to the Batcsh affair, where Germany demanded indemnities from Haiti and seized two boats in 1872. Upon receiving the money, he left on the boats the Haitian flag, covered with German feces.*

6 *Revolutionary leader, assassinated by U.S. Marines in 1919.*

Immigration (Standard English)

The silly immigration officer grabbed my collar
He said, "You aren't a citizen."
He asked "Where is . . ."
I said "What?"
He continued, ". . . your green card?"
They steal, and they kill
They put Duvalier in power,
He who caused me to flee Haiti.[1]
Now, I'm on Broadway[2]
They immediately scream out "Stop him!"
My, my! Tell me . . .
When the *Spanish* came . . .
And the Taino[3] were placed under submission,
Did Cristobal Colón have a residency card?
My, my! Tell me . . .
When the *French* came before 1804
Did Sonthonax have resident status?
My, my! Tell me . . .
When that shitty Capt. Batsch soiled the Haitian national flag,
My, my, Tell me . . .
Did the *German* gunboat have a residency card?

My, my! Tell me . . .
During the Occupation when they killed Péralte,
Did the *Americans* have a residency card?

Back home, they shred our skin
Over here, they smash our bones

Everywhere, they are in total control.
We're not the burden on the big wigs,

It's the big wigs who are on our back
But, one day the little guy
Will become the big shot[4]

For another 1804[5].
Submachine guns will rattle off . . .
The Americans will back off.

And then, in the cemetery,
They won't need a residency card.

—*KJ*

[1] *During the reign of both François Duvalier and his son, Jean-Claude Duvalier, many Haitians went into exile. This phenomenon became known popularly as the plight of the "boat people." Scholars have distinguished between waves of refugees by denoting the "Boeing people"—those who were in the upper class and had the money for a plane ticket to leave—and the "boat people"—those who left in the 1980s and later.*

[2] *The U.S. Immigration and Naturalization Service is located on Broadway, in New York City.*

[3] *The indigenous people of* Ayiti *in the 15th century.*

[4] *Using the Haitian expression "ti katkat," Trouillot plays off the Haitian diminutive "ti" and the English "cat" to show the process of maturation with the next line's reference to "gwo chat."*

[5] *The year of Haitian independence. This marked the formation of the first African-American country in the Western hemisphere. It also marked the first time in colonial history where "slaves" successfully fought for their independence. This year is consistently referred to as a point of pride for Haitians.*

Many of the footnotes that provide background to meaning-rich phrases come from examinations of a wide spectrum of knowledge. In order to better understand this poem, we include additional historical and anthropological information to contextualize it. Any historical information not otherwise noted is from Heinl.

Temporally, Trouillot paints seven "moments." By using the word "moment" (hereafter, not in quotes), we mean to concretize an event or series of events to open them for analysis within a theoretical framework. The first of these occurred when the immigration officer confronts the narrator. This sets the stage of the poem. The second involves the epoch of the Duvalier regime. This lasted from 1957 to 1986, when Jean-Claude Duvalier, son and hereditary heir to the throne of his father, François, left Haiti permanently. The manner in which the Duvaliers symbolically and physically controlled the country has been laid out elsewhere (see Trouillot 1990 or Jayaram 2001). The third era of history involves the moment in 1492 when Spanish colonial forces came to Haiti (then, *Ayiti*), which led to eventual decimation of the Taino and Ciboney inhabitants of the island by sword and by disease. The Spanish held claim to the area of Haiti until 1697, when it was ceded to France under the Treaty of Ryswick. The brutal treatment of people under the French crown has been described by Vastey, who was counselor to Henri Christophe (see Vastey 1969). Thus, the fourth moment involved French colonial influence, which lasted until the masses rose up and gloriously declared their independence in 1804. The contrast between Sonthonax's declaration of abolition and the date 1804 suggests a disdain for the words of the colonizer and respect for the actions of the Haitian masses. The fifth moment involves the period in the late 19th century when a rising German nationalism led to an interest in establishing colonies, Haiti being one goal. This showed the utter disrespect and racism the Germans dealt the Haitians. The sixth moment involves the first United States occupation of Haiti, from 1915 to 1934. The United States took control of the island and set up governments friendly to foreign interests, while simultaneously reinstituting a form of slavery known as a *kòve* in order to build roads. Charlemagne Péralte led a group of people known as *cacos* in armed rebellion against the racist U.S. occupying forces. After killing Péralte, U.S. marines tied his body to a door upright, Christlike, to discourage further rebellion. Rather than stifling dissent, the image has been used (during the 1915 occupation and the 1994 occupation) as a power point for anti-imperialism. From the second occupation, the United States played (and continues to play in 2003) a major role in shaping Haitian politics, either by coercing government officials or by withholding foreign aid to the country until the politicians reflect a pro-U.S. stance.

Up to this point, Trouillot has laid out a series of moments in his poem, all underlined by the theme of unjust domination. The final moment comes with the phrase "one day," indicating a future. During this moment, the oppressive forces of the United States and by extension all imperialist forces—foreign or domestic—will be put to rest by an invisible army of justice. This suggests that the same *mawonaj*, or guerilla tactics used by escaped Africans during the era of slavery, will present itself again to liberate the people in order to have another 1804.

Beyond the historical context, the reader needs to understand issues of transnationalism. By transnationalism, I draw upon the definition put forth in an essay by Haitian scholar Michel Laguerre of a *transnational political field*:

> The transnational political field means a system in which the political process of the nation state encompasses actors who live inside as well as those who live outside its legal and territorial boundaries. (Carolle Charles in Laguerre 1997, 170)

Throughout the poem, most specific references showed the transnational field of Haiti dominated by individuals and states that have no respect for the people *in* Haiti. Thus, the overriding notion suggests a disdain for those *outside* of Haiti who seek to change Haiti.

However, the narrator is in fact a part of the Haitian diaspora, one of the many people who left the country to reside elsewhere. So given the first idea of skepticism on the part of those *outside* of Haiti, we could assume that Trouillot resents his own position as a neo-colonialist, being from the "tenth department."[1] Community leader and musician Sanba Zao has termed this type of person a *kolon pèpè*,[2] or foreign colonist as opposed to a *kolon kreyòl*, or indigenous colonist. Trouillot's position actually is to the contrary. Rather than being an outside force, he uses symbolic and cultural capital afforded to him in order to wage his critique. His cultural capital in Haiti is based upon being an educated person, and the same holds for cultural capital in the United States (Trouillot taught at Johns Hopkins University, and now teaches at the University of Chicago). His symbolic capital in Haiti derives from his residence in the United States, and in the United States from his Haitian roots.

This provides for at least two conclusions. Firstly, it suggests that Trouillot holds "outside insider" status that exempts him from being a part of the transnational entities he is critiquing in the poem. Secondly, it is possible, and perhaps more likely, that he is renegotiating the concept of Haitian identity in the United States in light of existing negative views of Haitians (see discussions of such stereotypes in Stepick 1998, Glick-Schiller, & Fouron, 1990, Haiti Films, n.d.). These views have been fostered by the ridiculous claims that Haitians (or even all people who have been in Haiti) have a predisposition to contracting AIDS and by the problematic representations of Haitian "boat people" on television and in the U.S. news, which fail to contextualize the images within a transnational political economy.

—*KJ*

[1] *Haiti is divided into nine departments, as the United States is in fifty states. The "tenth department" is the Haitian diaspora in the United States, Canada, and France. This group adds much to the economy of Haiti through its remunerations.*

[2] Pèpè *in Haitian refers to poor quality, imported wares. When referring to a person, it pejoratively refers to a Haitian who returned to Haiti from abroad.*

Immigration (Poetic English)

The immigration idiot put his hand on my collar
He said: *"You're not a citizen"*
He said: *"Where's—?"*[1]
I said: "What?"
He said: *"Your alien card"*[2]
They steal, they kill
They defend Duvalier
He who caused my exile
Today, I'm on Broadway
They all call: *"Halt"*
My god,[3] I say . . .
When the Spanish disembarked
When the Indians fell back
Did Christopher Columbus have an alien card?
My god, I say . . .
When the French landed before 1804[4]
Was Sonthonax a resident?
My god, I say . . .
When they fouled the flag with Captain Batch's shit,
Did the German ship have an alien card?

My god, I say . . .
During the occupation when they killed Péralte,
Did the Americans have an alien card?

Back home, they shred our skin, here, they crush our bones

Everywhere they rule, it's not us on the bull's back
It's the bull on ours
But one day the kitten[5]
Must become a big cat
For another 1804
Sub-machine guns go "Crack!"
The Americans will fall back
Then, in the cemetery
No one needs an alien card

—*KO*

1 In the original, Trouillot parodies the English-speaking voice: "Wèriz?" He does the same for the next line, "Wat?"

2 Although the author was representing French through Haitian orthography, the English word "card" is "kat," pronounced "kaht," bringing a harsh beat to the end of many lines.

3 We have translated Trouillot's "mezanmi" as "my god," since it's used as an expletive. But in Haitian, the ear hears the word as "my friend." "My god" is a convenience that compromises meaning because it misreads the speaker's appeal to his human listener.

4 When spoken, the date here ends with "kat," or "four" (compare the French "quatre")—paralleling "kat" for "card."

5 Here "kitten" to translate "katkat," a double-rhyme for "kat," or "card." As for "katkat," according to the Haitian dictionary, "katkat" referred to "tikatkat," meaning "toddler" or "little child." However, with Trouillot's play on words, we think "tikatkat" can be understood as child but translated as "kitten."

L'immigration

Il m'a saisi au collet, le salaud de l'Immigration
Il dit: t'es pas citoyen, mon gars
Il dit: "Montre . . ."
Je dis "quoi donc . . ."?
Il dit: "Ta carte de séjour . . ."
Ils volent, tuent
Nous foutent Duvalier au cul
Celui qui m'a fichu en exil
Me voilà maintenant sur Broadway
Et ils crient tous: Stop!
Mon frère, que je me dis
Lorsqu'ils sont venus, les Espagnols
Et lorsque les Indiens, ils sont tombés
Est-ce qu'il avait une carte de séjour, le Christophe Colomb?
Mon frère, que je me dis
Les Français là même, lorsqu'ils sont arrivés en 1804
Leur Sonthonax était-il résident?
Quand ils ont poissé le Drapeau avec la merde du capitaine Batch
Les Allemands-là, avaient-ils leur papier?
Oh frère, que je me dis
Pendant l'occupation, quand ils ont trucidé Péralte
Les Américains avaient-ils papier?
Chez nous ils nous dépiautent, ici ils nous cassent l'os
Là où ils règnent, nous ne montons pas la bête
c'est la bête qui nous chevauche
Mais le jour viendra où petit chaton
Deviendra gros chat
Pour un autre 1804
Les mitrailleuses feront ratatatata
Les Américains s'abattront
Et dans le cimetière
Personne n'aura besoin de papier

—AI

NOTE FOR POETIC FRENCH: In this rendition of Trouillot's poem, I basically tried to use the colorful way Africans speak French—which involves, for instance, dropping articles like in line 22: "Les

Américains avaient-ils papier," instead of "leur papier," which would be more "grammatical French." Or by saying, instead of simply "Les Français," (The French)—which is the concise way the French speak, this: "Les Français là même" ("Those very French," but said in a very un-grammatical Afro-French that would be literally translated like this: "Those same French here"—to insist on the inequity. In this line, I translated "my God" not by "mon Dieu," but by "mon frère" (my brother), which I think directly corresponds to the Haitian exclamation ("mezanmi") in African French. What I tried to translate was not the language, with its tricks and peculiar sonorities (something that is dubious in a French version of an English version of a Haitian original), but the emotion, as I felt it. In the first line, for instance, I translated "idiot" by "salaud," which would mean "bastard" (and, for someone with an intellectual French education, the choice of this particular word makes all the more sense because Jean-Paul Sartre used it to generically designate people who mechanically serve a system because it is a system, regardless of its evilness: civil servants, collaborators, and soldiers in the colonial wars in particular). There are other instances of that "emotional" translation that follow similar patterns.—AI

Immgarasion

A nay di gindi ga, Immgarasion nyanioka *[the immigration mother fucker put his hand on my collar]*
A ne: "niyo manti ne haray boro no" *[he said: you're not from around here]*
A ne: "cabe . . ." *[he said: show . . .]*
Ay ne "Ifo . . ."? *[I said: what . . .]*
A ne: "Ni cat de sejuro . . ." *[he said: your alien card . . .]*
Iga zey ga wi *[they steal and kill]*
Ina Duvalier gisi ir bon *[they put Duvalier on us]*
Aro kan nay garay *[he who chased me from home]*
Sohon ay ne ya Broadway *[and here I am on Broadway]*
Nankul kan ay gana, gay ne ya, gi kati ay ga: Kay! *[And everywhere I go they shout: Halt]*
Hey ay arme, gune ka di me *[dear brother, look at this]*
Spanyoley, kan i ka *[the Spaniards, when they came]*
Ga Indienyey zeri *[and knocked the Indians down]*
Cristof Colombo din, a gon da cat de sejur? *[did their Christophus Columbus have an alien card?]*
Hey ay arme, guney se *[dear brother, look at it]*
Fransborey din, kan i ka 1804 *[those French, when they came in 1804]*
I Sonthonaxo, ne bor no? *[was their Sonthonax a resident?]*
Kan ina drapa zibandi di kapten Batch toso *[When they stained the flag with Captain Batch shit]*
Almanyan din, igon da cat? *[did the German have a card?]*
Hey ay arme, ci ay se *[tell me, my dear brother]*
Wato kan i nir kwara di, ga Peralt wi *[When they took over our country and murdered Péralte]*
Amrikenyey din, igon da cat? *[Did the Americans have a card?]*
Ir kwara ra i mir mursey, ne haray i mir tutubu *[Back home they wreck us, here they crush our bones]*
Nan kan iga may ir sa karu bario bon *[Where they rule we do not mount the horse]*
Bario no ga karu ir bon *[It is the horse that mounts us]*
Amma hanno ga to kan mageyzo *[But the time will come when the kitten]*
Ga bar ga te musu beeri *[Will become a lion]*
1804 fo ga ka *[There will be another 1804]*
Malfey ga te katkatkatkat *[Machine guns will go "Crack!!!"]*
Amrikenyey ga kan *[The Americans will fell back]*
Saara ra mo *[And in the cemetery]*
Bor kul si goy da cat *[No one will need cards]*.

—*AI*

NOTE FOR SONGHAY: Here, too, the remarks I made about the French translation hold. "Idiot," in the first line, becomes "motherfucker." It is the exact same insult in Songhay, Hausa, and Wolof, and it is used in Africa as much as it is used here, and in precisely this kind of context: The word "nyanioka" is "nya" (mother) "nioka" (fucker). We also see where the use of "my brother" in African French comes from, since the word I use to translate "my God" here is "arme," which means brother in a generic way—I specify generic because there are two other words for brother, one that means "younger brother" and another that means "older brother." Those two latter words have to do with family relations, whereas the word "arme" may be used in any instance where you just want to be affectionate with someone, but it does mean "brother" or "brotherly friend." There is a feminine equivalent, "wayme." The roots are "ar" (male) and "way" (female). The Songhay language is known for its epic oral literature, too. Whenever I try to translate poetry into Songhay, I am compelled by the reminiscence of those epic poems to use certain kind of images and words (to wreck, horse, lion, etc.), which are recurrent in the grandiloquent wickedness of epic poetry.—AI

FINAL NOTE: The text itself contains much information regarding the process. We started by selecting a poem. Isadora Del Vecchio first provided a literal English translation, based upon her language skills and the dictionary by Bryant Freeman. Next, Kiran Jayaram took Del Vecchio's work and, by examining it with the original Haitian, used his language skills to derive the standard English version. He followed with historical and anthropological notes to explain references. Karen Ohnesorge then created a version of the poem that respected elements of the original Haitian. She based this upon her own study of the language, as well as information she borrowed from Kiran. Next, Abdourahmane Idrissa created a French (his second language) version based upon Karen's version primarily, and secondarily on Kiran's notes, Isadora's version, and the original poem. Although he hasn't studied Haitian, he was able to see parallels between it and French. After that, Abdourahmane translated the French into Songhay, his first language.

Freeman, Bryant, and Jowel Laguerre. 2002. Haitian–English Dictionary *(4th ed.). Lawrence: University of Kansas, Institute of Haitian Studies.*

Glick-Schiller, Nina, and Georges Fouron. 1990. "Everywhere We Go, We Are in Danger": Ti Manno and the Emergence of a Haitian Transnational Identity. American Ethnologist *17(2), 329–347.*

Haiti Films (n.d.). Bitter Cane. *Crowing Rooster Arts: New York, NY.*

Heinl, Robert Debs, and Nancy Gordon Heinl. 1996. Written in Blood: The Story of the Haitian People 1492–1995 *(2nd ed.). Revised and expanded by Michael Heinl. Lanham: University Press of America.*

Jayaram, Kiran. 2001. Of the Blood of Biasou and Boukmann: Haitian Resistance to the Duvalier Regime. *Presented at the 22nd Conference of the Institute of Latin American Studies Students Association, University of Texas.*

Laguerre, Michel S. 1997. "The Role of the Diaspora in Haitian Politics." In Haiti Renewed: Political and Economic Prospects, *ed. Robert I. Rotberg. Washington D.C.: Brookings Institution.*

Stepick, Alex. 1998. Pride and Prejudice: Haitians in the United States. *New Immigrant Series, Nancy Foner, ed. Boston: Allyn and Bacon.*

Trouillot, Michel-Rolph. 1990. Haiti: State Against Nation. *New York: Monthly Review.*

Vastey, Pompée-Valentin, baron de. 1969. An Essay on the Causes of the Revolution and Civil Wars in Hayti ... *(original, 1823). Translated by W.H.M.B. New York: Negro Universities.*

PADCHA TUNTHA-OBAS

Translation in Six Steps: Thai to English

“ชูใจเกาคอลีเทาเบาๆ
ลีเทาชูคอพอใจ
มานีหัวเราะ
โตมาหามานี
มานีเกาหัวโต
โตชูคอดีใจ
ชูใจหัวเราะ
มานีพอใจ”

1

choojai kaow kor seetaow baow baow
seetaow choo kor porjai
maanii hua-ror
toe mahar maanii
maanii kaow hua toe
toe choo khor deejai
choojai hua-ror
maanii porjai

(ชูใจ)(scratch)(neck)(ลีเทา)(gently)(gently)
(ลีเทา)(raise)(neck)(satisfied)
(มานี)(laugh)
(โต)(approach)(มามี)
(มานี)(scratch)(head)(โต)
(โต)(raise)(neck)(happy)
(ชูใจ)(laugh)
(มานี)(satisfied)[1]

[1] *In elementary school, there lived these two friends,* maanii *and* choojai*, and their friends,* seetaow *the cat and* toe *the dog. Their textbook-world translated into our world, their language arose into ours, Thai.*

(when)(study)(level)(elementary) ตอนเรียนชั้นประถม
(used (to))(harmonize)(group)(acquaintance) เคยเกลียวกลมกลุ่มผองเพื่อน
(Maanii)(persistent)(visit) มานีเพียรเยี่ยมเยือน
(world)(like)(in)(lesson) โลกเลมือนในบทเรียน

2

choojai kaow kor seetaow, baow baow.
seetaow choo kor, porjai.
maanii hua-ror.
toe mahar maanii.
maanii kaow hua toe.
toe choo khor, deejai.
choojai hua-ror.
maanii porjai.

(ชูใจ)(scratch)(neck)(สีเทา), (gently)(gently).
(สีเทา)(raise)(neck)(satisfied).
(โต)(approach)(มานี).
(มานี)(laugh).
(มานี)(scratch)(head)(โต).
(โต)(raise)(neck), (happy).
(ชูใจ)(laugh).
(มานี)(satisfied).[2]

[2] *But we learn, in English, people pause (,) and stop (.). A friend asked how I know a sentence ends. Straightforwardly, I answered, "It says all it wants to say*

(study)(English), (end)(sentence), เรียนอังกฤษจบประโยค
(as if)(be)(luck)(exist)(mark). ราวเป็นโชคมีเครื่องหมาย
(full stop), (comma)(line up). มหัคภาคจุลภาคเรียงราย
(in)(Thai), (change)(no)(want). ในไทยกลายไม่ต้องการ

and ends."

3

Choojai kaow kor Seetaow, baow baow.
Seetaow choo kor, porjai.
Maanii hua-ror.
Toe mahar Maanii.
Maanii kaow hua Toe.
Toe choo khor, deejai.
Choojai hua-ror.
Maanii porjai.

(Choojai)(scratch)(neck)(Seetaow), (gently)(gently).
(Seetaow)(raise)(neck)(satisfied).
(Maanii)(laugh).
(Toe)(approach)(Maanii).
(Maanii)(scratch)(head)(Toe).
(Toe)(raise)(neck), (happy).
(Choojai)(laugh).
(Maanii)(satisfied).[3]

[3] *My friend continued, "No capitalization either?" "No." "How can you tell it is a sentence?" "Straightforwardly, it says all it wants and is a sentence." Sympathized, I said,*

(English)(think)(type)(different). อังกฤษคิดพิมพ์ต่าง
(Small)(big)(letter)(create). เล็กใหญ่อักษรสร้าง
(Start)(sentence)(begin)(sketch), ขึ้นประโยคเริ่มร่าง
(different)(clear). แตกต่างชัดเจน

4

Choojai kaow*s* kor Seetaow, baow baow.
Seetaow choo*s* kor, porjai.
Maanii hua-ror*s*.
Toe mahar*s* Maanii.
Maanii kaow*s* hua Toe.
Toe choo*s* khor, deejai.
Choojai hua-ror*s*.
Maanii ***is*** porjai.

(Choojai)(scratch***es***) (neck) (Seetaow),
(gently)(gently).
(Seetaow)(raise*s*)(neck)(satisfied).
(Maanii)(laugh*s*)
(Toe)(approach***es***)(Maanii).
(Maanii)(scratch***es***)(head)(of)(Toe).
(Toe)(rais***es***)(neck), (happy).
(Choojai)(laugh*s*).
(Maanii)(***is***)(satisfied).[4]

4 *Excess is complicated. For example, in Thai, there is no need for the dutiful "S's" in order to make* sense.

(In)(English), (different)(time) means ในอังกฤษต่างเวลา
(different)(world) and *(different)(letter).* ต่างหล้าต่างอักษา
(In) a *(sentence), (add)*ed *(things) (come)* ในประโยคสิ่งเพิ่มมา
(so)(that) we *(can)(communicate).* เพื่อว่าได้สื่อความ

5

Choojai kaow*s* kor of Seetaow, baow baow.
Seetaow choo*s* **its** kor, porjai.
Maanii hua-ror*s*.
Toe mahar*s* Maanii.
Maanii kaow*s* hua of Toe.
Toe choo*s* its khor, deejai.
Choojai hua-ror*s*.
Maanii ***is*** porjai.

(Choojai)(scratch*es*) (neck)(of)
(Seetaow),(gently)(gently).
(Seetaow)(raise*s*)(its)(neck),(satisfied).
(Maanii)(laugh*s*)
(Toe)(approach*es*)(Maanii)
(Maanii)(scratch*es*)(head)(of)(Toe).
(Toe)(rais*es*)(its)(neck), (happy).
(Choojai)(laugh*s*).
(Maanii)(***is***)(satisfied).[5]

[5] *"Or prepositions and possessive adjectives to tell that parts of a body belong to the body."*

(Different)(language) means *(different)(value).* ต่างภาษาต่างค่า
(Different)(world) has (different)(meaning). ต่างหล้าต่างความหมาย
To (be) a (translator), one (transform)s (body) เป็นคนแปลแปลงกาย
but (not) to (change)(far), the (person)(same). มิได้กลายไกลตนเดิม

Choojai (kaow)***s*** (kor) *of* (Seetaow), (baow)(baow).
(Seetaow) (choo)***s*** *its* (kor), (porjai).
(Maanii) (hua-ror)***s***.
(Toe) (mahar)***s*** (Maanii).
(Maanii) (kaow)***s*** (hua) *of* (Toe).
(Toe) (choo)***s*** *its* (khor), (deejai).
(Choojai) (hua-ror)***s***.
(Maanii) ***is*** (porjai).

Choojai scratches Seataow's neck
quite gently.
Seataow purrs, satisfied.
Toe approaches Maanii.
Maanii laughs.
Maanii scratches its head.
Toe raises its head, happy.
Choojai laughs.
Maanii is satisfied.[6]

[6] *My friend, unentertained but interested, asked that I stop and just translate. So I did.*

Thai Passage from: Ministry of Education. (1984). Thai Language for Grade 1: Book 1. *Bangkok: The Thai Teachers Association.*

CHRISTIAN WOLFF & CRAIG DWORKIN

Taking "Taking Chances"

The first one of us, however, who really went in for indeterminacy in performance was Feldman with those pieces written on graph paper where the range of the instrument is divided into high, middle, and low, and the performer can pick any note from the specified register. Feldman has dropped indeterminacy nowadays, and he must always have looked at it very differently from Cage. I think this interest had to do with his interest in painting.

—*CW*

tempo=94
10
20

30
40

50
60
70

80

Taking "Taking Chances" is the translation of part of an essay by the composer Christian Wolff. Each letter of the source text was translated either into its note name equivalent (for the first seven letters) or a quarter-note rest (for any other letter). Duration and articulation were determined by where the letter came in a word and where the word came in a sentence; the essay's punctuation determined accidentals. Dynamics are left to the performer. The left-hand line was created from the second half of the essay in a similar manner, but taking the spatial distribution of letters as the basis for the score.—CD

HERIBERTO YÉPEZ

Translation as Matricide (The Sequel!)

When somebody commits a crime,
he hides—just like the translator does.

—An epigraph

1

The first rule of traditional translation is to make two languages
Become
The second one.
(Domination).
(Disappearance of the first language).
(Conquest: Erase the Native!).
(Delete The Other, and then . . .
declare the "Other" has been translated).
(Mission Accomplished).
(¡Us!). (Nosotros!).
[Cool = Ajúa!]
(Translation Awards Needed Here). 1521 + 1847 = XXI
(Translation as cultural Communication with the *Other*—Remains to be seen).
(Chinese Emperor Looking for Hot Latina).
Translation should become the transformation of one first language into (at least) two other languages.
Translation as the practice where the permanent presence of the first language takes place in the context of a second language.
Co-presence of tongues.
(Good intentions?)
Translating the word *Translation* into Inglich results in:
1. Trans-nations.
2. Tranny Tongue.
3. Trans | Late | Nation.
I am not writing in English. I am recycling it.
Mexico (†) never had a mother tongue. Spanish was brought there and it meant the disappearance of dozens of mother tongues. Spanish was not a first language.

I'm recycling it.
That's why writing in English is Arte Povera for me.
(I am not a Chicano. Too easy a mix).
A big pro-translation culture is cannibalistic.
Imperialism employs huge quantities of translators. Builds universities for them.
Departments.
(We all work in them).
Recycling it.
(Domination).
Translators should quit.
Too easy a mix.
Translating A into B makes A feel it is now obliged to continue talking to B, even though B doesn't understand A.
To talk to A, B transforms A into B.
B talking to B.
Monologue.
In translation A feels it is in a conversation [was forced into a conversation] in the terms of B.
B always wins.
Translation gathers.
Gathers cultures into B.
B always wins.
Too easy a mix.

2 (Ajúa!)

Well,
In *my* case
I didn't decide to translate American Poetry into Spanish because I felt we had neglected that field. (But we have) (But "my" dislike of "our" Mexican reluctance toward American Culture was NOT the reason | why | I decided | to | translate American Poetry). I decided it because I knew it was time to.
It was time to
Translate | American poetry
Into Spanish.
Translate it
Before
History

Politics
"*The* Economy"
Makes
"Us"
    Enemies.

[I wrote the last text *after* reading a comment by Dubravka Djuric made for *Chain* 9 magazine. I also wrote it *before* the *Wall Street Journal* (Oct 29, 2002) called Mexico—because of its position on the war in Iraq—"Saddam's friends South of the Border." So, it appears we are now beginning to become enemies.
Translation-Time just went by.
Game Over.]

¿3?

Translation makes the reader feel At Home.
AT home.
Welcome.
        Welcome to Mexico (†)
[Bienvenidos, am(b)ig(u)os!]
—Translation sucks—
Makes the Reader feel AT Home.
Welcome Again!
"Transparency" | "Absorption".
"Oh, nice prose"
"Those lines even sound like Duncan!".
Translations should be uncomfortable.
(Viva Babel):
Unreadable.
Why do translators | writers in general | think so much about the Reader?
Is he paying them
            OR WHAT?

4 (or 6)

Translation should be A becoming A, B & C.
In translations A is never present. Just B. It does *not* make much sense.

Fast food, Hush Puppies and Brazilian poetry.
"Translation" represents a case of hermeneutical violence.
Even (date) rape.
A is forced to have a child with B.
A is left behind.
HTML made going from Here to There possible. But HTML is a (secret English) lingua franca—meaning: going from Here to There is always
an English Based Operation.
The troops.
English | Behind | The scenes.
(The Internet is the United States through other means).
Total Translation would really mean returning to the first tongue. Make translators write in the language they began wanting to disappeared from the face of the page.
Special Effects.
(Continuará . . .)

CHAIN TRANSLATION CHAIN

The first issue of *Chain* began with a series of chain letters. We asked artists and writers to write something, send it on to someone else, and then for that person to write something in response and send both pieces on to someone else, etc. Our goal was to open *Chain* up to writers that were new to us.

This translation chain was done in that same spirit. I sent out a version of the following letter:

> I am working on a sort of "chain mail" project for the next issue of *Chain* on translation.
>
> Ammiel Alcalay sent us an email shortly after we started work on this issue saying that our call for work seemed frivolous in such trying times.
>
> At first I felt annoyed with him. But then I realized that he had a point. We were not really addressing the politics of translation all that much in our call. We feel lucky, however, that we got some good and political work in the mail. But I still wanted to highlight the political potential of translation in these times.
>
> With that history, would you be interested in translating the following passage for us into [insert name of language here]?
>
> "In the face of this approaching disaster, it behooves men and women not yet overcome by war madness to raise their voice of protest, to call the attention of the people to the crime and outrage which are about to be perpetrated on them."
>
> This passage is from Emma Goldman's, "Preparedness, The Road to Universal Slaughter," *Mother Earth*, December 1915. I've chosen it because of its obvious message, because Emma Goldman is super cool, and because of the recent attempt by Berkeley to stop The Emma Goldman Papers from using it in their fundraising (details: http://sunsite.berkeley.edu/Goldman/Features/emma_news.htm).
>
> I am trying to get this into as many non-colonial languages as possible. If you've got any connections or suggestions, please let me know as soon as possible.
>
> Thanks.
>
> —Juliana Spahr

What follows are the results. The language spread is arbitrary, but it does encircle the globe. I am grateful for friends, and friends of friends, and parents of friends for help with this project. Special thanks to Rosa Alcalá, Maria Damon, Chris Daniels, Linh Dinh, Omar Gatto, Monica Ghosh, Mariana Hildesheim, Walter Lew, Laura Lyons, Bhanu Kapil Rider, S. Shankar, Lee Siegel, Caroline Sinavaiana, David Treuer, and Juliette Valéry.

I have started the chain with Hawai'i's languages and then moved out across the globe in a wandering path.

I ke alo o kēia 'ōuli weliweli e hiki mai ana, pono nā kāne a me nā wāhine i 'ōkā 'ole ai me ka 'ino kehena kaua, e ho'onui pū i ko kākou leo kū'ē i ka 'ino, a e ho'onānā ai i nā kānaka i kēlā 'ino e ho'omauka'alina iho ana iā kākou.—*Ku'ualoha Ho'omanawanui (HAWAIIAN)*

Wen look like everyting going come all buckaloose and maybe going get war, ees up to da bruddahs and sistahs who get da cool head, dey da ones gotta say someting for protess da crime and da outrage das going be perpetuated on top a-dem.—*Lee Tonouchi (PIDGIN/HAWAI'I CREOLE ENGLISH)*

A o lafoia le ataata o lenei taua le maalofia, e ta'u leleia alii ma tamaitai e le o aafia i talitonuga fiafia i taua, ina ia alagaina le leo faatuiese, e faailoa atu ai i tagata ia solitulafono ma tulaga matuia o le a faaooina ia i latou.—*Fepuleai Vita Tanielu (SAMOAN)*

Mwohn kahpwal laud en mahwen me koakoadohn eh pahn wiawi, eh wia ire kesempwal laud ohng ohl oh lih akan koaros me sohte utung kemwekid kamasepwehk wet ren kasalehda me re uhweng de sohte utung kemwekid wet, oh re anahne kaweid ki aramas koaros me dihp laud ehu met oh mahwen wet pahn kieng aramas koaros nan kahpwal laud.—*Emelihter Kihleng (POHNPEIAN)*

Mā te parekura nui e whakatata mai ana e whakatairanga ake i ngā tāne me ngā wāhine, kāre anō kia warea e te riri, kia whakaputa i ā rātau whakahē, ki te whakatūpato hoki i ngā iwi puta noa i te ao ki ngā hara me ngā hākiki ka mahia nei ki a rātau ākuanei.—*Robert Wiri (MAORI)*

Sa harap nitong nalalapit na kapahamakan, nararapat na magprotesta ang mga taong di pa nagagapi ng kahibangan ng digmaan, upang tawagin ang pansin ng sangkatauhan sa krimen at karahasan na isasagawa sa kanila.—*Eric Gamalinda (TAGALOG)*

予期される惨事を前に、戦争の狂気にまだ狂わされていない者は、戦争による残虐な殺人行為に人々の目を向けさせるため、その完全な不支持を叫び続けなければならないのです。—*Cyrille Marlin & Maiko Sakamoto* (JAPANESE)

현재 다가오는 재해에 맞서 아직 전쟁광기에 빠지지않은 사람들은 이제 반드시 항쟁의 목소리를 높여야 하고 그들에게 가해질 범죄와 폭력에 대중의 주목을 끌어야 한다. —*Jung Yeon Sohn* (KOREAN)

面临将近的灾祸、尚未被战争的疯狂压倒、进行呐喊抗争的男男女女、有责任提请人们对将会降临他们头上的罪恶和凌辱密切注视。—*Tian Chenshan* (CHINESE)

Đối mặt với tai hoạ đang đến gần này, điều cần làm đối với những người đàn ông và đàn bà vẫn còn tỉnh táo trước cơn điên loạn hiếu chiến, là phải cất tiếng nói phản kháng, kêu gọi sự quan tâm của con người trước tội ác và sự xúc phạm đang chuẩn bị bạo hành lên họ.—*Phan Nhien Hao* (VIETNAMESE)

ในช่วงเวลาแห่งภัยพิบัติอันใกล้มาถึงคือความเหมาะลมและจำเป็นที่ประชาชนชายหญิงผู้ตระหนักได้ถึงความบ้าคลั่งแห่งสงครามจะประกาศคำประท้วงและเรียกร้องให้โลกเห็นถึงอาชญากรรมและการทำลายล้างที่กำลังจะเกิดขึ้นกับตนเองและพลโลก—*Padcha Tuntha-obas* (THAI)

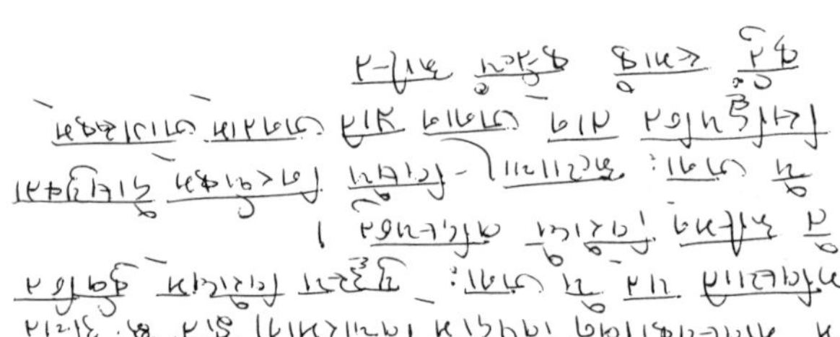

—*Ravi Sharma* (SANSKRIT)

इस आगामी संकर को ध्यान में रखते हुए। यह उचित होगा कि जिन स्त्रीपुरूषों पर अभी तक जंग का पागलपन ह्यभूतह सवार नही हुआ है वे इसके विरोध में आवाज उठायें और जो इस प्रकार के अपराध तथा अत्याचार लोगों पर थोपे जाने वाले हैं।—*Ravi Sharma* (HINDI)

பேரழிவு நம்மை எதிர் நோக்கியுள்ள
இத்தருணத்தில், யுத்த வெறியில் இன்னமும்
சிக்காத ஆணும் பெண்ணும், தங்களின் எதிர்ப்புக்
குரலை எழுப்ப வேண்டும். மக்கள் தம் மீது
சுமத்தப்படவுள்ள குற்றத்தையும்,
அக்கிரமத்தையும் புரிந்து கொள்ளுமாறு
அவர்களின் கவனத்தை ஈர்க்க வேண்டும்.

எம்மா கோல்ட்மேனின் "தயார் நிலை, உலகத்தின் பேரழிவுக்கு வகுக்கும்வழி."

தமிழாக்கம்
கி. ஸோ. சுப்பிரமணியன் —*K. S. Subramanian (TAMIL)*

Перед лицом грядущей катастрофы, мужчины и женщины, еще не зараженные безумием войны, должны поднять голос протеста, должны привлечь внимание человечества к преступлению и произволу, которым оно вот-вот будет подвергнуто.—*Matvei Yankelevich (RUSSIAN)*

Fronte al tiu ĉi alproksimiĝanta katastrofo, endas al tiuj viroj kaj virinoj kiuj ankoraŭ ne venkiĝis per la militfrenezo levi la voĉojn proteste, atentigi la popolojn pri la krimo kaj perforto kiuj estos truditaj al ili. —*Walter K. Lew (ESPERANTO)*

Uprkos nesreće koja nam se približava, muškarci i žene, oni koje ludilo rata još nije obuzelo, moraju podići svoj glas u znak protesta i upozoriti ljude na zločine i nasilje koji će se nad njima izvršiti.—*Dubravka Djuric (SERBIAN)*

Mod denne kommende katastrofe må mænd og kvinder, som endnu ikke er overvundet af krigsgalskab, hæve deres stemmer i protest, så folk bliver opmærksomme på den skændsel og forbrydelse, der snart vil blive begået mod dem.—*Mette Moestrup (DANISH)*

Di fronte a questo disastro che si avvicina, conviene che gli uomini e le donne non ancora presi dalla follia della guerra alzino la loro voce di protesta per richiamare l'attenzione del popolo sul crimine e l'oltraggio perpetrati contro di loro.—*Sharon Dolin (ITALIAN)*

Face au désastre qui s'annonce, il appartient aux hommes et aux femmes que la folie de la guerre n'a pas encore gagnés de clamer leur total désaccord afin d'attirer l'attention des peuples sur les crimes et les atrocités qui menacent d'être perpétrés contre eux.—*Juliette Valéry* (FRENCH)

I bhfianaise na hanachana seo chugainn, tá se de dhualgas ar a bhfuil d'fhir agus de mhná fós saor ó bhuile na cogaíochta a rún agóide a nochtadh, aird an phobail a tharraingt ar an éagóir agus ar an bhfeillbheart atáthar ar tí a ndéanta orthu.—*Katie Kane* (IRISH)

Yaklasan felaket karsisinda, savas çilginligina kapilmamis erkek ve kadinlara dusen sey, savasa karsi olduklarini soylemek ve bu sayede, kendilerine karsi islenecek suç ve katliamlara dunya halklarinin dikkatini yoneltmektir.
—*Levent Yilmaz* (TURKISH)

لم اللذين النسأ و الرجال من يقتضي تية الا المصيبة أمام
،اعتراضآ اصواتهم يعرفوا ان بعد العرب جنون عليهم يتولى
الفاحشة الى ،الجريمة الى جميعآ الناس انتباه يستدعوا
.ضدهم تقترف ان وشك على هي اللتي
—*Omar Gatto* (ARABIC)

נוכח האסון המתקרב, חובת גברים ונשים שדעיין לא נכנעו לשגעון המלחמה להשמיע קולות של מחאה על מנת לקרא תשומת לבם של העמים לפשע והזבעה שמתכננים נגדם.
—*Benjamin Hildesheim* (HEBREW)

Katika wakati huu ambao mathara yanakaribia, inabidi wanaume na wanawake ambao hawajashindwa na ukichaa wa vita kutoa mwito wa upinzani ili kuwajulisha watu juu ya uhalifu na ubaya ambao ukaribu kuenezwa kwao.—*Charles Tunai* (KISWAHILI)

Gonkaaga eno amabebe gatotachereye, ng'otakerwa ere iga abasacha na abakari bare batarakerwa nigichuro kirihii baimokere basumache gosauti emwe kori abanto bonswi bamanye amabebe gare gahangi gokorwa abanto.—*Charles Tunai* (IGIKURIA)

Fasa deblozay sa a, chak moun ki poko soufri anba tèt chaje lafoli lagè a bije rele poteste, pou fè lòt moun konnen nan ki kalite krim ak atwocite yo pral pase.—*Kiran Jayaram* (HAITIAN)

Diante do iminente desastre, homens e mulheres ainda não tomados pela loucura da guerra devem levantar sua voz de protesto e alertar para o crime e o ultraje que estão prestes a ser perpetrados contra todos.—*Josely Vianna Baptista (PORTUGUESE)*

En vista de este desastre que se aproxima, todos los que no han sucumbido a la locura guerrerista deben alzar la voz en protesta y alertar al pueblo sobre el crimen y el ultraje que están al perpetrarse contra ellos.—*Jorge Guitart (SPANISH)*

Tá:we' o:nen ki:ken na'teiotenonhianihton, ronón:kwé tánon' konón:kwé iáh tehoti'nikonhrahrí:'on ase'kén ronateri:ióhkwe' nahón:ne' shehró:ri iorakaréni, akwé:kon, enhserihwá:ronke' atokénhtshera tsi tá:we' ne tahonatenonhianihtén:ni'.—*James Thomas Stevens (MOHAWK)*

Wii-ani-miigaading egwanji'igoosigwaa nishkaadiziwin ininiwag miinawaa ikwewag odaa-aagonwewetaanaawaa i'iw ayi'ii maanaadak waa-toodawindwaa.—*Anton Treuer (OJIBWE)*

WHERE TO LOOK NEXT . . .

ANDRÉS AJENS . . . Poet, essayistnarrator, translator. Has published *Más íntimas mistura* (Intemperie, Santiago, poems, 1998), *Lecturas meridianas* (essays on Latin American culture, 1998), *Poemas inconjuntos y otros poemas* (translation of Alberto Caeiro, Fernando Pessoa, 1996), *La última carta de Rimbaud* (poem essay, 1995), *Conmemoración de inciertas fechas y otro poema* (poems, 1992). His *O entrevero* (poems and essay stories) and *Cobra Norato* (translucination of the poem of the same name by the Brazilian Raul Bopp) will appear shortly. In 2002, he coordinated the first South-Southern writers' conference, Poesíalteridad, in Córdoba, Argentina. Started his birth in 1961, in La Concepción, in the south of Chile. ⋆ AMMIEL ALCALAY is a poet, translator, critic, and scholar; he teaches in the Department of Classical, Middle Eastern, and Asian Languages and Cultures and in the Medieval Studies Program and Comparative Literature Department at the CUNY Graduate Center. His latest work, *from the warring factions* (Beyond Baroque, 2002), is a book-length poem dedicated to the Bosnian town of Srebrenica. *Poetry, Politics, and Translation: American Isolation and the Middle East*, a lecture given at Cornell, was published in 2003 by Palm Press. His other books include *After Jews and Arabs: Remaking Levantine Culture* (University of Minnesota Press, 1993), *the cairo noteboooks* (Singing Horse Press, 1993), and *Memories of Our Future: Selected Essays, 1982–1999* (City Lights, 1999). He has also translated widely, including *Sarajevo Blues* by the Bosnian poet Semezdin Mehmedinovic (City Lights, 1998), and *Keys to the Garden: New Israeli Writing* (City Lights, 1996). Current projects include translation of a new book by Semezdin Mehmedinovic, *Nine Alexandrias*, due out from City Lights in fall 2003; a Hebrew novel, *Outcast*, by Shimon Ballas; and a book of essays, *Politics and Imagination*. He has been a regular contributor to the *Village Voice*, and his poetry, prose, reviews, critical articles, and translations have appeared in *The New York Times Book Review*, *The New Yorker*, *Time* magazine, *The New Republic*, *Grand Street*, *Conjunctions*, *Sulfur*, *The Nation*, and various other publications. ⋆ FRANCISCO ARAGÓN was born and raised in San Francisco. His poetry has appeared in the anthologies *Under the Fifth Sun: Latino Literature from California* (Heyday Books/Santa Clara University, 2002), *American Diaspora: Poetry of Displacement* (University of Iowa Press, 2001), and *Inventions of Farewell: A Book of Elegies* (W. W. Norton & Company, 2001). He is the author of *Light, Yogurt, Strawberry*

Milk (The Chicano Chapbook Series, 1999), *In Praise of Cities* (momotombito, Chicago, 2002), and the bilingual chapbook *Tertulia* (BOOKLYN, New York, 2002). He holds a B.A. and an M.A. in Spanish from U.C. Berkeley and New York University, respectively. He lived, worked, and traveled in Spain for many years before returning to the United States to pursue an M.A. in English from U.C. Davis, where he was awarded an Academy of American Poets Prize in 1999. His works as a translator include six books, among them his collaboration on *Lorca: Selected Verse* (Farrar, Straus & Giroux, 1995) and four collections by Francisco X. Alarcón, most recently, *From the Other Side of Night: New and Selected Poems* (University of Arizona Press, 2002). His poems, as well as his translations of the Spanish poet Gerardo Diego (1896–1987), have appeared, or are forthcoming, in various publications, including *Chelsea, Nimrod, Puerto del Sol, The Journal, Zyzzyva,* and the online journals Jacket and Electronic Poetry Review. The founding editor and publisher of Momotombo Press, his first full-length collection of poems, *Puerta del Sol*, is forthcoming from Bilingual Press. ⋆ SHIMON BALLAS was born in Baghdad in 1930 and emigrated to Israel in 1951. A major novelist, Ballas has published fifteen works of fiction, several important studies on contemporary Arabic literature, and numerous translations from Arabic. Although he began his career in Arabic, Ballas switched to Hebrew in the mid-1960s. Since then, Ballas, perhaps more than any other Israeli writer, has opened a window onto the political and psychological life of the contemporary Arab world, both at home and in exile. His works consistently defy categorization, from the first Israeli novel to depict life amongst the Arab Jewish immigrants of the 1950s (*The Transit Camp*, 1964) or the portrayal of a Palestinian architect returning home for a visit after years in Europe (*A Locked Room*, 1980), to the depiction of a community of Middle Eastern political exiles in Paris (*Last Winter*, 1984) or the ruminations of a Jewish historian converted to Islam in Baghdad of the 1980s (*Outcast*, 1991). Other books by Ballas include *Facing the Wall* (1969), *Esav from Baghdad* (1970), *Clarification* (1972), *Downtown* (1979), *The Heir* (1987), *Not in Her Place* (1994), *Solo* (1998), and *Tel Aviv East* (1998). His important study *Arab Literature Under the Shadow of War*, which began as his doctoral thesis for the Sorbonne, appeared in 1978. He continues to write critical works in Arabic, the most recent of which, *Secular Trends in Arabic Literature*, appeared with the Iraqi-exile publishing house al-Kamel Verlag, in Cologne, Germany. Ballas retired from the Department of Arabic Literature at Haifa University and now spends part of the year in Paris, where he does most of his writing. ⋆ CAROLINE BERGVALL is a poet based in London. Her books include *Eclat* (1996) and *GoanAtom: Doll* (2001). She has collaborated on a number of performances and installations, including *Ambient Fish* (Hull Time Based Art, 1999), *About Face* (Berlin, 2000, and Bard College, New York, 2001), and *Say Parsley* (Exeter, 2001). She is an associate research fellow at Dartington College of Arts and an associate writer at Cardiff University. Her critical work is chiefly concerned with bilingualism and cross-media forms of writing. She has recently edited the *Performance Research Issue on Translations* (summer 2002). Some of her work is available online at epc.buffalo.edu/authors/bergvall. ⋆ CHARLES BERNSTEIN's most recent books are *Republics of Reality: 1975–1995* (Sun & Moon), *With Strings* (University of Chicago Press), *My Way: Speeches and Poems* (Chicago), and *Let's Just Say*, a pamphlet from Chax. He teaches at the University of Pennsylvania. Home page at epc.buffalo.edu. ⋆ Composer ALLA BORZOVA has rapidly been gaining prominence in the West after arriving in the U.S. from Minsk, Belarus, in 1993. Two-time winner of the All-Union Composition Contest before her emigration, and the first-prize winner of the Delius Composition Contest, she is also a recent recipient of the Goddard Lieberson Fellowship from the Academy of Arts and Letters. She has also received awards, grants, and fellowships from ASCAP, the Susan Rose Fund, the Jerome Foundation, the American Music Center, and Yaddo, among others. She holds a doctorate in music composition from Moscow Conservatory and has done further doctoral work at the CUNY Graduate Center. In addition to composing for various commissions, she maintains an active career as pianist, organist, and conductor. She became an American citizen in 2001. ⋆ HAROLDO DE CAMPOS, one of the major figures in Brazilian literature, lives in São Paulo. *Novas—Selected Writings of Haroldo de Campos*, edited by A. S. Bessa and Odile Cisneros, is forthcoming in 2004 from Northwestern University Press. ⋆ INGER CHRISTENSEN, born in 1935 in Vejle, Denmark, is one of the leading figures in modern Scandinavian literature. Christensen's first novel, *The Painted Room*, translated by Denise Newman, is available from Random House. Christensen's *Alphabet*, translated by Susanna Nied, was recently published by New Directions, and a second volume of Christensen's poetry, *Butterfly Valley: A Requiem*, is forthcoming. Her works have been translated into over a dozen languages. She lives in Copenhagen. ⋆ CHUANG TZU is the greatest prose writer of the Chou Dynasty and a notorious slanderer of Confucius. Several translations of Chuang Tzu, including those by Burton Watson, are online at www.geocities.com/dao_house/zztrans.html. ⋆ ALLISON COBB's poems are featured in recent issues of *Ixnay Reader* and *Primary Writing* and in the full-length collection *Born Two* from Chax Press this fall. Her work has also appeared in *Lungfull!*, *Snare*, *Torch*, *Can We Have Our Ball Back?* (www.canwehaveourballback.com), at theeastvillage.com, and elsewhere. She is co-editor of *Pom2* magazine (www.pompompress.com). ⋆ JENNIFER COLEMAN lives in Brooklyn, New York, and is co-editor of *Pom2* magazine (www.pompompress.com). Her poems appear at www.theeastvillage.com/v12.htm, www.speakeasy.org/subtext/poetry/jencoleman, and http://poets9for9.blogspot.com. ⋆ MICHAEL CUEVA was born in Pampanga, a province in the Philippines, and spent his early childhood in a town called Floridablanca. His father was in the U.S. Navy, thus he moved between Guam, California, and the Philippines, finally settling in Hawai'i. He graduated from James Campbell High School in Ewa Beach and received a B.F.A. in graphic design from the University of Hawai'i at Manoa. He currently lives his life as a graphic designer in a partnership called no.3 design. ⋆ DANTE, a thirteenth-century Italian poet, is best known for the epic poem *La commedia*, later named *La divina commedia* (*The Divine Comedy*). ⋆ RUBÉN DARÍO was born in 1867 in Nicaragua. His first mature work, published in Chile, was a mixed-genre collection—prose and poetry—titled *Azul*, which appeared in 1888. The poet found himself in the Chilean capital, working as a journalist at the time, and it was as a journalist that he made his living throughout most of his life, though he sometimes enjoyed brief stints as a Nicaraguan diplomat in Europe. He resided in both Paris and Madrid, working in the Spanish capital for the Argentinean daily *La Nación*. Darío's work is often cited as the most important poetry of so-called *modernismo*. But this is not to be confused with the "modernism" of the Eliot/Pound/Joyce variety. "Modernismo" is to poetry in Spanish what "symbolism" is to poetry in French. Other important volumes of verse include *Prosas Profanas* (1896), *Cantos de vida y esperanza* (1905), *El Canto errante* (1907), and *Canto a la argentina* (1910). After the sudden death of his wife in 1892, his personal life fell into disarray. He is said to have married a second time under the influence of alcohol. His inability to have this second marriage annulled led him, according to some biographers, to lead a bohemian life with incessant travel for the rest of his days. His drinking led to ill health, and he went back to Nicaragua in 1916 to die. His influence on poetry in Spanish at the turn of the century, and beyond, is monumental. A seminal anthology of Spanish poetry—edited by Gerardo Diego in Madrid in 1935—which introduced readers to the poets who went on to become *la generacion del '27* and includes Federico García Lorca, begins with Rubén Darío. ⋆ ADAM DEGRAFF is currently putting an artist's playground together with his brothers in Old Town, Arvada, Colorado, called the d note. The most recent places his poems can be found are in *All This Will Be Dust in Just Three Minutes*, from David Larsen and Beth Murray's We Have a Fax

Machine Press, and in *No Man's Sleep*, from Lytle Shaw and Emilie Clark's Shark Press. ⋆ A. ISADORA DEL VECCHIO has a B.A. is anthropology from the University of Kansas and is beginning her graduate work at the University of Florida. ⋆ ALBERT FLYNN DESILVER is editor/publisher of The Owl Press (www.theowlpress.com). His poems have appeared fairly recently in *Volt*, *Columbia Poetry Review*, *Zyzzyva*, *New American Writing*, *Combo*, *Hanging Loose*, *Tinfish*, *Slope*, *Web Del Sol*, *Exquisite Corpse*, *The Hat*, *Lungfull!*, *Skanky Possum*, *Can We Have Our Ball Back?*, and elsewhere. Also try a google search under "Albert Flynn DeSilver." ⋆ CRAIG DWORKIN edits Eclpise (www.princeton.edu/eclipse) and the UbuWeb Anthology of Conceptual Writing (www.ubu.com/concept); his book *Reading the Illegible* is available from Northwestern University Press. ⋆ Some recent and forthcoming essays by BRENT HAYES EDWARDS appear in *Critical Inquiry*, *Cultural Studies*, *Positions*, and *Representations*. His book *The Practice of Diaspora* was published in May by Harvard University Press. ⋆ KARI EDWARDS is a poet, artist, and gender activist, winner of New Langton Art's Bay Area Award in Literature (2002), and the author of *jduna* (O Books, 2003), *a day in the life of p.* (Subpress, 2002), *a diary of lies* (*Belladonna* 27 by Balladonna Books, 2002), *obLiqUE paRt(itON): colLABorationS* (xPress(ed), 2002), and *post/(pink)* (Scarlet Press, 2000). She is also the poetry editor of I.F.G.E's *Transgender—Tapestry: An International Publication on Transgender Issues*. Her work has been exhibited throughout the United States, including at the Denver Art Museum, the New Orleans Contemporary Art Museum, the University of California–San Diego, and the University of Massachusetts–Amherst. ⋆ RAINER GANAHL is based in New York and represented Austria in the 1999 Venice Biennial. He has been widely shown in museums and galleries in Europe, Asia, and the United States. Recent one-person exhibitions include Baumgartner Gallery, New York, and Galerie Nächst St. Stephan, Vienna. See his work on the Web at http://www.ganahlmarx.com/, http://www.ganahlmoney.com/, and http://www.ganahl.info/. ⋆ NADA GORDON's latest book, *V. Imp* (Faux Press, 2003), has been described as "mood-riddled hijinx and impudent lyric protest" and "nonsense galore, as in a bathhouse." With Gary Sullivan, she is the author of *Swoon* (Granary Books, 2001), a nonfiction e-pistolary multiform novel. She published two other books in 2001: *Are Not Our Lowing Heifers Sleeker than Night Swollen Mushrooms?* (Spuyten Duyvil) and *Foriegnn Bodie* (Detour), a collection of poems written during her eleven years in Tokyo. Ongoing obsessions include song, odalisques, ornament, and all forms of life. Her more-or-less daily musings on life and poetics can be found at http://ululate.blogspot.com. ⋆ KU'UALOHA HO'OMANAWANUI is a kanaka maoli who proudly traces her Hawaiian lineage to the islands of Kaua'i, Maui, and Hawai'i, and is a descendant of both chiefly and kahuna families in the districts of Kohala Ka'u and Puna on the islands of Hawai'i. She received her B.A. in Hawaiian studies and M.A. in Hawaiian religion from the University of Hawai'i at Manoa, where she is currently a Ph.D. candidate in English. She is a lecturer in Hawaiian mythology at the Center for Hawaiian Studies, as well as a co-editor of *'Oiwi: A Native Hawaiian Journal.* ⋆ PAUL HOOVER has published nine poetry collections, including *Totem and Shadow: New and Selected Poems* (Talisman House, 1999), *Rehearsal in Black* (Salt Publications, 2001), and *Winter (Mirror)* (Flood Editions, 2002). He is also editor of the literary magazine *New American Writing* and the anthology *Postmodern American Poetry* (W.W. Norton, 1994). ⋆ ABDOURAHMANE IDRISSA is the author of two essays in *Orange Light*, a Dakar cultural magazine, on local languages, Nigerian popular drama, and on the character of the African city, both in French: "Mais à quoi peut penser Malam Zourou?" (January 2000) and "Nos rustiques poliorcètes" (June 2000). Two papers on African politics are to be published soon: "A Decade of Transition: Institutional Experimentation and Inter-Elite Competition in Niger," in collaboration with Leonardo Villalón (October 2001) and "Modèle islamique et modèle occidental: le conflit des elites au Niger" (October 2002), both in books recording the transactions of the conferences at which they were presented. In addition, a travelogue, "Sahel Est-Ouest, Août 1999," will be published in the spring issue of the University of Kansas French magazine *Chimères.* ⋆ BRENDA IIJIMA's book *Around Sea* is forthcoming from O Books. An essay titled *Color and its Antecedents*, published as a chapbook, is forthcoming from Yen Agat Books. Together with Alan Davies, she publishes a chapbook series. A compact disc of Friedrich Hölderlin's poems read in German by Erika Uchman and in English (using Richard Sieburth's translations) by Iijima will be released shortly by Portable Press at Yo-Yo Labs. ⋆ KIRAN JAYARAM is the author of *Digging the Roots and Cultural Politics and Identity in the Mouvman Rasin in Haiti* (Institute of Haitian Studies, Occasional Papers Series, Bryant C. Freeman, editor, forthcoming). He is a Ph.D. student in anthropology, currently at the University of Florida, and an instructor of the Haitian language. ⋆ MATT KALEIALI'I KA'OPIO has been a mouth painter since a swimming accident at Waipahe'e Falls on Kaua'i left him a quadraplegic in August 1994. Born and raised on the island of Kaua'i and a 1990 graduate of Kamehameha Schools, Matt is currently a graduate student in Pacific Islands studies at the University of Hawai'i at Manoa. ⋆ J. N. KAPIHENUI was a Kanaka Maoli (Native Hawaiian) who resided in Kailua, Ko'olaupolo, O'ahu, Hawai'i, when he (or she) published the story "He Mo'olelo no Hi'iakaikapoliopele" (A Story of Hi'iaka-in-the-bosom-of-Pele) in the Hawaiian-language newspaper *Ka Hoku o ka Pakipika* in 1861. No other biographical information is known at this time. ⋆ ADEENA KARASICK is the author, most recently, of *The House That Hijack Built* (Talonbooks, 2004) and also of *The Arugula Fugues* (Zasterle Press, 2001), *Dyssemia Sleaze* (Talonbooks, 2000), *Genrecide* (Talonbooks, 1996), *Mêmewars* (Talonbooks, 1994), and *The Empress Has No Closure* (Talonbooks, 1992). "The Wall" is forthcoming in *Poetry and Cultural Studies: A Reader*, edited by Maria Damon and Ira Livingston (Wesleyan University Press). Check out www.adeenakarasick.com for more details. ⋆ JAKE KENNEDY's poetry and fiction have previously appeared, or are forthcoming, in a number of literary journals, including *Pom2*, *Descant*, and *The Malahat Review*. ⋆ LEEVI LEHTO, born 1951, Finnish poet and translator, author of five collections of poems, most recently *Ääninen* (Lake Onega, 1997), and a novel, *Janajevin unet* (Yanayev's Dreams, 1992). Authors translated range from Althusser, Deleuze and Guattari, and Lyotard (philosophy) to Keats, Ashbery, and Bernstein (poetry). Some work of his is available in English at http://www.leevilehto.net/default.asp?a=8, and his "Google Poem Engine" at www.leevilehto.net/google/patterns.asp. See also his section in a new online anthology of contemporary Finnish poetry at http://www.electricverses.net/sakeet.php?poet=17&poem=-1&language=3. ⋆ LI YU was a Chinese poet and the last ruler of the Southern T'ang dynasty (937–978). In 975, he was taken into captivity and died three years later, having been poisoned. His work is often separated into pre- and post-capitivity poems, the former known for their sumptuous pursuit of his own desires and the latter for their melachonoly edge and poignancy. "Night Crow Calls" is a post-captivity poem. ⋆ ABRAHAM LINCOLN was the sixteenth president of the United States (1861–1865). ⋆ R. ZAMORA LINMARK divides his time between San Francisco and Manila. He is the author of *Rolling the Rs* and the forthcoming *Leche*. Most recent poems will appear in *Zyzzyva*, *Indiana Review*, and *Hyphen*. ⋆ ERNESTO LIVON-GROSMAN is an assistant professor at Boston College, where he teaches Latin American poetry and literary theory. He is editing, together with Cecilia Vicuña, an anthology of five hundred years of poetry in translation, to be published by Oxford University Press in 2004. His *Geografíías Imaginarias* (Beatriz Viterbo), dedicated to travel writing, will be coming out this fall in Argentina, and an anthology of José Lezama Lima's poetry in translation (University of California Press) will be published next spring. ⋆ PAMELA LU was born and raised in a provincial region of Southern California and studied mathematics at the University of California, Berkeley. Since 1995, she has worked as a technical writer in Silicon Valley. She is the author of *Pamela: A Novel* (Atelos Press, 1999). ⋆ Other sections of SCOTT MACLEOD's *Tales of the OOtd War* can be found at http://www.burningpress.org/va/pote/potet26.html and (with other work) at http://www.muse-apprentice-guild.com/scottmacleod/home.html. Some poetry is available (as PDFs) at http://www.brokenboulder.com/catalog.htm, and there are some texts on the Web site www.seriousprojects.com. "ãauditoruimaä," a long poem, is forthcoming from Potes & Poets. ⋆ LOREN MADSEN is a New York–based artist with thirty years' experience creating large-scale installations, human-scale sculpture, and commercial and government commissions. See members.bellatlantic.net/lmadsen/home.html for more work. ⋆ JILL MAGI's recent work can be found in *Pierogi Press* 8, *Can We Have Our Ball Back?* 12, and at www.sonaweb.net. Her prose has appeared in *The Brooklyn Rail*, *Murmur*, and *Global City Review*. *Threads*, which she hopes to publish in January 2004, is a collection of poems, prose, and works on paper, and, in its electronic form, will also include sound and video (see sonaweb.net to find out more). Jill runs Sona Books, a community-based chapbook micro-press that brings works by new writers and artists into print. She lives in Brooklyn and teaches at the City College/CUNY Center for Worker Education, an interdisciplinary liberal arts program for working adults. ⋆ ANN E. MICHAEL is a poet, essayist, and librettist living in northeastern Pennsylvania. She is a 1998 recipient of a Pennsylvania Council on the Arts Poetry Fellowship and a recent M.F.A. graduate of Goddard College. Her work has been widely published in literary journals such as *Natural Bridge*, *The Coe Review*, *Minimus*, and *Poem*. She has written or translated libretti for Ivan Salinas, Elaine Erickson, and Alla Borzova. ⋆ MONCHOACHI's recent work includes *La Case où se tient la lune* (Bordeaux: William Blake & Co., 2002) and Creole translations of Beckett's *Waiting for Godot* and *Endgame*. He lives in Martinique. ⋆ ERÍN MOURE's (or Erin Mouré's or Eirin Moure's) latest books are *O Cidadán* (Toronto, Anansi, 2002), a philosophico-poetic exploration of what it means to be a "citizen," and *Sheep's Vigil by a Fervent Person: A Transelation of Alberto Caeiro/Fernando Pessoa's O Guardador de Rebanhos* (Toronto, Anansi, 2001, www.anansi.ca). She has published nine other books of poetry in the past twenty-five years, and her work has received many prizes. She is currently translating Chus Pato's indispensable *m-Talá* from Galician and working on a new book of poems and a book of poetics essays, mostly in her house in Montréal. ⋆ Arab and Western scholars are divided on whether there was an actual QAYS IBN AL-MULAWWAH, of the Beni 'Amir tribe, who lived and wrote in the seventh Christian (first Muslim) century. Verses that are attributed to him were collected a century later, and a written corpus existed by 1245 C.E. ⋆ KISHWAR NAHEED is considered one of the foremost poets writing in Pakistan today. She has been writing poetry in ghazal and free-verse format on social and political issues since the 1960s; her influence, as one of the first women poets to use and popularize the free-verse form in Urdu poetry, is far-reaching in contemporary Urdu literature. She is a social activist and has tirelessly worked for human rights and women's equality in her capacity as a civil servant and NGO worker. Naheed was a vocal critic of the draconian policies enforced during the martial law rule of General Zia and has faced the wrath of the authorities on numerous occasions for her articulation of social dissent; for instance, in 1983, her Urdu translation of Simone de Beauvoir's *The Second Sex* was banned and became the basis of charges of obscenity filed against her, which were later challenged and repealed. Naheed has written nine volumes of poetry, an autobiography, and a travel memoir; she has also translated poetry from other languages into Urdu and has edited anthologies and essay collections about women's roles in literature and society. Naheed's poetry, along with that of her compatriots Fahmida Riaz and Sara Shugafta, was featured in *We Sinful Women: Contemporary Urdu Feminist Poetry*, edited by Rukhsana Ahmad (London, Women's Press, 1991), and the latest translation of her work has appeared in editor Asif Farrukhi's compilation of her work, *The Distance of a Shout* (Oxford University Press, 2001). ⋆ MARCI NELLIGAN has an M.F.A. in creative writing from Mills College and has published in *Syllogism*, the Free Lunch young writers series, and the *Walrus*. ⋆ DENISE NEWMAN's collection of poetry *Human Forest* was published by Apogee Press, and her translation of Inger Christensen's novel *The Painted Room* is available from Random House. ⋆ SUSANNA NIED is a writer and literary translator whose most recent publications are *Selected Poems* by Søren Ulrik Thomsen (Poetry New York) and *Alphabet* by Inger Christensen (New Directions). She was the winner of the 1981 PEN/ASF translation award. ⋆ MARK NOWAK is the author of a poetry collection, *Revenants*, co-editor with Diane Glancy of the anthology *Visit Teepee Town: Native Writings After the Detours* (both from Coffee House Press), and editor of the journal *XCP: Cross-Cultural Poetics*. (http://bfn.org/~xcp). ⋆ DOUG NUFER is the author of *Never Again* (ubu.com and forthcoming from Black Square Editions), a novel where no word appears more than once. "The Gettysburg Variations" are from his constraint-driven novel-in-progress *Circus Solus*, parts of which also appear in *Monkey Puzzle* magazine and at the Muse Apprentice Guild Web site. His novel *Negativeland* is forthcoming from Autonomedia. ⋆ KAREN OHNESORGE's poems have appeared in *Ploughshares* and *Mudfish*. Her current research concerns image-and-text combinations by U.S. artists and writers of color. ⋆ OSKAR PASTIOR was born in 1927 in Hermannstadt, in Siebenbürgen, the German-speaking part of Romania. After World War II he, along with other young Romanian-Germans, spent five years in a Soviet labor camp as part of Romania's reparation for having sided with Hitler. This experience, he says, provided him with his thematic tonic: "the small—but significant—scope between freedom and determinism." Then, after taking a university degree and working for Bucharest radio, he managed, in 1969, to come to Berlin, where he has gained a considerable reputation as a poet, performer, and the only German member of Oulipo. His many honors include the Ernst-Meister Preis (1986), the Hugo-Ball-Preis (1990), and last year's Erich-Fried Preis. His volumes of poems include *Anagrammgedichte* (1985), *Lesungen mit Tinnitus* (1986), *Jalousien aufgemacht* (selected poems, 1987), a volume of palindromes, *Kopfnuss Januskopf* (1990), and *Das Hören des Genitivs* (1997). Available in English: *Poempoems*, translated by Malcolm Green (London, Atlas Press), and *Many Glove Compartments*, translated by H. Mathews, Christopher Middleton, and Rosmarie Waldrop (Providence, Burning Deck). ⋆ JOAN RETALLACK's most recent publications are *The Poethical Wager* (University of California Press), *Memnoir* (Wild Honey Press), and *Mongrelisme* (Paradigm Press). ⋆ THOMAS SCHEIBITZ lives and works in Berlin and Dresden. His work has been exhibited in numerous galleries, including the London Institute of Contemporary Art, the Berkeley Art Museum, the Tanya Bonakdar Gallery, and the Walker Art Center. ⋆ Some new poems by ALAN SEMERDJIAN can be found at www.whalelane.com, www.canwehaveourballback.com, and www.rattapallax.com/fusebox, and in *Ararat*. Some of his musical escapades can be found at www.milquemusic.com and www.surrealmusic.com, and essays on music can be found at www.longislandmusicscene.com. ⋆ MAHWASH SHOAIB is a Pakistani-American poet. As a poet and scholar, she is interested in avant-garde, experimental, political, and multilingual forms. She also translates contemporary Urdu poetry into English, and her translations of the Urdu poetry of the Pakistani poet Kishwar Naheed have been featured in the journal *connect*. She is an English doctoral candidate at the CUNY Graduate Center and also teaches at Queensborough Community College and Hunter College in New York. She is currently working on her dissertation on the transnational poetics of twentieth-century American and Asian poets. ⋆ MARA LEIGH SIMMONS is a writer and musician. Her recent work can be found in *Glottis: New Writing* (out of New Zealand), *Nerve Lantern*, and *For Immediate Release* at www.poetz.com/fir/. In 2002, she was the poetry editor of *Bombay Gin*. She is currently working on a critical essay titled, "Dimensions of a Palimpsest: Memory, Time, and

Stream of Consciousness in H.D.'s Prose," which, among many themes, explores the effects of writing memory during the disorientation of wartimes. ⋆ CAROLINE SINAVAIANA was born in the village of Utulei in Tutuila, Samoa. Her poetry and scholarship have appeared in national and international journals. Her book of poetry *Alchemies of Distance* came out last year from Subpress. Current projects include co-editing a mixed-genre collection of indigenous writing by Pacific women and a new collection of poetry and essays, *Nuclear Medicine*, exploring some of the metaphysical landscape(s) of breast cancer, "illness," and healing. ⋆ ANDRÉ SPEARS is the author of *Xo: A Tale for the New Atlantis* (on the Web at pangaeapress.com) and, in collaboration with Swiss artist Gilgian Gelzer, *Letters from Mu* (Part I) (Voix Editions, France, 2000, distributed through printedmatter.org), excerpts of which have been published in *First Intensity* and *Pierogi Press*. His translation of the infamous 1949 Rimbaud forgery "La chasse spirituelle" appears in *First Intensity* 15. ⋆ AMY STALLING is most recently the creator of forty artist books for The Grid Project (Buffalo, Elevator Project, 2003). ⋆ JONATHAN STALLING's "Translating as Reading/Translating as Writing" is in *Verdure* (2002). His review of *Transpacific Displacement* by Yunte Huang appeared in the *Boston Review*, fall 2002. Links and current projects can (often) be found at www.acsu.buffalo.edu/stalling/. ⋆ GERTRUDE STEIN (1874–1946) was an American writer. ⋆ JAMES THOMAS STEVENS is the author, most recently, of *Combing the Snakes from His Hair* (University of Michigan Press). ⋆ ESZTER SZUCS studied urban sociology in Columbia University's doctoral program. She recently returned to Budapest, Hungary, to seek employment. Her suitcases were laden with books by Pierre Bourdieu and Bruno Latour on the voyage back to her country of origin. ⋆ LORENZO THOMAS is a professor of English at the University of Houston–Downtown, where he teaches American literature and creative writing and is director of the university's Cultural Enrichment Center. His poetry and criticism have appeared in *African American Review*, *Arrowsmith*, *Blues Unlimited*, *Living Blues*, *Partisan Review*, *Ploughshares*, and *Popular Music and Society*. A regular book reviewer for the *Houston Chronicle*, he has also contributed scholarly articles to the *African American Encyclopedia*, *American Literary Scholarship*, *Gulliver* (Germany), and the *Dictionary of Literary Biography*. His books include *Chances Are Few*, *The Bathers*, and *Es Gibt Zeugen*, collections of poetry, as well as *Sing the Sun Up: Creative Writing Ideas from African American Literature*. His most recent book is *Extraordinary Measures: Afrocentric Modernism and 20th-Century American Poetry* (University of Alabama Press, 2000). ⋆ MÓNICA DE LA TORRE is a poet and translator. She edited and translated a volume of selected poems by Gerardo Deniz published by Lost Roads. With artist

Terence Gower, she is co-author of the artist book *Appendices, Illustrations, and Notes* (Smart Art Press). Her writing about art, poems, and translations have appeared or are forthcoming in journals such as *Art on Paper, Bomb, Boston Review, Cabinet, Mandorla, Pierogi Press, Review: Latin American Literature and Arts, Ten Verses*, and *The Germ*. With Michael Wiegers, she edited *Reversible Monuments: Contemporary Mexican Poetry*, published by Copper Canyon Press in 2002. She is the poetry editor of *The Brooklyn Rail*. ⋆ The TRADUCTION COLLECTIVE À ROYAUMONT took place during the Atelier Cosmopolite at the Foundation Royaumont, near Paris, in the summer of 1995. Format Américain is a series of chapbooks directed by Juliette Valéry within the framework of the association Un bureau sur l'Atlantique. ⋆ MICHEL-ROLPH TROUILLOT's publications in English include *Silencing the Past: Power and the Production of History* (Beacon, 1995), *Open the Social Sciences* (with I. Wallerstein et al., Stanford University Press, 1996), *Peasants and Capital: Dominica in the World Economy* (Baltimore, John Hopkins University Press, 1988), and *Haiti, State Against Nation: The Origins and Legacy of Duvalierism* (New York, Monthly Review Press, 1990). Trouillot's most recent work considers the history of Haiti from colonial times through the present day. He is the author of the first history of Haiti to be written in Krio, the language spoken by 95 percent of the nation. ⋆ PADCHA TUNTHA-OBAS is a graduate student at Mills College's M.F.A. program. She comes from Thailand and travels home every year. This is her first nationally published work. ⋆ ROSMARIE WALDROP's recent books of poems are *Reluctant Gravities* (New Directions, 1999) and *Split Infinites* (Singing Horse Press, 1998). Two new volumes are forthcoming in fall 2003: *Blindsight* (New Directions) and *Love, Like Pronouns* (Omnidawn). She has translated fourteen volumes of Edmond Jabès's work. Her memoir, *Lavish Absence: Recalling and Rereading Edmond Jabès*, is just out from Wesleyan University Press. For more information, see http://epc.buffalo.edu/authors/waldropr. ⋆ BURTON WATSON is one of the world's best-known translators from the Chinese and Japanese. His translations include *The Vimalakirti Sutra, Chuang Tzu: Basic Writings, Ryokan: Zen Monk-Poet of Japan, Saigyo: Poems of a Mountain Home*, and *The Columbia Book of Chinese Poetry: From Early Times to the Thirteenth Century*, all published by Columbia. ⋆ CHRISTIAN WOLFF came to prominence in the 1950s as an associate of John Cage, Morton Feldman, Earle Brown, and the other American experimentalists of that period, later working with Cornelius Cardew and Frederic Rzewski. His work has gone through many transformations, including minimalism (the early 1950s), indeterminancy, open form, and works connected with political issues. ⋆ HERIBERTO YÉPEZ (b. Tijuana, 1974) currently teaches philosophy at the Autonomous

University of Baja California. Writings by him have appeared in recent issues of *Shark* and *XCP*. Duration Press will soon release a chapbook by him titled *Babellebab. Non-Poetry on the End of Translation*. Weblog: www.hyepez.blogspot.com.

EDITORIAL INFORMATION

Jena Osman
Department of English
Temple University
10th Floor, Anderson Hall (022-29)
1114 West Berks Street
Philadelphia, PA 19122-6090

Juliana Spahr
Mills College
5000 MacArthur Boulevard
Oakland, California 94613

Since 1993, *Chain* has been publishing a yearly issue of work gathered loosely around a topic. The topic allows us to switch the editorial question that we ask each piece of work submitted from "is this a great piece of art" to "does this piece of art tell us something about the topic that we didn't already know." This makes *Chain* a little rougher around the edges, a little less aesthetically predictable. Within the frame of the topic, we tend to privilege mixed media and collaborative work and work by emerging or younger artists. We welcome submissions from readers. Please see our call for work on the following page.

Archive . . . http://www.temple.edu/chain

CALL FOR WORK

Chain *11: Public Forms*

As long as art is the beauty parlor of civilization, neither art nor civilization is secure.
—John Dewey, *Art as Experience*

Nobody knows who the public is or what it wants or needs.
—David Antin

We invite interested readers to submit work to *Chain* 11, on the topic of "public forms." We are interested in pieces that address what is commonly called public art—visual artworks that are publicly displayed and frequently supported by public funds—but also various forms of art that happen outside of usual performance and publication contexts, such as street art, political speeches, poster campaigns, architectural design, mail art, community theater, speaker's corners, poetry written for specific public occasions, etc. In other words, this issue will investigate art that is created for communities or "the public" in its broader definitions.

We also encourage a variety of "reports from the field," where artists observe how public art functions in their local environments. Such reports could take any genre or form, visual or textual. Reports from outside the United States are especially welcome.

Please be aware that we can only print visual images in black and white.

Send two copies of your submission and two copies of your cover letter to:

Chain (c/o Jena Osman)
Department of English
Temple University
10th Floor, Anderson Hall (022-29)
1114 West Berks Street
Philadelphia, PA 19122-6090

Deadline: December 1, 2003

If you have questions, send them to josman@temple.edu and spahr@hawaii.edu. But, please, NO email submissions (we tend to lose them).

Enclose a self-addressed, stamped envelope if you would like your work returned. Do not send us originals.

We read work in December and then contact everyone in early February at the latest.

More details at http://www.temple.edu/chain . . .

PLEASE SUBSCRIBE

The continued existence of *Chain* is dependent on subscriptions and contributions. Please donate and/or subscribe!

I enclose:

_____ $20 for two issues, starting with *Chain* 11

_____ $12 for *Chain* 9, dialogue

_____ $12 for *Chain* 8, comics

_____ $12 for *Chain* 7, memoir/antimemoir

_____ $12 for *Chain* 6, letters

_____ $12 for *Chain* 5, different languages

$ _____ donation to keep *Chain* going

Name ______________________________

Address ______________________________

____

____

Send to:

Chain (c/o Jena Osman)
Department of English
Temple University
10th Floor, Anderson Hall (022-29)
1114 West Berks Street
Philadelphia, PA 19122-6090

Please make check out to Chain Arts.